# THE SOUND OF WELSH PATAGONIA

# THE SOUND OF WELSH PATAGONIA

## PERFORMANCE, SUBJECTIVITY AND MUSIC IN Y WLADFA, PATAGONIA, ARGENTINA

### LUCY TROTTER

UNIVERSITY OF WALES PRESS

2025

© Lucy Trotter, 2025

Reprinted 2025

All rights reserved. No part of this book may be reproduced in any material form (including photocopying or storing it in any medium by electronic means and whether or not transiently or incidentally to some other use of this publication) without the written permission of the copyright owner except in accordance with the provisions of the Copyright, Designs and Patents Act. Applications for the copyright owner's written permission to reproduce any part of this publication should be addressed to the University of Wales Press, University Registry, King Edward VII Avenue, Cardiff CF10 3NS.

*www.uwp.co.uk*

*British Library Cataloguing-in-Publication Data*
A catalogue record for this book is available from the British Library.

ISBN 978-1-83772-219-8
eISBN 978-1-83772-220-4

The right of Lucy Trotter to be identified as author of this work has been asserted in accordance with sections 77 and 79 of the Copyright, Designs and Patents Act 1988.

This book is freely available on a Creative Commons CC-BY-NC-ND licence thanks to the kind sponsorship of the libraries participating in the Jisc Open Access Community Framework OpenUP initiative.

For GPSR enquiries please contact:
Easy Access System Europe Oü, 16879218
Mustamäe tee 50, 10621, Tallinn, Estonia.
*gpsr.requests@easproject.com*

Typeset by Marie Doherty
Printed and bound by
CPI Group (UK) Ltd, Croydon, CR0 4YY

*For my son, Matteo*

# Contents

|  | List of figures | ix |
|---|---|---|
|  | Acknowledgements | xi |
|  | A note on translation | xiii |
| Chapter 1 | Introduction: Musical encounters | 1 |
| Chapter 2 | A little Wales away from Wales | 17 |
| Chapter 3 | 'Eisteddfodamos': Eisteddfod as ritual performance | 47 |
| Chapter 4 | Performing Patagonia under the gaze of the Welsh other | 87 |
| Chapter 5 | Mirror, mirror on the wall, who is the most Welsh of them all? | 117 |
| Chapter 6 | 'The community is a family, and the choir is the glue': Performing Patagonia for the ear of the Welsh other | 149 |
| Chapter 7 | Conclusions: Sound and the subject | 185 |
|  | Notes | 197 |
|  | Works cited | 225 |
|  | Index | 247 |

# List of figures

1. Map of Argentina — 5
2. Map of indigenous populations — 25
3. Chubut River — 31
4. Chubut River at sunset — 31
5. A view over Gaiman village — 37
6. A wintery sky in Gaiman — 37
7. Sign for Capel Bethel — 42
8. Esquel — 52
9. An evening in Esquel — 53
10. Welsh road signs in Gaiman — 55
11. Welsh and Argentinian flags — 108
12. Welsh and Argentinian bunting — 109
13. Capel Glan Alaw — 143
14. Arriving at Capel Glan Alaw — 143
15. Gaiman Music School — 156
16. The main rehearsal room in Gaiman Music School — 157

# Acknowledgements

*The Sound of Welsh Patagonia* began in 2014 as a PhD project at The London School of Economics and Political Science (LSE). The research was funded by a scholarship from the Economic and Social Research Council of Great Britain (ESRC) and a maternity leave grant from the ESRC from April 2018 to April 2019. The ESRC also supported an event 'A Piece of Wales in Patagonia' as part of their annual Festival of Social Science in November 2018. The research, in its various stages, was presented at conferences and events in Aberystwyth (2015, 2018, 2019), Leicester (SLAS 2019) and London (2019). I remain indebted to my PhD supervisors, Mathijs Pelkmans and Harry Walker, for their academic rigour, good humour and consistent support throughout the project, to colleagues in the anthropology department at the LSE, who always inspired me to 'find the causes of things', and to my thesis examiners, Nick Long and Magnus Course, whose detailed feedback was instrumental in shaping this book. I am also immensely grateful to Llion Wigley, Dafydd Jones and an anonymous peer reviewer at University Wales Press for their patience, engagement, constructive feedback and support throughout this process. Additional thanks must also go to the Higher Education Funding Council for Wales (HEFCW) who funded the publication of this book, to the OpenUP Early Career Researcher Monograph Initiative who generously funded its Open Access publication, and to Efa Lois who illustrated the cover.

I joined Aberystwyth University's School of Education as a lecturer in August 2019. The final manuscript of this book was completed during a period as interim head of department of the School of Education (2023–4). I would like to extend my warmest thanks to colleagues in the School of Education for their support. Ruth Fowler, Dave Smith, Catrin Wyn Edwards, Beck Edwards, Colin McInnes, Lucy Taylor, Sarah Wydall, the FASS HoDs and colleagues in the Women in Research Network have also been incredibly supportive.

This book could not have existed without the participation of my interlocutors in Chubut. To my friends in Patagonia, who welcomed me into their community and lives with open arms as though as I was one of their own, thank you, for all that you taught me and continue to teach me, for the time we spent together, and for trusting me to tell your story. As always, I am especially grateful to my family. My three sisters Sarah, Sophie and Penny have been there through thick and thin. I express my deepest thanks to my mother Allyson Trotter, for her unwavering love and support, and to my much-missed father, David Andrew Trotter (27 July 1957–24 August 2015), who would have been delighted to see this book published. Finally, my wonderful son Matteo simply makes everything worthwhile, and this book is dedicated to him.

# A note on translation

Fieldwork was conducted through the medium of Welsh, English and Spanish. The book contains snippets of each language throughout to convey the linguistic diversity of conducting anthropological fieldwork in Welsh Patagonia. All translations between Welsh, English and Spanish are the author's own. Whilst great care has been taken to ensure that the meaning and nuance is not lost in the process of translation, any remaining errors are the author's own.

# 1

# Introduction: Musical encounters

'Singing was an essential part of social production and reproduction. It re-established the clarity of spatial domains, temporal durations, and certain forms of human relationships. Singing enabled individuals to create and express certain aspects of self, it established and sustained a feeling of euphoria characteristic of ceremonies, and it related the present to the powerful and transformative past'[1]

## Introduction: A Patagonian choir rehearsal

'Sopranos, *por favor*, watch the rhythm in bar forty-six. Ok, tenors solo from bar twenty ... Shh, *escuchen* (listen)! *Por favor*, sopranos, *escuchen*, so that you don't come in early!'

The light of the evening sun glinted through the window of the main hall of Gaiman Music School, throwing shadows on the tiled floor. The sound of the four-part choir resonated through the building, accompanied by the echoes of a backing track from a large, square speaker, the intermittent sounds of tapping feet, the scrambling turning of pages and the occasional interjection from the choir director, Maria, a strong, enthusiastic Welsh Patagonian woman with short curly hair, who never missed a beat. It was a Monday evening in spring, and the choir were rehearsing 'Môr a Mynydd' ('Summit to Sea'), which was a swing-style song written about Aberystwyth, a coastal university town in west Wales. Alberto, a local Welsh Patagonian composer and musician who had written the piece, stood at the edge of the rehearsal room in his characteristic combination of fleece and shorts, his glasses balancing precariously on the end of his nose, grinning widely.

The dotted rhythm of the swing beat combined with the first few moments of harmonious humming were what gave this song its lazy, finger-clicking feeling. The imagery invoked by the lyrics complemented this rhythm, as we sang in Welsh of young romance, 'lovers are whispering like the sun', 'the world wondering along the prom', of 'the waves lick[ing] the distant mountains', of 'waves like fields of wheat whispering in the bay', and of a still, tranquil presence in nature. These themes intertwined throughout the piece and the resulting musical message was simple: life is pretty good in Aberystwyth:

> Mae'r llyn mor agos heno [The lake is so close tonight],
> Mae'r byd yn crwydro hyd y prom [The world is wandering along the prom],
> Cariadon yn sibrwd fel yr haul [Lovers are whispering like the sun],
>   And waves like fields of wheat are whispering in the bay.
>     There are a thousand and more stories and histories
>       to tell ... to repeat and repeat, ha ha ha.
>
> Everyone is searching for some faith,
> They are like children with their ice-cream smiles.
> The lake is so close tonight,
>   And the world is wandering along the prom,
>     Lovers are whispering like the sun ...
>
> Mae'r llyn mor agos heno,
> But the distance is the same today and tomorrow.
>   There is nothing but movement and stillness of the water,
>   And the picture here is changing over time.
>
> The waves lick the distant mountains,
> As people greet each other on the prom.

Most – though not all – choir members could understand and speak at least a couple of sentences of Welsh. Even so, when a new piece of music with Welsh lyrics was distributed during our weekly rehearsals, we usually went through the lyrics together to reach an agreed translation. Maria stood up. '*Oes gyda chi eich pensiliau yn barod?*' (Have you got your pencils ready?) We nodded obediently. A woman sitting to my left stifled a yawn and I felt some fidgeting behind me. '*Bueno, excelente, vamos*, we will start from the start. "*Llyn mor agos*" means that the lake is close. *Se entienden?*' (Do you understand?) There was a pause, followed by the sound of pencils scribbling frantically. We continued like this, diligently, until we had reached a mutual understanding on the full translation of the piece. Geographically, the song was familiar to a few: some members of Gaiman girls' choir had visited Aberystwyth in 1997, and a couple of others had visited independently. However, the majority had to use their imagination, filling the disjuncture between context and music to sing about a place to which they had never been. Despite the initial efforts with translation, during the rehearsals that followed, whispers of '*Qué significa?*' (What does it mean?) and '*Dónde? Ble?*' (Where?) fluttered through the rows of choir members.

A month later, I was dressed in a black formal outfit, standing with the other choir members at the side of the stage in the Chubut Eisteddfod, holding our music folders, waiting to compete in the mixed choir competition. When we were called, we made our way in single file to the stage, where the squeaking of the benches underneath our feet seemed deafeningly loud in the full, silent hall. Maria pressed 'play' on the backing track, before stepping back to her place in front of the choir and raising her arms with a grin. We sang with great energy and enthusiasm, painting an idyllic image of Aberystwyth: seaside dreams full of beaches, promenades, ice cream, romance and happiness. The audience, largely made up of locals and tourists visiting from Wales, clapped vigorously when we finished our performance. We grinned and bowed collectively before returning to our seats, to listen to the other performances, and to eagerly anticipate the words that we had all been hoping and waiting for: '*Mae'r wobr gyntaf yn mynd i* [The first prize goes to] ... Escuela de Música Gaiman!'

This book focuses on the formation of Welsh subjectivity in the Chubut Province of Patagonia, Argentina, and draws out the importance of the creation, circulation, performance and enjoyment of music in that formation. The book therefore seeks to unpack the multiple, multisensory ways in which identity is constructed in this context. In doing so, the chapters that follow analyse a series of what Rosello and Covington-Ward (p. 9) have termed 'performative encounters' to consider the usefulness and limitations of theoretical concepts that have been developed and used to theorise the self, such as subjectivity, subjectivation, performance, performativity and self-cultivation.[2] I argue that in the context of the Welsh Patagonian settler colony, these concepts are theoretically valuable for the ways in which they draw attention to the role of power in shaping who people are and how they see themselves. In other words, some encounters in the settler colony *can* be usefully analysed as visual subjectivation. In Gaiman, however, the creation of Welshness was not only explicitly foregrounded in performances for tourists under an imagined Welsh gaze, but also, as in the vignette above, for a Welsh ear, with subjectivities created and re-created through musical encounters in different contexts.

The key ethnographic puzzle, therefore, that the book seeks to address is: how can we best understand the myriad ways in which subjectivity is constituted in Welsh Patagonia? The argument put forward here is that the Welsh Patagonian context, and critically, the significance of music in this context, adds a new dimension to visual tropes or metaphors that have typically been relied upon to theorise the process of subjectivation.[3] In the context of Welsh Patagonia, the choir rehearsal described above, for example, when considered as an encounter between different individuals in the field, had the capacity to performatively create Welshness as an image, along with feelings of unity and belonging, a process that was inevitably related to power structures in the community. These performances had different implications in terms of our understandings of the process of subjectivation and the subject. The book argues that whilst the element of recognition was key to subjectivation under the gaze, sonic interpellation worked best when my interlocutors were fully immersed in, and engaged in, the music or sound, therefore enabling an attention to the kind of self that was formed in multisensory contexts of encounter and to the power dynamics involved in that formation.

## Fieldwork context and methodology

Y Wladfa is one of five provinces in the region of Patagonia, south of Argentina, and is home to a community of around 5,000 Welsh-speaking individuals following a series of migrations from

Introduction: Musical encounters

Figure 1: Map of Argentina

Wales to the area in the late 1800s after Argentina opened its borders to immigrants. The largest group of individuals (153 men, women and children) migrated in 1865, on a tea-clipper called the *Mimosa*. This initial migration was followed by a series of smaller migrations, which ceased in 1914.[4] They live predominantly in the village of Gaiman, and have connections with the nearby town Trelew, as well as the surrounding areas of Puerto Madryn, Rawson, Dolavon, and the village of Trevelin near the town of Esquel in the Andes mountains. With a

5

population of 12,711, the village of Gaiman is small in comparison to Trelew and Rawson, which have a combined population of 146,620 as per the 2022 census.⁵ It is important to note, however, that Gaiman has grown rapidly over recent years. Nearby cities include the administrative city of Rawson, the seaside town of Puerto Madryn and the smaller seaside resort of Playa Union.⁶

This book is based on eighteen months of ethnographic fieldwork conducted between 2015 and 2017, with some evidence also drawn from fieldwork that took place between July and August 2013, on my first trip to the field as an anthropology undergraduate student. During fieldwork, Welsh culture, music and language were visibly thriving in Y Wladfa. The year 2015 was particularly significant, with celebrations of 150 years since the establishment of the settler colony intending to further strengthen the connections between Wales and Argentina. Gaiman was my main research location, and at the time of my fieldwork it was a small but rapidly expanding village. I travelled regularly by bus to Trelew to teach English in a private language institute and to meet with friends. I also visited Trevelin in Esquel for a brief fieldwork stint in November 2015, when I travelled with friends from both Wales and Welsh Patagonia to celebrate the anniversary of the founding of the village. Most of the data which informs the book was obtained from in-depth participant observation, formal and informal interviews, and focus groups with my interlocutors, though in January 2018, I also conducted archival research at the National Library of Wales. Finally, to complement the fieldwork conducted in the eisteddfodau in Patagonia, in August 2018, I conducted fieldwork at the National Eisteddfod of Wales, in Cardiff.

In terms of my methodological approach to writing the book, readers might wonder why I am so present in the dialogues and encounters presented throughout the chapters that follow. Even in a context where anthropologists have long moved away from the idea of an objective ethnography, this may be considered an unusual approach. However, Townsend and Cushion have argued that whilst focus on the agency of the researcher can be problematic, it is possible to work towards a more specific method of reflexivity, which includes, as Waquant puts it, 'a methodological reflection on the act of objectification itself'.⁷ This more in-depth reflexivity involves transparent discussions of the specific conditions that shape the research practice.

As Kaaristo notes, 'The qualitative researcher ... needs to constantly scrutinise both their own and the research participants' influence on the fieldwork process, choice of methods, particularities of knowledge creation and data analysis'.[8] Following this line of thinking, my reasons for this approach are twofold.

First, I believe that not shying away from including our own interactions in our work is key to an ethnography of encounters in that it foregrounds the dialogical nature of fieldwork in the analysis, situates us within the power relations in the field and in relation to our interlocutors, and enables us, in addition to our interlocutors, to be open to the interpretation and critical analysis of readers.[9] Funder highlights the importance of making power explicit and open to interpretation, arguing that we can do this through exposing 'efforts to engage other actor's perceptions of the researcher's biases and interpretations' and by paying 'attention to the role and implications of the power relations and associated world views and epistemologies of which the researcher forms part at home and in the field'.[10] In my fieldwork situation this was also made more complex by my background as being Welsh. This book therefore considers ethnography as a 'data co-creation process'.[11] In doing so, it includes my own reactions and emotions in conversations or situations with others, presented here as an 'interplay of voices', reflections on the research practice itself and discussions of both my interlocutors' perceptions of me as a researcher and the role of my own bias in shaping the research.[12]

Secondly, Clifford describes 'the predominant metaphors in anthropological research [as being] participant-observation, data collection, and cultural description, all of which presuppose a standpoint outside – looking at, objectifying, or, somewhat closer, "reading" a given reality'.[13] One of the key arguments of the book is that there has been an over-reliance on the visual in theorising the subject in the social science disciplines, which has obscured the specific means by which subjectivation through music occurs – often alongside, or sometimes instead of – visual subjectivation. In Gaiman, alternatively, becoming a subject happened in some contexts through processes of gazing or looking, but was also about music and sound. Following Clifford, my intention here is to embed a personal narrative within the description to present an ethnography that is more in line with the personalisation of sound, whereby 'once cultures are no longer prefigured visually – as objects, theatres, texts – it becomes possible to think of a cultural poetics that is an interplay of voices, of positioned utterances'.[14] Ultimately, to write an objective and detached ethnography which is based – however subtly so – on visual metaphors of research, writing and data presentation would go against the very argument of the book.

## On being a Welsh, white woman in Argentina

As Fetterman puts it, anthropologists 'enter the field with an open mind, not an empty head'.[15] My subjectivity and unconscious biases influenced the data collected and therefore the argument of the book. I already had my own political views about what were controversial themes in the field, such as the debates on the legalisation of abortion, gender dynamics or the power differences between the Welsh Patagonians and local Argentinians. Navigating the balance between cultural relativism, productive data collection and my own desire to argue for what I believe in presented some difficult (yet anthropologically revealing) fieldwork situations, defined by Guillemin and Gillam as 'ethically important moments'.[16] Furthermore, I grew up in Wales and am a fluent Welsh speaker, and these two factors were both an asset and a hindrance to this project. They were an asset in the sense that I was readily welcomed into the community, and my presence was not deemed threatening in any way in a context where the community were familiar with receiving (white) tourists from Wales. The mutual language was also a great help during the early months of fieldwork whilst I learnt Spanish. However, in some ways, this immediate identification as Welsh also made it more challenging to connect with my local Argentinian interlocutors. The conflation of me with a Welsh tourist generated another logistical challenge which was how to clearly demonstrate to my interlocutors the concrete differences between tourism and anthropology. This was especially significant given that the majority of what my interlocutors would consider to be visible 'work' took place behind closed doors – my fieldnotes were written up from scratch-notes late at night, when the days' activities were long over.

As a cellist and singer, my place within Gaiman Music School was established within days of my first trip to the field in 2013, and I slotted back into this role easily upon my return in 2015. Most of the fieldwork revolved heavily around activities related to the music school. I participated in the mixed choir and the girls' choir, sung in various groups for the eisteddfod, played cello in the string ensemble, accompanied choirs on cello, played in smaller ensembles for several concerts in various chapels, performed solo cello concerts and attended a term of violin lessons. I also attended and participated in three end-of-year music school concerts. Ultimately, the impact of these musical skills on the project highlights the subjective nature of qualitative research. Without these musical skills, I would have been unable to fully participate in the activities, and this book would have looked very different.

Another key factor influencing my interactions in the field and therefore the data presented in the book is my gender as a woman. Whilst I could do little to escape the daily cat-calling on the streets, with a friend stating the reason for this as being 'you look different, you wear those boots [Dr Martens], that is why', it should be noted that living alone, renting a *quincho*, working as an English teacher in Trelew and owning my own bicycle offered me a higher level of independence in relation to many of the young women of my age whom I met during fieldwork.[17] I maintained this independence throughout the duration of fieldwork, which arguably limits my capacity to comment fully on the experience of being a woman in Argentina. Further, despite my best attempts at encouraging the more fluid gender boundaries that I had heard of anthropologists experiencing during fieldwork, this was challenging due to both the nature of qualitative research as a woman and the strict gendered spheres in Argentina.[18] As Moreno argues, 'In the field, it is not possible to maintain the fiction of a genderless self. In the field, one is marked.'[19] The name *la chica galesa* ('the Welsh girl') stuck, and throughout fieldwork many spheres, such as rugby, poker nights and especially football, were inaccessible to me.[20] Ultimately, however, my identity as a white female smoothed access to certain spheres of social life, and my independence meant that I was allowed into women's worlds without being entirely confined to them.

## Key concepts

The concept of 'encounter' is central to the book, and my use of it draws largely on the work of Sartre, Lacan and Althusser, who each, in their own ways, emphasise a metaphorical interaction between the self and an 'other', highlighting the power relations embodied in subjectivation.[21] Levinas, though he is not often considered alongside these scholars, took this beyond the abstract to develop a theory of a face-to-face encounter, which he described as a relationship that helps us to escape the 'solitude of being'.[22] Morgan explains that for Levinas,

> the face-to-face encounter between the self and the other person ... is not an idea or concept, nor a type of action or event. It is a concrete reality, an event; it occurs. Furthermore, it occurs as utterly particular: the self is a particular person, and the face-of-the-other is a particular revelation of a particular person.[23]

Levinas's focus is on the ethical dimension of this encounter, and on our mutual responsibilities. For Levinas, 'every encounter between one person and another, is always *already* such a nexus of plea, command, and inescapable responsibility, *before* it is anything else – which it always is'. Whilst his account has been criticised for its extreme view of ethics, it is valuable to consider his focus on the engagement of concrete individuals with one another, and the implications of these encounters in terms of responsibility, not only to each other, but also to the broader community.[24]

Faier and Rofel argue that 'ethnographies of encounter ... consider how culture making occurs through everyday encounters among members of two or more groups with different cultural backgrounds and unequally positioned stakes in their relationships'.[25] The book explores a series of concrete encounters in the Chubut Province of Patagonia, Argentina, taking as foundational the ways in which interactions with others were *constitutive* of Welshness rather than reflective of a stable pre-existing Welsh essence. Subjectivity is considered throughout as both an individual and a collective concept.[26] The encounters focused on here are those that occurred between Welsh tourists and local Welsh Patagonians (chapter 4), between performers and their performance on film (chapter 5), between music and the community, and between the self and the ideal musical 'I' (chapter 6). The analysis of these encounters follows a preliminary exploration of encounters which occurred historically between the Indigenous

Tehuelche and Mapuche communities and the Welsh settlers (chapter 2), and of encounters between the Welsh Patagonian community and locals and tourists in formal performance contexts – namely the Chubut Eisteddfod (chapter 3). Ultimately, the book argues that subjectivity was constituted differently through the power dynamics of seeing and being seen, and of hearing and being heard.

## Performativity, performance, subjectivity and subjectivation

The theoretical concepts of performativity, performance, subjectivity and subjectivation are pushed forward in the book, and it is important to clarify these in terms of how they specifically relate to the context of Welsh Patagonia. Performativity (daily habits and actions which constitute identity) and performance (larger cultural performances) are taken as interrelated terms, enabling a consideration of the relationships between everyday acts and more formal performances.[27] Chapter 3, '"Eisteddfodamos": eisteddfod as ritual performance', which considers the eisteddfod in its broader social, historical and political context, is where this interrelation is at its most explicit. Likewise, subjectivation and subjectivity are viewed as interrelated, with subjectivation used throughout to refer to the process by which subjectivity is constituted. The latter is defined by Ortner as 'the ensemble modes of perception, affect, thought, desire, fear, and so forth that animate acting subjects… [in addition to] the cultural and social formations that shape, organise, and provoke those modes of affect, thought, etc'. This definition focuses on understanding the interactions between culture and the individual, what Ortner calls the 'inner states of acting subjects', which also includes an element of 'collective sensibility'.[28]

Four key metaphors and allegories which speak to these key concepts are fundamental to understanding the first part of the book, which explores encounters between tourists and Welsh Patagonians and during film nights organised in the village. Each of these examples, in their own ways, argue that subjectivation – that is, coming into being as a subject – occurs when subjects are interpellated by either the power of the gaze, or an imagined gaze.

First, Foucault, in *Governmentality*, draws on Bentham's idea of the panopticon to argue that the prisoners are controlled through the constant possibility that they are being watched.[29] According to this theory, prisoners in cells in a circular room can never be sure if the guard in a tower in the centre of the room is looking at them, and therefore the sheer possibility that they could be being watched at any time serves to discipline them.[30] Secondly, Sartre, in *Being and Nothingness*, argues that when an individual is caught engaging in a socially unacceptable activity (in his example, peering through a keyhole), that individual becomes aware of themself as a subject under the gaze of the other.[31] Sartre focuses specifically on the feelings of shame involved in this – the individual caught looking through the keyhole feels a deep sense of shame, knowing how they must appear to the onlooker. Thirdly, Althusser develops a useful allegory of a police officer shouting 'Hey, you!' at an individual on the street.[32] He argues that when an individual turns around in recognition of and response to the police officer, they are brought into being as a subject of state ideology. This, of course, depends on the individual seeing the police officer, and recognising his or her uniform as a visual symbol of state authority.[33] Finally, Lacan, though he is not often considered alongside Foucault, Sartre or Althusser also develops a theory of subjectivation of which looking is a central component.[34] In his mirror stage theory, he argues that an infant, at around the age of 18 months, develops a sense of self through seeing his or her body and actions in a mirror or reflected in a caregiver.[35] The infant recognises the gap between the self as experienced and the ideal 'I' reflected in the mirror, viewing the ideal 'I' as something to work towards.[36]

A consideration of Lacan's work alongside Sartre's ideas enables us to account for the element of desire or awareness involved in becoming a subject (as opposed to a sole focus on shame), or for the ways in which people do, to some extent, fashion – and desire to fashion – themselves.[37] These elements of desire, awareness and mastery in subjectivation are explored in detail in chapter 4, 'Performing Patagonia under the gaze of the Welsh other', which argues that Welsh Patagonia was created as a concrete entity when it was performed to, imagined by and watched by Welsh tourists and officials. What became clear during fieldwork was that performance and performativity could invoke feelings of Welshness even whilst there was an awareness of the performative element of this. In fact, the recognition or self-awareness of visual subjectivation – understanding that Welsh tourists had a particular image of what the Welsh community would be like and performing that image consciously – was key to its success. Covington-Ward argues that this is central to performance, stating that 'performance is reflexive and involves manipulation of behaviour, based on the awareness of being observed'.[38] In Welsh Patagonia, Welshness was often performed to outsiders, with the moment of encounter between the gaze of the Welsh other and the performers serving to constitute the very subjectivity that was being performed. Key to this chapter is an analysis which follows work in Critical Tourism Studies, allowing for the consideration of the performative tourist interactions in their broader structural context.[39]

Lacan's concept of the mirror stage has been foundational to film theory, and his theory enables us to further consider the concepts of desire, self-awareness, the mutual gaze and the role of documentary films in the valley in the process of subjectivation. Chapter 5, 'Mirror, mirror on the wall, who is the most Welsh of them all?' builds on this work, focusing on film nights that were held in the Casa de Cultura (arts centre) in Gaiman, events at which my interlocutors gathered for social evenings to view their own performance as Welsh Patagonians in films that had been created in and about the settler colony.

Much of the work focusing on the constitution of subjectivity in relation to power structures has focused on the power dynamics of seeing and being seen, and in doing so has drawn primarily on visual metaphors to consider the ways in which gazing, looking or imagining the look of another plays a role in subject formation.[40] Looking is central to Althusser's analysis (the individual on the street must turn around and see the police officer, wearing, no doubt, a uniform which acts as a visual symbol of power and social position), but interpellation is also mediated through language – the police officer shouts, 'Hey, you!'[41] For Foucault and Sartre, coming into being in relation to the gaze, or the imagined gaze of the other does not require sound. Lacan's mirror theory similarly depends on an infant looking at his or her own mirrored image rather than hearing his or her own voice. For each of these theorists, the element of recognition is also important. For Sartre, the individual peering through a keyhole becomes a subject at the exact moment in which they realise the presence of the other. Althusser and Lacan both argued (in different ways) that whilst subjectivation is not momentary but permanent, the key moments of recognition, interpellation and encounter are still significant, in that subjects must turn around, look up or see themselves in a mirror to continually reaffirm themselves as subjects.

Whilst my intention here is not to do away with the importance and value of these theories of visual subjectivation, the focus on rehearsing and performing Welsh music in the province meant that much of the work of constituting subjectivity challenged these visual tropes as it occurred in a musical context. Chapter 6, '"The community is a family, and the choir is the glue": performing Patagonia for the ear of the Welsh other', is about the specific role of music in creating Welshness in Welsh Patagonia. It considers the role of music in the creation of Welshness and belonging, in addition to unpacking the relationship between music and power in the Welsh Patagonian context. Other scholars have pointed to non-linguistic sound, music, music lessons and musical structure as contributing towards subject formation.[42] Rice, in his ethnography of an Edinburgh hospital, argues that the formation of the 'patient-self' takes place in response to being interpellated by hospital sounds which structure the patient's experience of time and space in the hospital.[43] McClary discusses the way in which gendered subjects are created through nineteenth-century operatic discourse, and Mills discusses the ways in which pupils in schools are discursively constituted through the labelling of them by teachers as either 'musical' or as 'non-musical'.[44] Others have focused more broadly on music and its relation to power, relating musical practice or structure to gendered ideology or class structures.[45] The key role of music in Welsh Patagonia emphasises the necessity of allowing space in our analysis for a multisensory theory of subjectivation and subjectivity in which the power of music, and what Weidman has termed 'the poetics and politics of spoken and sung forms' can be acknowledged.[46]

The final part of the book is concerned with the way in which the senses have been theorised within subjectivity studies, whilst acknowledging the work that has already been done in terms of theorising sound in the anthropology of the senses, ethnomusicology and with the concept of soundscape.[47] The book argues that the concept of seeing and being seen is useful to understand *some* encounters in Welsh Patagonia, but it cannot fully account for subjectivation in relation to music. In Welsh Patagonia, many of the encounters were musical encounters in that they that occurred during choir, orchestra or string group rehearsals, in addition to during concerts, performances and festivals. These encounters between music and the community and between music and the self means that understanding what it means to be Welsh in Welsh Patagonia necessitated a consideration not only of the ways in which performativity and subjectivation were central to self-cultivation but, critically, how this was musically realised.

For my interlocutors in Welsh Patagonia, key to subjectivation through music was the moment of 'flow' – an experience of complete absorption, engagement with and immersion in the act of listening to or playing music.[48] Flow in musical performance is characterised by a lack of self-consciousness.[49] Hackert et al. have argued that flow 'can (and should) be investigated as an emergent state of groups', highlighting the ways in which group flow consists of a 'peak group state and a collective state of mind'.[50] The suggestion here is that, in contrast to interpellation through the gaze, for which an element of recognition or self-awareness was necessary to subjectivation, in the context of music, interpellation was at its most successful during this moment of flow, and this exists at both an individual level and at a group level, such as during choir rehearsals or performances.[51] The distinctive contribution of the book is in the foregrounding of the importance of the specific 'others' in relation to which subjectivation occurs, and in the attention to the multisensory nature of performative encounters. Ultimately, the book explores how performing Welshness for a Welsh ear or a Welsh gaze changes our understanding of the power dynamics involved in these encounters, pointing towards a self that is more relational, more porous and more permeable than is implied in visual and discursive theories.

# 2
## A little Wales away from Wales

> It was not like the dear land of Wales, but brown and barren with sparse, tufted, coarse grass and stunted bush expanding in every direction. The cliffs on either side of the Bay were whitish under thin dark caps of struggling growth in the grip of midwinter. The immigrants stood mute before a landscape of mystery. Expressions of disappointment essayed the landscape.[1]

### Introduction: #Paithlife

> Look, do you see to the left? Nothing! Nothing! It is like this between Gaiman and Trelew and Madryn ... empty. So different to Wales. Those big green hills – we have a shock arriving in Wales. We have ... become used to it, the flat land ... *viste*? We have become so used to the difficult land, dry land. We love it! That is the land that the original settlers arrived on, so it is in our blood. That is why there aren't loads of animals or plants there; they can't *live, viste* ... no ... it's impossible. But in the middle of the *paith* there are some big spiders, pumas and snakes. Sometimes they come down to Gaiman in the summer to look for shade. Be careful!

I gulped. Rosario glanced at me from her driver's seat and proceeded to howl with laughter as we made our way to Trelew. 'Are you enjoying the guided tour?' she asked, bursting into laughter again. Rosario was great fun – an intelligent, quick-witted, down-to-earth woman who became a close friend during fieldwork. Her great-great grandfather was one of the first settlers to arrive in Chubut on the *Mimosa* tea-clipper, but she tended to distance herself socially from the Welsh Patagonian community, preferring to spend time with her Argentinian friends outside work hours. We first met in 2013, when she worked as an English teacher in Ysgol yr Hendre, the bilingual Spanish and Welsh primary school in Trelew. Since meeting her she had become a mother, and at the time of my fieldwork, was taking a break from work to look after her 2-year-old son before later beginning a new job at Ysgol Gymraeg y Gaiman (the Welsh medium primary school) in Gaiman. We soon stopped at a traffic light and glancing at me again she opted for a more reassuring tone, '*No te preocupes*, don't worry, you can come to my house, and we will drink *mate* if a big spider ... especially a tarantula ... goes in your house.' I laughed too, 'I think I might have to!' She shook her head, laughing, and a long wisp of dark hair fell across her face as she turned the local radio on.

The light turned to green. We continued. Rosario looked ahead, humming along to a tune on the radio, which was barely audible beneath the crackle, and I turned my attention to the right to the residential area between Gaiman and Trelew. I could see rows of houses, closely spaced together, and made from tin, wood, stones and pieces of cloth. There were people cycling, children walking, large stray dogs running free and run-down cars parked outside some of the homes. 'Who lives there?' I asked Rosario. Her response was quick. 'It is a *barrio* for poor people. Why do you ask? Don't say you want to live or work there? *Estás loca*. For a clever girl you are sometimes *muy pelotuda*. *Por favor*. You'll get robbed in two ... three minutes, or worse.' I took her word for it. Yet, in the days, weeks and months that were to follow, whilst travelling past, my eyes would be drawn to the windows of buses and cars for glimpses of life in this other *barrio*. As I watched mothers hanging their children's washing, neighbours talking amongst themselves and children playing football in the streets, I would wonder who lived there, and what their stories were.

A few months later, I found myself on a bus from Gaiman to Puerto Madryn with Amy, an English-speaking Welsh tourist who was visiting Gaiman for a couple of days. We had met at the beginning of her visit and were going to spend the afternoon at the beach before she travelled on to the Andes. Using her mobile phone, she quickly snapped a photo out of the window of the open *paith* and showed it to me. 'Do you like it? I might upload it to Instagram.' The photo showed the bus curtain, the slightly dirty window, and beyond that, the enormity and vastness of the *paith*. The flatness of the land and clarity of the blue sky were perhaps what made it characteristically Patagonian. I shrugged, and responded, 'Yeah, I like it, it is a good photo.' She smiled, 'Great, glad you like it, I'm uploading it now. What hashtag shall I use? Hashtag Patagonia ... hashtag *paith* ... hashtag goingtothebeach. Oh my gosh, I've just thought of a really good one. What about hashtag paithlife? Let's get it *trending*.'

Both these encounters, despite being a few months apart, embodied key themes that resonated with the politically complicated history of the establishment of the Welsh settler colony in the Chubut Province. Amy's photo of the empty landscape, which she considered to be the perfect representation of Patagonia to share on social media, and Rosario's comment about the neighbourhood between Gaiman and Trelew, both obscured, in different ways, the diversity of Chubut by focusing, however subtly, on the Welsh descendants as being the only meaningful inhabitants. Ultimately, the photo and the comment both reproduced the dominant historical narrative of the arrival of the Welsh settlers to the settler colony (which largely focused on arrival to an empty, barren terrain which they transformed into a fruitful agricultural province) whilst also touching on more current themes of visual representation and social media, which were key elements in portraying Patagonia to potential tourists and therefore fundamental in the present-day construction of Welsh Patagonia.

This chapter provides an historical and sociological contextualisation of Welsh Patagonia, in doing so arguing that the establishment of Welsh Patagonia as a tangible and separate place has rested on, and relied on, specific political representations of Indigenous people – as absent, friends or dangerous. Following an overview of the dominant narrative of the landing of the settlers, it discusses the ways in which this narrative of the establishment of Welsh Patagonia is challenged by an historical overview from the 1800s to the time of the research (between 2015 and 2017), which considers the establishment of the Argentine state, immigration policy in Argentina between the late 1800s and 1900s,[2] the Conquest of the Desert, and the changing political position of the Welsh and the Welsh language in Patagonia in relation to Indigenous groups. Finally, the fieldwork context is considered. One of the dominant discursive tropes at the time of the research was an emphasis on European descent, or what Lublin has referred to as the 'myth of whiteness', which was a key means by which the settler colony was depoliticised during the time of fieldwork.[3]

In contextualising the chapter in relation to the remainder of the book, it is important to draw attention to the most obvious limitation of the book. Despite the focus on the encounter between the Welsh settlers and the Tehuelche in this chapter, with the argument being that they were made absent in historical representations of the establishment of the settler colony, they remain relatively absent for the remainder of the book too. Whilst this chapter seeks to provide an historical and geographical contextualisation, and to de-romanticise the beginnings of Welsh Patagonia, the remainder of the book focuses on a specific period of fieldwork between 2015 and 2017, and on the role of the gaze, music and other processes of subjectivation in the creation of Welshness in that context. The book, therefore, does not make any claims to analyse present-day relationships between Welsh settlers and Tehuelche or Mapuche, in part because there was a silence around discussions of Tehuelche and Mapuche groups within the Welsh Patagonian community,[4] and in part because present-day interactions between these groups – and thus the data collection on them – were not a feature of fieldwork. Therefore, the remainder of the book, whilst it builds on the historical context outlined in this chapter, seeks to analyse interactions that were organically present in fieldwork – those between the Welsh Patagonians, tourists from Wales and local Argentinians.

This chapter explores the political significance of the way in which the initial establishment of Welsh Patagonia as a place has been discursively constructed through representations and omissions of the relationship between the Welsh settlers and the local Indigenous people through various media: the press, popular literature including children's books, the Welsh curriculum and museums in Patagonia. It demonstrates how the dominant popular construction of the historical encounters between the Welsh settlers and local Indigenous people (specifically the Tehuelche and Mapuche) must be taken into consideration in relation to the present-day continuous construction of the subjectivity of the colony as a separate and pure place of Welshness, as illustrated in the fieldwork vignette with which the chapter opened. In sum, the chapter argues that the construction and performance of the Welsh settler colony was dependent – albeit sometimes in subtle ways – on specific representations of Indigenous people, and that the narratives explored in the chapter have also worked to obscure the structural violence that enabled the construction of the Welsh settler colony.

### The landing: 28 July 1865

> Though I have never seen a ship,
> And though my years are quite four score,
> If God permit, I'll join this trip,
> For Patagonia's distant shore![5]

On 28 July 1865, the *Mimosa*, a tea-clipper, pulled into the shores of Puerto Madryn. On board were a group of 153 Welsh men, women and children, who had boarded the ship in Liverpool two months earlier, and emigrated to Argentina, under the leadership of the independent minister Michael D. Jones.[6] The motivations of these 153 Welsh men, women and children who emigrated to Chubut can only be understood within the context of the social dynamics of nineteenth-century Wales.[7] The social relations of the Welsh and English (broadly speaking) who were living in Wales at the time were strained: 'despite the vigorous survival of the Welsh language ... there was no such place as Wales'.[8] Schools operated exclusively in English, and individuals caught speaking Welsh were made to wear the 'Welsh Not', a wooden plaque worn around the neck to symbolise shame.[9] In the workplace, those in positions of seniority tended to be English-speaking whereas the workers were Welsh-speaking, serving to economically reinforce these hierarchical divisions.[10] In the religious domain, the Welsh settlers dreamt of 'religious liberty' to maintain their evangelical Welsh-language religious practice in the chapels away from the influence of Roman Catholicism.[11] Michael D. Jones 'believed that the Welsh language was so inextricably linked to the national identity that losing it was virtually equivalent to being left without Welsh customs, values, and religion, which was what prompted him to act'.[12]

In nineteenth-century Wales, the 'basic ... thesis [was one] of the classless Welsh "gwerin" [variously tenant-farmers, slate quarriers, etc.] suffering from oppression at the hands of the English'.[13] It was in response to this increasing anglicisation of Wales that another group of around 2,000 migrated to Pennsylvania in North America. Despite their best efforts towards independence, they became rapidly integrated with US society, and quickly spread beyond Pennsylvania to other states, especially Ohio and New York.[14] To board the *Mimosa*, to develop a new colony in the Chubut, would be to preserve and strengthen Welsh culture and language in isolation from what was perceived to be the otherwise inescapable Englishness of Wales.[15] As noted in a London newspaper article published in 1867:

> Some Welsh patriots have lately spent some thousands of pounds in an effort to preserve their race and language. For this purpose they selected Patagonia as a favourable site for a colony, *being sufficiently removed from the contagion of the English-speaking races* ... One or two hundred Welsh men and women have been living there for a couple of years, speaking Welsh, no doubt, with the utmost purity, but obliged to subsist on the charity of the Argentine Government. It is doubtful whether they may not in time succeed in making their own living, *but the chances seem to be against it*. If it fails, the last hope of preserving a distinct Welsh nationality will probably disappear; the Welsh will have to reconcile themselves to the prospect that their language will gradually cease to be a living one.[16]

The move to Chubut, as well as being a response to the tentative relations between the Welsh and English, was also, at least in part, a response to the rapid assimilation in North America, which was viewed by the settlers as a failure on the part of the North American migration. Central to the move was a determination to maintain cultural independence in Argentina, where they had secured an offer from the Argentine government of 100 square miles in the Chubut Valley. As Lublin argues:

> The only way to preserve Welshness was to streamline migration to a single settlement where the Welsh would be the dominant 'formative' element rather than the 'assimilative' one, which led to a favouring of Patagonia over locations such

as Vancouver, Palestine or Brazil because of its isolation from a potentially dominant non-Welsh majority culture.[17]

Settling in the Chubut Province was to do with the hope for a better life, with one of its foundational principles being to preserve and strengthen the Welsh language and culture away from the threat of the English, a preservation which the previous migrants who left for North America had, in the eyes of these 153, failed to achieve.[18] In addition to its relationship with Welshness in nineteenth-century Wales, the migration from Wales to Argentina cannot be considered outside the rapidly changing Argentine context. The migration to Argentina followed a period of political upheaval within the country: 1816 saw the end of colonial rule and independence from Spain, which was followed by decades of civil war and turmoil under the repressive dictatorship of Juan Manuel de Rosas. Rosas was initially the governor of the province of Buenos Aires, who pushed to 'enhance the economic, political, and military power of Buenos Aires'.[19] By 1848, he was the ruler of Argentina.

Political resistance to Rosas followed in the form of a push to create a centralised government. A national government took shape in 1853 but dissolved in 1861.[20] Due to his then-position as the governor of Buenos Aires, Bartolomé Mitre was automatically made the first president of the Argentine Republic, with his term lasting from 1862 until 1868. He did not resist the unification of the country, though he made sure that he only supported it in such a way that would benefit Buenos Aires. Mitre was very much focused on economic modernisation through the expansion of railway services, and through immigration.[21] Lewis argues that during this time, Argentina's 'political system ... appeared more stable and democratic than it was in practice: violence, systematic fraud, and corruption left the concerns of the majority without representation'.[22]

Between the 1800s and 1900s, the population of Argentina grew rapidly, with immigration from Europe being key to this demographic transformation.[23] As Lewis puts it, 'settlers and investors came to see Argentina as a land of opportunity. Its open spaces seemed rich with potential'.[24] Immigration policies at the time also provided an incentive for immigrants to enable them to settle, including food, shelter and space.[25] Germani and Meter both emphasise the impact of European immigration on the demography of Argentina, in economic and social terms, highlighting that the modification of the population was a key goal of the Argentine government.[26] This increased communication and connection remained the case even whilst some communities (including the Welsh settlers) sought to segregate themselves. As Germani notes, 'Even if they have not lost all emotional ties with their fatherlands, they show an increasing identification with their home country.'[27] Ultimately, this was the political backdrop on 28 July 1865, when 'after much suffering and many perils, both on Sea and Land, the [Welsh settlers] found themselves together on the banks of Chubut in Patagonia, some 7,000 miles distant from the old home'.[28]

### The arrival: empty landscape or friendly relations?

In discussions of the arrival to Patagonia, the Welsh settlers have often been depicted as arriving at an empty, *desierto* (desert) and *vacío* (empty) landscape, whereby the settlers were 'shunted aside in a lonely valley, in the solitude of the illimitable expanse of the Patagonian plains'.[29] There has been the argument, often seen in children's books, popular literature, memoirs, local museums, documentary films, radio programmes and in the Welsh curriculum taught in primary and secondary schools in Wales, that the settlers arrived at an empty landscape, whereby they were presented with further difficulties due to the wilderness of the terrain.[30] The terrain was tough – in contrast to the 'paradise' promised, the soil was 'dry [and] brittle'.[31] Here, the emphasis has tended to be on the idea that the Argentine government provided the Welsh settlers with land, and that they struggled initially, but enjoyed relative independence thereafter.[32] The land is described as difficult terrain, but the depiction of the relations of the Welsh settlers and Indigenous people are often vague, absent, or described as being reciprocal and positive.[33]

When the relations between the Welsh settlers and the Tehuelche *have been* included in the dominant narrative, they have often been discussed in terms of friendship. E. Wyn James, for example, in a discussion on BBC Radio 4 emphasises the reciprocal relations between what he refers to as the 'nomadic Indigenous people' and the Welsh settlers.[34] Whitfield likewise states that 'the Welsh lived peacefully in Patagonia alongside the native Tehuelche, trading with them and

Figure 2: Map of indigenous populations

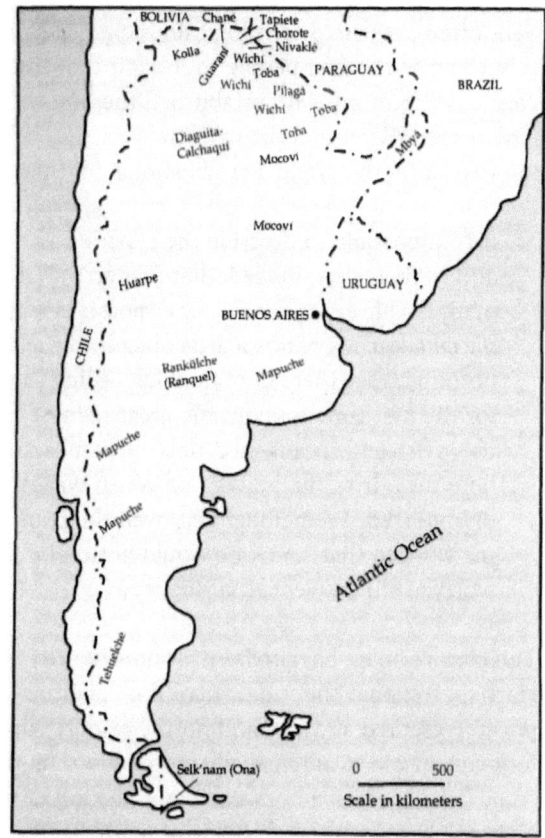

learning survival strategies from them'.[35] Rhys notes that 'the Colonists treated the natives consistently with much consideration and with wonderful patience and indulgence'.[36] The inclusion in terms of friendship, whilst potentially an accurate depiction of the individual relations between the Welsh settlers and Indigenous Tehuelche, remains problematic, in that it obscures the specific political and historical context, leading to an idealistic and romanticised picture of the establishment of the settler colony.

These narratives of arrival of the Welsh Patagonian community remained prominent in the more recent context too and were influential with regards to the perceptions of Welsh Patagonians and tourists from Wales, as evident in the two short vignettes with which this chapter opens. Within museums in the valley, historical narratives were often presented teleologically, acknowledging the Indigenous Tehuelche as the first people to inhabit the land, but depicting the Welsh as the 'group who established the first *permanent* and *lasting* settlements'.[37] Consider the narrative of arrival below from 1981, over 100 years after the original establishment of the settler colony:

> It is impossible to describe the experience of arriving at the airport at Trelew. Indeed, that first arrival in 1981 is still one of my big life experiences. The airport is in an *extreme desert in the middle of the prairie* a little outside of the city and there is nothing to see there but brambles. Seeing the endless prairie for the first time brought me great sadness … To think that the Welsh left a beautiful country to come to such a place. But here they drowned in a sea of Welsh voices and all sadness disappeared. I remember very well the tears that first time, me worried that someone would notice, but I didn't have to worry at all; we were all crying.[38]

This curious image has also been prominent in depictions of Amazonia. Harris states that the Amazonian floodplain has been 'traditionally [mis]represented as a vast and hostile resource domain', arguing that to focus on the social instead is to realise that 'the floodplain landscape [is] a lived one, born of the interaction of people and places'.[39] Nugent likewise draws on his work with a community of Sephardic Jews who have been resident in Amazonia since the 1820s to counteract 'the view … that Amazonia is fundamentally a natural resource domain lacking a significant social presence'.[40] More recently, Bartles has drawn on analysis of Argentine film to argue that the recurring focus in film on empty spaces and vast uninhabited landscapes serves to revitalise essentialist tropes whereby Argentina is depicted as a desert.[41] In each of these diverse Latin American contexts, the emphasis on the empty land obscures the local inhabitants, which risks justifying their exploitation.

### The political context: the Conquest of the Desert and political dichotomies

This dominant narrative, however, is challenged by academic discussions of the settler colony.[42] These alternative critical analyses have recognised the complexity of the Welsh Patagonian situation, highlighting that when the Welsh settlers arrived in Chubut, the land was already occupied, with Indigenous Tehuelche.[43] Lucy Taylor's work describes the changing relations between the Welsh settlers and the local Tehuelche.[44] According to her analysis, the two groups did, at the beginning, enjoy brief cooperative relations, insofar as after the 'Welsh arrival the [Tehuelche] autonomy was largely untroubled, their language and cultural life was unchallenged'.[45] During the first years in the Chubut Province, the Welsh settlers and the Tehuelche maintained their own separate systems of education, economics and their own local political and religious institutions. This remained the case despite the Welsh settlers receiving support from the Argentine government. The Tehuelche, reportedly, 'deemed the Welsh less of a menace than the Argentine government and were contented to see [the Welsh settlers] colonize on the Chupat, as trading with them would be easier than with the 280-mile distant Carmen de Patagones'.[46]

However, in the 1870s, when General Julio Argentino Roca sought to establish state control over Patagonia, the Welsh were essentially required to 'take sides' and, due 'to their geographical origin and skin colour, they were drawn into the category of Argentine civilisation'.[47] As Taylor puts it:

> far from being benign ... 'friendship' can legitimise colonisation by stripping it of the obvious violence associated with political domination, asset appropriation, and cultural oppression. Clothed in the warm and fuzzy sensations of camaraderie and mutual help, shared campfires and fair trade, colonialism becomes veiled in kindness.[48]

Lublin notes that 'winds of change were blowing in Patagonia, as the infamous "Conquest of the Desert" (1879–1884) spelt the end of successful trade between the Welsh and the Tehuelche with its systematic persecution, imprisonment, and murder of Indigenous populations'.[49]

The Welsh settlers were involved in a broader political project, and in doing so were complicit in oppressing the Tehuelche, a point which is often overlooked in popular or media depictions of the settler colony. As Bletz puts it, we must consider the ways in which identities are created in the historical context of the country which are hosting them.[50] Taylor's analysis likewise points to a very different outlook of the history of the Welsh settlers, one which is more in line with Veracini and Johnston and Lawson's perception of 'settler colonies' as perpetuating more subtle oppression in terms that are not necessarily physical.[51] Military occupation (the 'Conquest of the Desert') served to consolidate these dichotomies, with the state seeking to violently eliminate Indigenous groups. In this context:

> Insofar as the nomadic habits of Patagonia's Indigenous people allowed the authorities conveniently to describe the region as a desert, the settlement of white northern European populations (the Welsh were virtually synonymous with the Anglo-Saxon from an Argentinian perspective) in the then frontier territory of Patagonia had a twofold objective. On the one hand, it was expected to plant the seed of civilisation in that remote corner of the country, contributing to the government strategy to counter Indigenous primitiveness with progress. At the same time, it was meant to realise the Argentine claim, until then merely nominal, to the region, under threat both from Chile's expansionist designs and from European imperialism.[52]

Gordillo and Hirsch, in their introductory article to a special issue of *The Journal of Latin American Anthropology* on Argentina, explain the offer of the 100 square miles of land in terms of the historical trajectory of Argentine state policies vis-à-vis Indigenous groups.[53] They argue that in the nineteenth century, whilst discourses of celebration of indigeneity were typical of other Latin American countries such as Mexico, Peru or Brazil, Argentina was contrastingly constituted on a discourse of homogenous Europeanness. Argentina had opened its doors to (white) immigrants in conjunction with a systematic attempt to eliminate its Indigenous populations. Endere describes how during this time, the government presented a unified culture based on defending religious (Christian) values and remembering historic heroes.[54] In this context, Indigenous populations, religious minorities and non-European immigrants were absent in official historical narratives and museums. Vom Hau and Wilde further note that prior to the 1980s, policies tended to be focused on class struggles, which was another factor contributing to the invisibilisation of Indigenous people.[55] Lublin highlights that key dichotomies were at play here, that of the 'Argentine nation' versus 'the desert' (used to refer to the Pampas, Patagonia and the Gran Chaco), and that of 'civilisation' (European immigrants) versus 'barbarism' (Indigenous groups).[56] As Lublin also notes, 'the frame of the civilisation/barbarism dichotomy [informed] Argentinian intellectual thinking'.[57] Following these dichotomies, European immigrants were heroic, adventurous, brave and a symbol of modernity, whilst Indigenous groups were taken to be dangerous, unpredictable, volatile and a symbol of backwardness. These dichotomies are encapsulated in a Welshman's farewell to his nephew who was travelling on the *Mimosa*:

> Since you will not be dissuaded from expatriating yourselves to that wild outlandish desert, I write to wish you a safe and pleasant voyage and much success in your new country. If the Indians do eat you up, I can only wish them a confounded bad digestion.[58]

Finally, some scholars working on Welsh Patagonia have chosen to theorise the group as a diasporic community.[59] Whilst those using the term 'diaspora' have attempted to acknowledge the historical inequalities between the Welsh settlers and the local Indigenous people, the term 'diaspora' cannot fully account for the colonial element of the settler colony.[60] The book moves away from the term 'diaspora' to refer to Welsh Patagonia as a 'settler colony' throughout, defined by Veracini as 'circumstances where colonisers "come to stay" and to establish new political orders for themselves, rather than to exploit native labour'.[61] Lublin further notes that the use of 'settler colony' also helps to navigate the issues of translation:

> The view of Y Wladfa as a settler colony is also particularly helpful in settling the dispute as to whether it should be referred to as a colony or a settlement. In Welsh, the term *gwladfa* is a bit of a riddle: the first translation suggested is 'colony' (*trefedigaeth*), followed by the equivalent of 'settlement' (*gwladychfa*), before a third entry explaining that, when preceded by the definite article, the word is used to

denote 'part of a province in South America with the name of Patagonia that was colonised by the Welsh in 1865'. The lack of a specific term in English has meant that those who sympathise with Y Wladfa tend to call it a 'settlement' and those who do not refer to it as a 'colony'.[62]

Ultimately, the book adopts the term 'settler colony' to highlight that the displacement of Indigenous occupants can take various forms and does not necessarily have to be physical, and in doing so broadens our concept of colonisation beyond a focus on overt control towards the realisation that settlement is a negotiation and a relationship, which can be enacted in symbolic, spiritual or cultural terms.[63]

## 1884 onwards

It is especially important to consider the role of the dominant narrative when considering the claiming of more land and the overall boom in the Welsh language and economy that occurred in the 100 years that followed the landing. This success story and 'golden age' has often been ascribed to the hard work and resilience of the Welsh on a difficult, wild terrain.[64] In Chubut the settlers irrigated an area three or four miles to each side of the 50-mile stretch of the Chubut River, creating fertile wheat lands. Williams has argued that central to this process of irrigation was the flow of Welsh information and the creation of Welsh institutions, in that it directly connected the Welsh with the historical experience of irrigation.[65] At this time, the settlers also began to move and settle further afield, in the Andes. By 1885, wheat production had reached 6,000 tons. At around the same time, in 1884, the Argentine congress authorised the construction of the Central Chubut Railway, and work began in 1886, coinciding with the arrival of another 465 settlers on the Vesta steamer.[66]

However, after the Conquest of the Desert, there was increasing pressure from the government on the Welsh community to become a more integral part of the project of building the Argentine nation: it had begun to dawn on government officials that 'the soil on its own did not magically create "Argentinians"'.[67] In other words, the Welsh were considered civilised, but what the government was really aiming for was civilised Argentinians. By the 1890s in Chubut, schools came

Figure 3: The Chubut River

Figure 4: The Chubut River at sunset

under Argentinian control and Spanish became the language of the public sphere: the schools, the streets, and so on. Althusser's model of subjectivation is useful here in that it offers a language with which to talk about the civilising project of the state. In his analysis, schools were a central means by which ideology could be interpellated into subjects. He argues that schools teach children a 'know-how', but in forms which ensure subjection to the ruling ideology or mastery of its 'practice'. In other words, they learn to read, count and write, but simultaneously, they learn 'the "rules" of good behaviour, in other words, the attitude that should be observed by every agent in the division of labour, according to the job they are "destined" for'.[68] In his view, the manipulation of these ideological apparatuses was central to the subjectivation of individuals as subjects of the state. In this light, speaking Spanish in schools could be viewed as an efficient means by which pupils became subjects of the Argentine state. Yet, the Welsh language continued, becoming ideologically associated with the private sphere: family, chapel and agriculture.

Alongside the changing schooling system, serious environmental damage was caused to the irrigation system, and to Gaiman in particular, by major floods that occurred in winter 1899 and July 1901, meaning that some of the settlers relocated to Canada, Colonia Sarmiento in Chubut and Choele-Choel in Rio Negro.[69] The impact of the floods, alongside the disagreements between the settlers and the Argentinian government due to the introduction of conscription, which was against the religious principles of the early settlers, caused some settlers to return to Liverpool on 14 May 1902, though some families later returned to Chubut.[70] The return to Wales was not uncommon amongst immigrants to Argentina. Germani argues that most immigrants never intended to stay but rather sought to emigrate to save money to purchase land at home upon their return.[71]

The years that followed were politically turbulent.[72] In 1925, a national secondary school (Spanish medium) opened in Trelew. Between 1930 and 1938, Argentina saw a successive stream of military governments, followed by a democratic spell (1938–43) before a more nationalistic regime. In 1940, non-Argentinian names became banned, in 1943, Catholicism became an obligatory subject in schools and, in 1945, the canals which had been irrigated by the Welsh settlers became nationalised. In this context, the Welsh settlers were becoming increasingly integrated into Argentinian culture, and it was becoming something of a 'paradox of history that Welsh Patagonians were eventually coerced into a culture more alien to them than the Anglicised Welshness that they had fled'.[73] The Peronist period that followed (1946–55) was founded on a discourse which 'emphasised the erasure of differences', and Argentina saw the collapse of conservative ideology and the acknowledgement of citizenship for Indigenous people.[74] As Adkin argues, 'With his first government, Peron granted citizenship rights to those Indians that still lacked them, and many of these people *received identification papers certifying their Argentine citizenship for the first time ever*.'[75] This time is recalled as a moment 'when they were elevated to the status of full, dignified members of the national community'; an elevation which lent itself to the beginnings of political mobilisation for Indigenous populations.[76] However, it is important to note that these changes were not because of specific Indigenous policies. Lenton further argues that 'any improvements that the indigenous communities experienced under Peronism were the result of general and social labour reforms and not of policies specifically designed for the indigenous population'.[77]

Peron's fall had further implications and in the following years, Indigenous groups were repositioned as needing development.[78] Simultaneously, the Welsh settlers were gaining increased recognition. Following the creation of the Chubut Province, Patagonians were granted the right to vote in 1955:

> [This was] a development which turned out to be very significant for the Welsh. The new government officials – a number of them of Welsh descent – adopted the Welsh feat as the foundational narrative of the province and established *Gŵyl y Glaniad* ('The Festival of the Landing') on 28 July as the first bank holiday in Chubut. As the Welsh pioneers gained recognition as Argentine founding fathers of sorts, their descendants regained pride in their heritage.[79]

The early 1960s marked the beginning of an increasingly prominent space for the Welsh language in Chubut. In 1965, a group of Welsh descendants created a committee to organise the celebrations marking the centenary of the landing, a celebration which served to strengthen the links between Wales and Patagonia.[80] As Lublin notes, 'while the more than seventy "Welsh pilgrims" who flew to Chubut marvelled at the survival of "a piece of Wales" at the other end of the world, Patagonians updated their notion of Wales as a modern, thriving country'.[81] That same year also saw the revival of the Chubut Eisteddfod, which had not taken place since 1950.[82]

From the 1980s, 'binational contacts thrived with the advent of new technologies, and a number of Welsh descendants in both the Chubut Valley and the Andean foothills set out to capitalise on their ethnic background by attracting national and international tourism'.[83] The year 1997 saw the strengthening of the links between Wales and Patagonia, with funding being secured for a Welsh Language Revitalisation project, coordinated by the Welsh government, the Wales-Argentina society and the British Council of Wales.[84] The key goals of this project are described as being 'the secondment of teachers to key communities, the development of native teachers, the establishment of structured courses and the promotion of Welsh language activities in Patagonia'.[85] These developments signal a significant shift from the challenges that faced Welshness in Chubut before 1950. The Welsh language and Welshness were being celebrated, and the connections between Wales and Patagonia were gaining in strength.

At the same time, from the mid-1980s, there emerged a 'demand for a new legal framework for Indigenous rights at a national level'.[86] From 1990, Indigenous movements began to gain increasing relevance and support, with a focus on the reconstruction of language and cultural practices. As Vom Hau and Wilde explain:

> During the 1980s, policymakers enacted several laws that treated Indigenous communities as legal subjects and granted them a number of special rights. A new national legislation, the *Ley de la Protección y Apoyo a las Comunidades Indigenas* passed in 1985 and ratified in 1989, established Indigenous communities as carriers of specific rights, guaranteeing them, among other things, the possibility to recuperate lands they had historical claims to. The 1994 constitutional reform confirmed these new legal norms by depicting Argentina as a pluricultural nation and encoding the ethnic and cultural pre-existence of Indigenous people.

In other words, in 1994, a constitutional reform granted specific rights to Indigenous people, based on a new definition of Argentina as being a multi-ethnic country, in contrast to the previous conception of Argentina as being a white nation of immigrants.[87] Ultimately, this implies that in a manner comparable to the increasing prominence for Welshness, there was also an increasing space for Indigenous communities centre stage, one which was now protected by legislation.

However, despite these seemingly positive changes, Barreiro et al. argue that, in practice, 'the current hegemonic narrative about the Conquest of the Desert denies not only the Argentinian state's responsibility for the injustices suffered by Indigenous people in the past, but also the ongoing existence of Indigenous communities in Argentinian territory in the present'. The new rights granted to Indigenous people did not translate into practice, and Indigenous people were still being made invisible. Barrerio et al. argue that the 'purported absence of Indigenous populations in Argentina does not correspond to the reality'.[88] Adkin further argues that whilst in the past two decades Indigenous groups have progressed from a position of invisibility – in which they were ignored by institutions and organisations – to participating in assemblies, forming political parties, and winning governmental positions, 'native populations have the strongest correlation with impoverishment, lack of education, marginalisation of any group in the region'.[89]

### Gaiman, Chubut and Patagonia: 2015–17

In Chubut, of the 420,137 inhabitants of the Chubut Province who are recorded as living in private homes for ten years or more in the 2010 census, 36,557 of these are defined as Indigenous or as having Indigenous descent.[90] In Argentina as a whole, the corresponding figures are 33,398,225 and 788,497, respectively. Whilst there are no corresponding figures for those of Welsh descent, with the 2010 census only recording as 'European' those who were born in Europe and were living in Argentina, a significant proportion of the population of both Chubut and broader Argentina are said to be of Welsh descent, without considering whether they speak Welsh.[91] In Patagonia, the figures of individuals of Welsh descent (with or without the Welsh language) were estimated to be around 50,000 at the beginning of the twenty-first century, which would make up around 25 per cent of Patagonia.[92] Given that these figures account for the whole of Patagonia (rather than only for Chubut) it would indicate that there are far fewer people with Welsh descent than Indigenous descent living in Chubut; it is estimated that there are 5,000 Welsh speakers and learners in Chubut, in comparison to 43,279 individuals of Indigenous descent in Chubut, 73 per cent of these being Mapuche.[93] Whilst the figures of individuals with Welsh *descent* (rather than speakers or learners) will inevitably be higher than 5,000, these figures remain striking.

Whilst there is limited recent data on the demography of Gaiman village, out of a total of 11,141 inhabitants recorded in the 2012 census in the department of Gaiman (which accounts for the village of Gaiman and the immediate surrounding settlements, including Dolavon, Veintiocho de Julio, Las Chapas, Bryn Gwyn and Villa Dique Florentino), 542 are recorded as being from other countries. Out of these, 471 are recorded as being born in neighbouring countries (with 292 being from Bolivia), sixty are recorded as being born in Europe and eleven as from another country.[94] Establishing a concrete figure of Welsh descendants in Gaiman is challenging. In the census, these inhabitants would all be recorded as Argentinian due to their place of birth, given that some Welsh speakers did not necessarily socialise within the Welsh-Patagonian community, and given that some members of the Welsh Patagonian community who were fluent Welsh speakers did not have 'Welsh descent' or identifiable Welsh surnames (such as Williams, Davies or Thomas, which were common in Chubut), making them harder to trace. Ultimately, however, Welsh Patagonians were a minority in relation to other inhabitants of the village, with approximately 1,000–1,100 individuals active in Welsh Patagonian culture during the time of fieldwork (regularly attending Welsh lessons, traditional Welsh dancing classes, choir, and so on). Despite Argentinians making up most of the demography of Gaiman, it is important to note that this category of 'Argentinian' as per the census would include Argentinians of Spanish, French, Italian and other European descent. It would also include Indigenous populations. Beyond this, there were two significant other demographic categories in Gaiman village – Chinese migrants who owned and ran local supermarkets, and Bolivian migrants who owned farms on the outskirts of Gaiman and who owned fruit and vegetable stores in the village.

Figure 5: A view over Gaiman village

Figure 6: A wintery sky in Gaiman

Despite Welsh Patagonians being a minority in a demographic sense, they were nevertheless an economically and socially powerful group in Chubut, where 28.5 per cent of the total population have been defined as living in poverty.[95] At the time of the research, the dominant economic activities in Chubut were oil and gas exploitation, trade, sheep farming and slaughter, wool production, fishing, aluminium production and tourism, among others.[96] In Gaiman, sheep farming and wool production were particularly significant. The farms, shops and supermarkets in the village were largely run by Argentinians, Chinese migrants and Bolivian migrants. Contrastingly, many of the Welsh Patagonians with whom I lived were largely involved – or had been, prior to retirement – either in the education sector (as nursery, primary or secondary school teachers) or the tourism industry (running their own businesses, such as guest houses, restaurants, teahouses, or museums). The standard of living, education and cultural capital (gained, for example, by travelling to Europe or the UK) was relatively high amongst Welsh Patagonians, and many were educated to undergraduate degree level. The tourism industry in Chubut was particularly significant, with the Argentine Ministry of Tourism and Sports noting that on average, Chubut receives 754,064 tourists annually, 112,987 of whom travel from outside Argentina.[97] Most of the tourists that I met during fieldwork who visited Gaiman were from Wales, with a minority travelling from the US, and some from other parts of Argentina. Tourism and the subsequent development of relationships between Welsh tourists and Welsh Patagonians was also the basis of new – often economically significant – opportunities for the Welsh Patagonian community. The Welsh Patagonian presence also manifested itself in the village through Welsh-medium road/cafe signs, and through Welsh flags adorning the nurseries and schools.[98] Additionally, the Welsh Patagonian community received financial support from the Welsh government in Wales – who, according to BBC News, invest approximately £56,000 per year in Welsh Patagonia[99] – and from the local Chubut government, who funded various projects, such as the conversion of a large wool barn to accommodate the visit of a Welsh orchestra and the extensive renovations of Welsh chapels in Chubut, and who were also often physically present at concerts hosted by the Welsh Patagonian community, adding to the prestige of those events.[100]

In terms of the Tehuelche and Mapuche in Patagonia, the political context of eighteenth-century Argentina has been said to lead to a 'Araucanization' of Tehuelche culture.[101] The 'National Indigenous Census' of 1966-8 notes that the majority of Tehuelche who remained most attached to their culture at this time were in the Santa Cruz Province (200 of whom are recorded in the census), and that the 278 individuals in La Pampa and Chubut were 'found Mapuchised'.[102] In terms of the Tehuelche language, the census notes 'fewer than ten speakers in the decade of 80', suggesting the near extinction of the language.[103] This 'Araucanisation' was both a political and discursive project.[104] Adkin argues that 'both national and provincial state institutions dismiss the claims of aboriginality by Argentine Indigenous groups [for example, their originality as Tehuelche] by stressing their lack of the traditional cultural markers [such as language] present in their foreign affiliates'.[105] In this context, then, Indigenous populations are in danger of either being accused of not being authentic, or of being 'declared extinct'.[106]

In the Chubut Province, at the time of the research, there were mixed communities of Mapuche and Tehuelche individuals such as the Mapuche Tehuelche Trelew Community and the Namuncurá Syhueque Community in Gaiman. Each year, on 9 August, Argentina celebrated the International Day of Indigenous People. In October, Columbus Day (a national holiday which officially celebrated the arrival of Christopher Columbus in the Americas) was firstly modified to Day of Race and more recently – in 2010 – to the more inclusive Day of Respect for Cultural Diversity. These days were all marked with a national bank holiday. However, as Berg has previously argued, the silence around discussions of the Indigenous Tehuelche and Mapuche presented challenges in terms of collecting data on the present-day perception of the Tehuelche or Mapuche, or on the Mapuche and Tehuelche communities in Gaiman and Trelew.[107] This silence was also apparent in the depiction of the establishment of the settler colony in the museums of the valley, which prioritised the place of the Welsh settlers in both the historical narrative and in terms of the objects on display.[108]

Contrastingly, in recent years in Chubut, Welsh language and culture have been increasingly prominent, with the opening of a bilingual (Spanish and Welsh) primary school Ysgol yr Hendre in Trelew in 2006, and the establishment of Menter Patagonia (which promotes Welsh activities in the valley) in 2008. Out of the estimated 5,000 Welsh speakers and learners in Chubut, a high number were living in Gaiman, and statistics on the numbers of Welsh learners enrolling on Welsh courses demonstrated that this figure was increasing annually in a consistent manner, with a total of 1,236 Welsh learners registered in 2018. This mirrored a trend in Wales where there was also an emphasis on increasing numbers of Welsh-language speakers. At the time of the research, in 2015, there were around 800,000 Welsh speakers in Wales according to the Annual Population Survey, and the Welsh government had released a target of achieving 1 million Welsh speakers and doubling the daily use of Welsh by 2050.[109] By the time of writing, figures for Welsh speakers aged three or older had reached 889,700, and the Welsh government had published an updated strategic plan for 1 million Welsh speakers for the years 2021–6.[110]

Number of Welsh learners (all ages) in the Chubut Province 2008–18.[111]

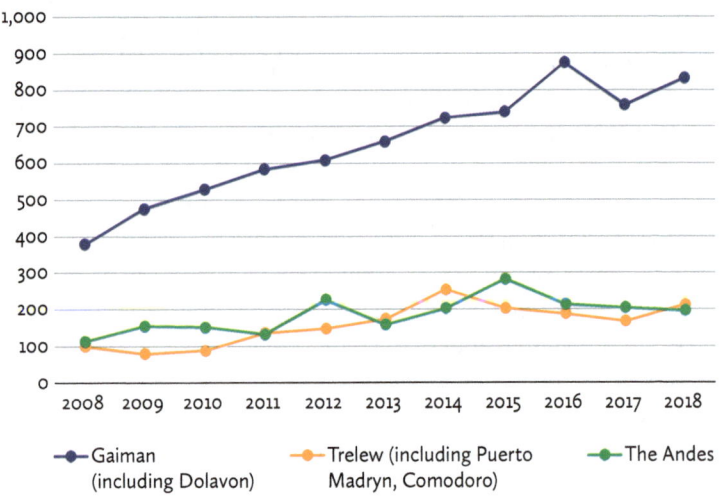

The Covid-19 pandemic had a significant impact on Welsh language and culture in Chubut. Whilst the total of Welsh learners (in Gaiman, Trelew and the Andes) in 2019 was 1,411, this figure more than halved in 2020, with 623 Welsh learners registered.[112] As noted in the British Council report on the Patagonia Welsh Language Project, the three language development officers who travelled from Wales to Patagonia in February 2020 left in May 2020 because of the pandemic. Lessons were moved online, which presented challenges due to internet connectivity issues and learners lacking appropriate hardware and IT skills to access classes. Statistics from the 2022 census indicate that out of a total of 215,257 homes in Chubut, 46,122 (21 per cent) are without internet. Of those with internet, 42,478 (25 per cent) are without a computer or tablet, and therefore rely on mobile phones to connect.[113] However, moving classes online made learning more flexible in other ways, with learners registering from across Argentina, including Buenos Aires and Neuquen. In the year 2021–2, no teachers were sent from Wales to Patagonia. The Covid-19 pandemic had further implications for tourism, social gatherings (such as choir rehearsals or *cymanfaoedd canu*) and events like the eisteddfod.[114] 2022 saw the revival of the Welsh Language Project following the pandemic, but recruitment of Welsh teachers has remained a challenge.

Given the impact of the pandemic and the ongoing recovery effort, it must be emphasised that the argument of the book, and the data upon which it is based, is reflective of a specific time of fieldwork between 2015 and 2017. Whilst the Welsh Patagonian community were fully integrated into Argentinian society, they did maintain their own traditions and institutions within this integration. In Gaiman, there was a Welsh nursery called Ysgol Meithrin Gaiman, a primary school called Ysgol Gymraeg y Gaiman (which taught pupils up to the age of nine), a primary school called Escuela 100, a secondary school called Ysgol Camwy, a small museum full of historical artefacts belonging to the original Welsh settlers, the Casa de Cultura (an arts centre which hosted concerts, film nights, lectures and photography exhibitions), three large Welsh teahouses,[115] a Welsh-language music school, and a bakery-cafe called Siop Bara (bread shop) in the centre of the village. Two Welsh teachers were sent annually from Wales to Gaiman and Trelew as part of the Welsh Language Project, to support Welsh-language development in the area. Gaiman's main tourist attractions were the 'first ever built Welsh house' and the disused train tunnel which had been converted into a museum, where visitors could listen to a spoken history of the old railway in Spanish and in Welsh. Across the *paith* in the Andes mountains was the village of Trevelin, with its Welsh chapels, traditional Welsh architecture, a recently opened (2012) bilingual (Spanish and Welsh) school called Ysgol y Cwm, Welsh traditional dancing groups and classes, a museum which displayed a variety of items used by the Welsh settlers, Welsh teahouses, and one teacher being sent annually from Wales with the Welsh Language Project to support language learning. The permanent learning co-ordinator of the Welsh Language Project also lived in Trevelin at the time of the research.

Religious buildings were a prominent presence in Gaiman – on the outskirts of the village there was a Welsh chapel called Capel Bethel, and in the centre of town there was a large Methodist church. At the time of the research, Christianity was the predominant religion in Argentina and the official religion of the state, with most of the population identifying as Roman Catholic.[116] Other religious affiliations in Argentina included Evangelism, Protestantism and Judaism (amongst others). In Gaiman, there were several Welsh Nonconformist chapels (with the most significant being Capel Bethel) and Roman Catholic churches. Most of my Welsh Patagonian interlocutors attended Capel Bethel every Sunday, whilst others attended the local Catholic church. Those who attended Nonconformist chapels or Catholic churches

Figure 7: Sign for Capel Bethel

regularly attended hymn-singing sessions together in the Welsh Nonconformist chapels. A minority of my Argentinian interlocutors attended Catholic church, but a large majority – though they identified with Catholicism ideologically – were not actively practising. Many of my younger Argentinian interlocutors identified as atheist.

Ultimately, whilst the Welsh Patagonian community lived alongside – and interacted with – other demographic, economic and religious groups – for example in the supermarkets, at vegetable stores or at local events, those who were active participants in the Welsh Patagonian community tended to socialise separately, by attending hymn-singing sessions, Welsh lessons, choirs, festivals and other Welsh-language events. Furthermore, whilst the Welsh-medium schools were open to other demographic groups, some of these schools (such as Ysgol yr Hendre in Trelew) were private schools and were thus unaffordable to many demographic groups in Gaiman and the surrounding areas. Essentially, then, despite being fully integrated to Argentinian society, the Welsh Patagonian community did maintain a degree of separateness in their day-to-day lives, and the sociological data indicates that whilst the Welsh Patagonian community was a minority in Patagonia, Chubut and Gaiman in comparison to Indigenous populations, they were a powerful minority, in an economic, political and cultural sense.

## Conclusions: empty lands, the myth of whiteness and the creation of Welsh Patagonia

> 'This is a land of exiles,' the legendary writer Jorge Luis Borges would respond with a half-smile when asked about Argentine identity. Aside from exhibiting his taste for eccentricity and puzzling his audience, in his answer Borges was in fact repeating one of Argentina's most powerful images: the idea that it is a modern country built from scratch through liberal economic and social policies and massive European immigration.[117]

Today, Argentina is often described as being a country made up of European immigrants, and many people living in Gaiman have French, Spanish, Italian or Welsh descent.[118] On the Day of Gaiman, which was an annual celebration of the establishment of the village, this multiculturalism was performed through a parade in which groups of individuals with different European descent walked through the main street of Gaiman dressed in traditional outfits representative of their culture or country. Guano points out that the typical description of Argentina (his specific focus is on Buenos Aires) as the 'most European of all Latin American countries' is a discourse which romanticises and depoliticises Argentina, obscuring the struggles of Indigenous groups, Asian groups, Arab groups, and what Hooker refers to as 'Afro-Latinos' in relation to those of European ancestry who occupy positions of relative power and prestige.[119] However, this emphasis on European descent, or the 'myth of whiteness' is problematic.[120]

In this respect, the Welsh Patagonian case resonates with other cases of European migration to and settlement in Latin America in fitting with the 'homogenisation promoted by the state in its construction of the country as white and European'.[121] However, between the late eighteenth and mid-twentieth centuries, Latin America also saw waves of migration from China, East India and Japan,[122] and from Syria, Lebanon and Palestine.[123] Between 1580 and 1640, at the height of the slave trade, many Africans were also relocated to Latin America.[124] This immediately 'rooted people of African descent in an immediate and direct environment of patronage and hierarchy'.[125] Despite this, Guano writes that 'even though in Buenos Aires a dark-skinned Argentine citizen can be arrested at any time under suspicion of being an illegal immigrant from another Latin American country, it is a commonly held belief ... that there is no racism in Argentina'.[126]

Hu-DeHart and López argue that whilst the history of Asian migration is barely registered in the history of Latin America, in practice, 4.5 million Latin Americans are of Asian descent, and 'Mexicans enjoy their *pan chino* with coffee for breakfast, Peruvians swear on their uniquely named *Chifa* restaurants that they have the best Chinese foods in the world, and Cubans love the lottery game they call *la charada china*'.[127] In other words, cultural diversity is deeply embedded within everyday life. In terms of the dynamics of the migration, the biggest wave of migration in the mid-nineteenth century from China were men who were sent as cheap agricultural labour.[128] In the last two decades, this gendered element has changed in the light of China's investment in capital in Latin America, and more recent migration has consisted largely of a female workforce to work in factories and to run supermarkets.[129] Further, Boas notes that in the late nineteenth to the middle of the twentieth centuries, Argentina, Mexico and Brazil saw a wave of migration from Syria and Lebanon, whilst Chile and Central America saw a wave of migration from Palestine.[130]

Whilst the Palestinian case resonates partly with the Welsh Patagonian case in that migration was, in part, concerned with a 'search for a better life', all these groups were ultimately marginalised and faced discrimination.[131] Boas argues, for example, that 'Arabs are called 'turcos' (Turks) all over Latin America, which they regard as insulting'.[132] Denardi argues that migration from China in the last two decades has largely been from lower income backgrounds, which contrasts with the relatively powerful economic position of the Welsh Patagonians in Chubut.[133] Whilst these migrations share with the Welsh Patagonian case the rough timeline of migration, the power dynamics and dichotomies at play were, and remain, different.

Wade's work has been central in this respect.[134] He argues that starting from the 1980s in Brazil, Columbia and Mexico, the discourse of multiculturalism placed populations of European ancestry on a pedestal, and Black and Indigenous populations became treated as a singular homogenous 'other'. Whilst the new framework of collective rights seemed, theoretically, to be inclusionary of both groups, Hooker argues that Indigenous groups have been far more successful in winning collective rights from the state.[135] In practice, then, multicultural citizenship reforms have deepened gaps between Indigenous and Black groups. It has been easier for Indigenous groups to formulate their struggles within the parameters of collective rights, insofar as such rights must be claimed in terms of connections to the land and an essentialised conceptualisation of identity.[136]

During my time in the field, Argentina was often described to me as a country made up of European immigrants. Once, whilst drinking a cup of coffee with one of my interlocutors in Trelew's shopping centre, relatively early on into fieldwork, she smiled sympathetically at me as I stirred my coffee and, in Welsh, asked me how I was. 'Sut wyt ti'n teimlo yma?' (How do you feel here?) I paused, and said, 'I feel good.' I explained to her that I had settled in easily and that I felt quite at home. 'Ahhh *si*,' she nodded, a knowing smile emerging, 'Do you know why? It is because Argentina is the closest Latin American country to Europe – it is a country made up of Europeans, by descent. For you, it is just like being in France. We are very mixed. Dyna pam rwyt ti'n teimlo'n dda.' (That is why you feel good here.) This emphasis combined with the discourse surrounding the landing of the Welsh to the 'empty land' is exactly what Guano refers to when he discusses the discourse of multiculturalism or sameness serving to obscure the place of Indigenous people in Argentina.[137] As Chamosa notes, 'In Argentina, [the] assimilation myth asserted that there were no ethnic or racial differences within the Argentine nation and that Argentines were homogenously white.'[138]

This chapter has sought to consider the establishment of the Welsh Patagonian settler colony within the context of broader Argentinian history, especially the establishment of the Argentine state, which paved the way for the arrival of the settlers, and the Conquest of the Desert, which saw the displacement of Indigenous people from their traditional lands to make way for what the military government saw as being a civilising force of Europeans. Whilst the Welsh settlers were largely motivated to emigrate to Argentina to create a community in which their language and culture could thrive in the 'desert', away from the influence of the English, they were nevertheless complicit in this civilising mission. Dominant popular stories have reinforced the idea that those 153 Welsh settlers arrived in Chubut to an empty land, in addition to the image of the 'heroic' Welsh, and the dichotomies of Welshness, Indigeneity, civilisation and barbarism. The discourse of 'European-ness' presented in this chapter demonstrates the recent significance of these ideas. The creation of Welsh Patagonia as a tangible 'thing' ultimately rests on the maintenance of these dominant narratives.

Following the political, geographic and historical context that I have described, the remainder of the book turns to the particularity of the present-day Welsh community to explore the significance of present-day performative encounters in Chubut, which occurred between local Argentinians, Welsh descendants and Welsh tourists, to consider in more depth how Welshness and the image of a homogenous community was continually created, performed and affirmed, both visually and sonically through music alongside a consideration of the power dynamics within this context.

# 3

# 'Eisteddfodamos':
# Eisteddfod as ritual performance

> The relationship between power and collective
> ideas is riddled with contradictions. The ideas that
> are most conspicuously present, that are most
> aggressively pushed, are also the most likely to
> collapse under their own weight ... In other words,
> the potency of ideology is rooted in its fragility.[1]

## Introduction: the work of enjoyment at the Eisteddfod

In August 2015, I arrived at a secondary school in Puerto Madryn which was being used as a site for the small annual 'Mimosa' Eisteddfod. I glanced up at the large Welsh and Argentinian flags hanging down over the entrance to the school and the smaller bunting flags lining the walls, and tentatively pushed open the double doors, unsure of what to expect on the other side. I was immediately welcomed enthusiastically in Welsh and Spanish by two women sitting behind a desk at the school reception. '*Croeso! Bienvenidos!*' they announced, almost in unison. They both grinned widely at me as they called me forward to the ticket office in the school reception booth. After buying my ticket, I went through into the main hall, where the competitions were already taking place. Rows of plastic chairs faced a stage at the front of the hall and, despite it being early, the room was busy. I glanced around. Groups of people were sitting on the chairs huddled against the gas heaters at the edge of the hall, sharing *mate* and *facturas* (small pastries), and chatting amongst each other whilst the competitions took place on stage.

The ambience of the room was one of light-hearted fun, with the constant stream of chatter in the background interrupted only by intermittent applause from the audience for the contestants on the stage. I scanned the room, relaxing as I noticed a group of friends whom I had known since 2013 from Gaiman Music School sitting towards the middle of the room. I waved and Alberto called me over. Alberto was an eccentric, kind Welsh Patagonian composer and an incredible pianist who was fluent in Welsh, English and Spanish. During fieldwork, he lived in Gaiman with his wife Sofia, who was a music teacher at Ysgol Gymraeg y Gaiman, and their little girl, Siwan. His mother, Eleanor, who also spoke fluent Welsh, was the leader of Gaiman girls' choir. Eleanor's brother, at the time of the research, lived with his family in Wales in a village close to Aberystwyth and visited Patagonia regularly. Likewise, Alberto and his family had also visited Wales regularly, where Alberto had taken part in the Gorsedd in Wales, performed in several concerts and had also been a judge in the Llangollen Eisteddfod.

He welcomed me to the group with a hug and explained the situation to me in Welsh:

> *Ni yma i fwynhau.* We are here to enjoy. Even the competing is all done in good spirits … we don't mind who wins. It is just fun to have an opportunity to get together, listen to music and drink *mate. Dydyn ni ddim yn llym* … We are not strict like the eisteddfod in Wales … you can see that because everything always runs over and we are late to *everything. Yn y diwedd, byddi di fel ni.* You'll be the same eventually.

He smiled warmly, and I settled into a chair, accepted the *mate* from him, and eagerly awaited my first Welsh Patagonian eisteddfod experience, one which, in many ways, would set the scene for the many other eisteddfodau that I would attend during fieldwork.

A month later, in September, I was sitting with my fellow choir participants in the main rehearsal hall in Gaiman Music School waiting for the weekly four-part choir practice to begin. My interlocutors were chatting about how much they were looking forward to the upcoming Chubut Eisteddfod when Maria, the choir director, bounced through the doors. Her bright red blouse and booming voice immediately filled the rehearsal room, in a seamless combination of Spanish and Welsh:

## 'Eisteddfodamos': Eisteddfod as ritual performance

*Un mis ac un diwrnod i fynd!* One month and two days to go! *No lo puedo creer* ... I can't believe how quickly it has come round again. Can you believe that a year has passed? Hands up if you know the pieces from memory yet? *Os nad ydych chi* ... If you don't ... then it's getting quite urgent so now is the time to begin learning them and to begin learning them quickly! [...] What about blouses? Have you all got your blouse ready? Do they still fit you nicely from last year? You all need a blouse, a black one, and a coloured scarf if you are singing in the girls' choir. People visiting ... Rhiannon, Lucy ... *gallwch chi fenthyg.* You can borrow. Black on the bottoms, remember. Who hasn't got trousers? *Bueno, empezamos con Croeso Patagonia?* Right, shall we start with *Croeso Patagonia*? *O, a peidiwch anghofio mwynhau!* Oh, and don't forget to have fun!

If you were to approach Gaiman from the nearby town of Trelew via Ruta 25, and to follow its main street, you would pass the museum, the hospital, a few houses, Siop Bara, kiosks selling chocolates, biscuits, beer and cigarettes, and a large petrol station, before reaching a set of concrete steps framed with two pillars leading down to double wooden doors – the entrance to a creamy yellow single-storey brick building with a low sloping roof; Escuela de Música Gaiman. Between 15:30 and 21:00, students could take classes of all kinds at the music school, including violin, cello, double bass, harp, percussion, guitar, music theory, electronic music production or piano. The musical repertoire varied greatly across these classes, with some groups leaning towards a Welsh repertoire, and others focusing on rehearsing and performing traditional Argentinian pieces and styles. The classes were open to all ages and registration took place annually in late January, towards the end of the summer holidays. The music school also provided a rehearsal space for Gaiman Music School's mixed choir and girls' choir, and the string instrument group. Other groups including recital groups and smaller ensembles also occasionally made use of the rehearsal space.

*Tymor yr Eisteddfod* or 'Eisteddfod season' in Welsh Patagonia was the most anticipated and important time of the year for the Welsh

Patagonian community, summarised on the official Chubut Eisteddfod website as 'one of the most relevant and representative events of the cultural tapestry of the country ... taking part ... creates the possibility of manifesting the values that enrich our lives'. As Eleanor (the director of Gaiman Music School's girls' choir) succinctly put it, this was the 'most important event of the year for us in Patagonia'.[2] The calendar year in the Welsh community and in the music school revolved around the Chubut Eisteddfod as an ultimate end goal to hours of learning pieces in rehearsals, practising alone to backing tracks at home, and performing in other smaller concerts throughout the year.

This is how it came to be that every year, following a brief post-eisteddfod respite in rehearsing to recuperate, attention in the music school turned, slowly but surely, to preparation for the next eisteddfod, interrupted only by the Christmas, summer and Easter holidays. From around November, new pieces would be introduced in the rehearsals amidst the usual repertoire. The intensity of rehearsals and the pressure to attend them increased in the months, weeks and days leading up to the eisteddfod and other big concerts. Whilst there was still no formal register taken, the expectation to attend additional rehearsals was quietly clear, with choir participants often leaving work early, taking time off work and postponing other commitments in the days leading up to the eisteddfod, as well as during the eisteddfod itself. Additional singing, reciting and music groups were also created in anticipation of the eisteddfod, often appearing as sub-groups of the already existing choirs. We worked hard, and preparation for competing took up most of our free time as the festival approached. In January, after the summer break, the Spanish and Welsh bilingual schools also turned their focus to learning and rehearsing pieces to perform in the eisteddfod. Its importance was often reflected in counting down to the big day, as Maria so often reminded us at the beginning of choir rehearsals, '*Tres* ...three ... *dos* ... *dau* ... one ... *una*... weeks until the eisteddfod!'

The Chubut Eisteddfod was the largest of the eisteddfodau in Chubut and was held in October. The diverse and carefully planned programme of competitions and performances ran over a few days, and ran late into the night. It closed with a large *cymanfa ganu* and an Argentinian *asado*. The ceremony of the Gorsedd, which served as the official opening of the eisteddfod, whilst closely connected to it, was theoretically a separate institution that, through its members (writers, poets, musicians and academics, to name but a few), celebrated and promoted literary scholarship and the creation of poetry and music. In both Wales and Patagonia, the Gorsedd was an important element of the eisteddfod. However, in Patagonia, the Gorsedd was younger, having been re-established in 2001 following a lull.[3] To become the archdruid (the head of) the Gorsedd you must have won one of the eisteddfod's two most important awards, either the chair (for poetry) or the crown (for prose). The role encompassed conducting the Gorsedd ceremonies which included opening the eisteddfod and presenting the chair and crown. In Patagonia, the opening ceremony was informally referred to as 'Gorsedd' and was held in a circle of stones in a square in the village, known as the 'Welsh Settler's Square'. This was a sacred space; within the square only Welsh was to be spoken.

I was in the field for two eisteddfod seasons – 2015 and 2016. In 2015, I attended the annual Mimosa Eisteddfod which took place over one day in a local school hall in Puerto Madryn, and the Chubut Eisteddfod which took place in an old wool barn that had been converted into a concert hall on the outskirts of Trelew. In 2016, I attended the Youth Eisteddfod which was held in Gaiman gym and the Chubut Eisteddfod which took place in St David's Hall in Trelew. My role in the Puerto Madryn Eisteddfod – a few days after my arrival in the field – was as a member of the audience, and I participated in the other eisteddfodau as a singer in choirs and other vocal groups, as a cellist accompanying choirs and ceremonies, and as an audience member. In both the official Gorsedd ceremonies for 2015 and 2016, I participated as a member of Gaiman girls' choir. Finally, in January 2018, I conducted archival research into the history of the eisteddfod at the National Library of Wales, Aberystwyth, reviewing newspapers from 1800 to 2017, and in August 2018, I conducted fieldwork at the National Eisteddfod of Wales in Cardiff Bay. This chapter draws on data gathered during those eisteddfodau (during the official Gorsedd ceremonies, the festival itself, the *cymanfaoedd canu* and the *asado* that marked the end of the eisteddfod) as well as from the rehearsals leading up to them, and from conversations with my interlocutors in their aftermath.

This chapter seeks to understand the role of the eisteddfod in identity construction in Welsh Patagonia. The eisteddfod, to an extent, represented the formalisation of the daily performative events and activities, such as singing together. It was viewed, in part, as the 'end goal' to several rehearsals and smaller events that took place throughout the year. However, in addition to being a performance, it was also performative. In other words, it was the scene of the creation of new relations of belonging and power. Covington-Ward has argued that 'performances, like many other forms of embodied movement, can provide a critical site of inquiry for examination of struggles for power and authority in multiple settings'.[4] In this context of heightened emotion, this site of encounter between Welsh tourists, local Welsh Patagonians from the Chubut Valley, Welsh Patagonians from Trevelin and Esquel, and local Argentinians was a key space in which contemporary power dynamics were navigated.

Keane defines a 'ritual performance' as a public and formal event which hides its creative potential.[5] In Welsh Patagonia, an event such as the eisteddfod might appear to be a representation of already existing social relations (between Welsh Patagonians and tourists, or between Welsh Patagonians and local Argentinians), but in its appearance, it simultaneously creates them. As Covington-Ward states, one

Figure 8: Esquel

'Eisteddfodamos': Eisteddfod as ritual performance

Figure 9: An evening in Esquel

'major characteristic of performance ... is its potential to transform social realities'.[6] Beyond a focus on the creative element of performance, Keane argues that paying attention to 'slippages', or moments at which the performative fails to function, is key to the understanding of ritual performance.[7] As Pelkmans argues in the context of state ideology, 'things can and do go wrong'.[8] This chapter argues that the context of the eisteddfod demonstrated that beyond the slippages that occur during ritual performance itself, we should pay attention to what I have termed 'moments of disgruntlement'. These moments, in which my interlocutors did not enjoy and complained about the festival, or in which they expressed doubt about what Pelkmans has referred to as the 'ideational power' of the eisteddfod, occurred largely in moments beyond the ritual performance itself and revealed different power dynamics to those revealed by slippages, in that they were related to the difficulties of organising and financing performance, and the connected issue of inclusion.[9]

First, the chapter will situate the eisteddfod in relation to two key theoretical concepts which shape this chapter – performance and performativity – before providing an historical contextualisation of the eisteddfod and a discussion of the present-day institution in both Wales and Patagonia. Following this, it explores Keane's concept of 'slippages' in relation to the ceremony of the chairing, one of the most prestigious ceremonies of the eisteddfod.[10] The chapter ultimately seeks to analyse the relationship between enjoyment, flow and power in the eisteddfod. It argues that beyond the slippages, attention to the moments in which my interlocutors expressed enjoyment of the eisteddfod – or conversely, in which they complained about it – which occurred during the festival but also in its lead-up and aftermath, were not only key to understanding the multilayered nature of the power dynamics in this context, but also in moving away from the objectifying nature of visual theories of anthropology toward a more subjective understanding of the relationship between performance and performativity, on the one hand, and towards a better understanding of the interactions between the themes of flow, enjoyment, power, accessibility and belonging, on the other.

## Performance and performativity

In Welsh Patagonia, two key elements contributed to the creation and continuation of Welshness. First, there were a series of large, formally staged performances of Welshness. These consisted of concerts with choirs singing in Welsh, performances of traditional Welsh dancing, dressing in Welsh traditional costumes, hosting Welsh teas, celebrations of various cultural holidays such as the Day of Gaiman and the Festival of the Landing, theatre performances of the establishment of the settler colony, concerts performed by orchestras or choirs from Wales, and the eisteddfod. These performances closely reflected what Turner termed 'cultural performance[s]', under which he included 'numerous genres ... ranging from ritual, to theatre, the novel, folk-drama, art exhibitions, ballet, modern dance, poetry readings, to film and television [...] games and sports, as well as festivals'.[11] Turner argued that cultural performances develop from and reflect the framework of social dramas, which he took to describe 'periodic social upheavals, such as political conflict, illness, war, or virtually any disturbance to the normative order'.[12] Others following him have pointed out that space must be maintained in analysis for performances as exercises in enjoyment.[13] The perspective that became clear in Welsh Patagonia was that performance and enjoyment were two complementary elements, with the performance being more effective when it was enjoyable.

Secondly, existing alongside the more dramatic spectacles of 'parades, festivals, and other such events' were a series of everyday acts, referred to by Kapchan as the 'patterns of behaviour, ways of speaking, manners of bodily comportment ... whose repetitions situate actors in time and space, structuring individual and group identities'.[14] In Welsh Patagonia, these everyday acts consisted of speaking Welsh, hosting tourists from Wales, attending Welsh choir rehearsals, Welsh traditional dancing rehearsals, music rehearsals and Welsh lessons, taking part in other regular events such as film nights or meals organised in the valley, attending the Welsh and Spanish bilingual schools, baking and eating traditional Welsh food (such as Welshcakes or Bara Brith), and listening to Welsh-language radio or music at home. Alongside these daily performative acts were several other displays of Welshness which could be considered to be more 'banal' in Billig's sense of the word, such as the presence of Welsh road signs, Welsh flags, wearing Wales rugby tops, and the red and green school uniform of the pupils

Figure 10: Welsh road signs in Gaiman

of Ysgol yr Hendre (a bilingual Welsh and Spanish primary school in Trelew).[15] These elements were key to setting the scene for more explicit performative acts. As one of my interlocutors said to me, early on in fieldwork, 'I remember feeling at home in Wales because of the Welsh street signs, I wonder if that is why the tourists feel at home here too.'

My use of the term 'performativity' throughout the book comes from Goffman and Butler.[16] In the Goffman model of 'homo performans',[17] the coherent organisation of everyday habits forms a social role whereby individuals adopt different social roles in different contexts.[18] Goffman's focus was on encounters and, more specifically, on the performances of day-to-day interactions.[19] Goffman's argument is grounded in the idea that the 'core self' remains stable throughout despite the changes to role.[20] Contrastingly, Butler moves beyond the idea that acts are expressive of an identifiable essence.[21] Building on Austin's concept of speech act theory, in which he argued that certain utterances bring about the very contexts which they invoke, Butler argues that gendered identity is created via the stylised repetition of acts which fabricates the appearance of a substance.[22] As Rollason notes, 'subjects appear in particular ways because the ways in which they are subjects can be reproduced continually by them, constituting their identities'.[23] In other words, we become who we are because of how we act.

This model of identity as a social construct can account for flexibility, change and power in a way that Goffman's cannot, as it opens the possibility of identity being constructed differently through encounters (rather than revealing a fixed essence).[24] Butler's argument, when considered in the context of Welshness, implies that to view an individual as having an identifiable 'Welsh' essence is itself a construction: there is no self as 'Welsh' who adopts various social roles of 'traditional Welsh dancer' or 'choir singer'.[25] It is the repetition of habitual activities, such as attending rehearsals and regularly performing as part of a Welsh choir, that creates the appearance of a stable Welsh identity.

The book considers performance and performativity as two distinct but interrelated concepts. This is a useful approach in the context of Welsh Patagonia, and particularly when thinking about the eisteddfod, because the daily performative acts were inextricably connected to the performances, with the performances often being the culmination of the daily activities, such as choir rehearsals. Furthermore, a strict distinction between performance and performativity is itself problematic, as Ebron notes:

> The distinction between performance and performativity is important only because of particularly positioned theories of subject-making. Eighteenth-century European philosophy established that conscious minds are different from unselfconscious bodies and that freedom is that which is not nature. It is within this set of distinctions that performance and performativity appear so different; they repeat the distinctions between body and mind, nature, and freedom.[26]

The approach taken in the book builds on the work of Keane, who argues that any performance has with it an element of performativity even if the very intention of the performance is to conceal the element of creation. In other words, performance is not taken here to be reflective of everyday performative actions, but rather is seen to have its own creative potential. Keane argues that 'when most successful, ritual performance works by a circular logic in which it creatively brings about a context and set of identities that it portrays as already existing'.[27] In Welsh Patagonia, concealing the element of creation was key to understanding the efficacy of large cultural performances and to understanding the relevance of viewing performance and performativity as two sides of the same coin. Many of the performances presented a polished version of Welshness, of a cultural context (of Gaiman as a place) and of a clear, defined community (of Welsh Patagonians), whilst in practice also creating these very concepts. Finally, by focusing on the daily performative activities which revealed the element of creation underlying the performances, quite literally so in the context of music rehearsals, and by considering how these created the social context in which they appeared embedded, a more nuanced picture can be drawn whereby it becomes possible to tease out not only the ways in which performances were formalised representation of daily performative acts, but also the ways in which they were connected to broader power structures.

## Contextualising the Eisteddfod: Wales

> What is a Welshman without his Eisteddfod? A poor unhappy mortal, more miserable than an Englishman without his cricket-field or a Scotsman without his haggis. The Welshman, however, takes care that he is not without his Eisteddfod ... If you are neither bard nor competitor, you cannot be a Welshman.[28]

The first eisteddfod in Wales was held in 1176, when Lord Rhys invited poets and musicians from all over Wales to a grand gathering at his castle in Cardigan, but the public did not form the role of an audience until 1789.[29] From the 1800s to 2017, trends and structural changes to the public perception of the institution of the eisteddfod have been reflected in national British newspapers. From the 1800s to 1900, the press focus was largely on issues of organisation and money.[30] During this time, the eisteddfod also appears to have been subject to ridicule and criticism in the English press, which reflected the broader power imbalance between the Welsh and the English,[31] something which was especially apparent after one eisteddfod held in London in 1888:

> Fortunately, the Bards had fine weather for their ceremony, and were not, as in November last, when London was 'proclaimed' as the next meeting-place, compelled to go through their ancient rites under the shelter of umbrellas.[32]

Despite this, as early as 1892, it was recognised that the eisteddfod 'no doubt does an excellent service in keeping alive interest in Welsh music and Welsh poetry'.[33] The eisteddfod continued to flourish; as noted in *The Saturday Review*:

> Our Welsh friends are at it again. They have been exposed to a fair share of ridicule, and as is generally the case, it seems to have done them good. In fact, of the two evils, an excess of ridicule and an excess of flattery, there can be no doubt that ridicule is by far the most favourable to a struggling institution.[34]

During the First and Second World Wars, the eisteddfod thrived in a context where music was considered indispensable in keeping spirits high. As reported in *The Musical Herald*, 'If anxiety and doubt and fear cast a gloom over the land, let us revive its fainting soul with the harp and with those intellectual distractions which cluster around the Eisteddfod.'[35] The introduction of rock music and wrestling contests in 1985 contrasted 'sharply with the measured solemnity of earlier events'.[36] From the 1990s, news articles have tended to celebrate the diversity of the modernised eisteddfod and its role in preserving and promoting the Welsh language.[37] Though most of the competitions appear to have remained the same, choral competitions for children and youth choirs became increasingly prominent, as did non-musical competitions, such as theatrical performances.

At the time of the writing, in Wales, the eisteddfod is a prestigious, annual cultural event, comprised of several different competitions with a specific focus on poetry, literature and music, defined by Barnard as 'a distinctly Welsh institution ... a veritable microcosm of Welshness'.[38] There are several eisteddfodau which occur annually in Wales, including the National Eisteddfod of Wales, which consists of eight days of competitions and performances in Welsh, alternating its location between north and south Wales. Approximately 6,000 individuals compete annually in the National Eisteddfod, with the overall attendance of the festival generally exceeding 150,000 visitors. Its overall philosophy remains consistent with Parry and Cynan's description of it as being 'first and foremost an institution for the safeguarding of the Welsh language and the promotion of Welsh culture'.[39] Since 1952 the competitions have all been held through the medium of Welsh, a vital element in the preservation of Welsh language and culture. As Brooks and Lublin elaborate:

> Once a year, Welsh native speakers and learners get a chance to immerse themselves in a unique atmosphere, while various institutions, businesses, government, and non-governmental organisations set up their stalls around the main pavilion and establish a more direct link with the thousands of visitors that make the Eisteddfod the biggest wandering festival in Europe.[40]

There is also an Eisteddfod yr Urdd (youth eisteddfod) which involves Welsh children from nursery age to 25 years old, and several other smaller-scale local eisteddfodau which are held throughout Wales, including within primary and secondary schools as part of the regular curriculum. Another important eisteddfod that is held in Wales is the annual Llangollen International Eisteddfod, which attracts choirs, singing groups and folk dancers from all over the world. Llangollen was established in 1947 in the aftermath of the Second World War, with the philosophy behind it being to promote world peace by uniting the nations, using what its organisers saw as the unifying force of music to do so. The competitions, at the time of writing, are mostly choral, vocal, dance and instrumental. Llangollen has grown into an eclectic celebration of international musical traditions, with competitions held during the day and concerts performed during the evening. The key message of global unity and of bringing people together in peace and harmony is still emphasised and materialises in the mixture of musical traditions. This message is highlighted during the week, through the diversity of competitions, evening concerts and events such as the international parade.

### Contextualising the eisteddfod: Patagonia

In Patagonia, although a few eisteddfodau were held between 1865 and 1875, it has been difficult to establish exact dates as to when they occurred.[41] The eisteddfod did not become an 'official' event until 1965, when seventy-three visitors from Wales, including several government officials, visited Patagonia to celebrate the centenary of the colony, a visit which led to its revitalisation.[42] Ap Aeron Jones's[43] discussion (p. 184), whilst a romanticised version, is one of the few documentations of the early Patagonian eisteddfodau:

> In the Chubut Valley the first Eisteddfod took place in 1875, in a small meeting place constructed with the boards salvaged from an old shipwreck that lay on the shore near Rawson. There the group sang, recited, danced and reminisced their *old and beloved country*. During the first years of consolidation of the groups, regardless of the adversity that they had to confront, the settlers celebrated new competitions every

year, maintaining the tradition of their 'Old Wales'. In the nineteen-forties, the Eisteddfod began to include presentations in the Spanish language. The descendants of the first Settlers could no longer maintain a linguistic isolation, not even in the Eisteddfods, even considering that in its prime objectives they wished to uphold Welsh language and traditions. In a short time, the two languages have come to share equally and fuse perfectly.

Brooks and Lublin agree with this analysis, arguing that during the early years of the settler colony, the eisteddfod suffered as 'a result of such a discouraging political and socio-economic context'.[44] At the time of fieldwork, the eisteddfod was an official, popular, fully bilingual annual event, organised by the Chubut Eisteddfod Association, who had offices in the centre of Trelew. The association defined itself as follows:

> The Eisteddfod Association of Chubut is a charity association that has as its main objective to organise the Youth eisteddfod and the Chubut Eisteddfod, complying in this respect with its proposal to strengthen the Welsh language and to enable the arts as a path towards a better world.

The association organised two large eisteddfodau during the year, the Eisteddfod de la Juventud ('Youth Eisteddfod') and the Eisteddfod del Chubut ('The Chubut Eisteddfod'). The competitions for both eisteddfodau were held in a mixture of Spanish and Welsh. The eisteddfodau were attended by many local individuals from Chubut, but eisteddfod season was also a peak time for tourism to the area. Many individuals and groups would travel from the Welsh-speaking communities of Trevelin and Esquel in the Andes to attend, and it also attracted Welsh tourists visiting from Wales (explored in depth in chapter 4). Buslads of tourists on package holidays from Wales would arrive annually to witness the display of the cultural tapestry – the perfect fusion of Argentinian and Welsh culture. A group of around twenty-five young people were also selected annually by the Urdd organisation in Wales to visit Chubut, following a rigorous application process in which they were required to demonstrate the ways in which they could contribute during their time in the valley (such as through singing, conducting, instrumental performances, or by providing accompaniment on the piano or harp). Their visit would coincide with the eisteddfod and they would take part in a variety of competitions over the course of the festival, often winning several first-place prizes.

In terms of attracting tourists from Wales, the smooth mixture of *tango*, *zamba* and Welsh traditional dancing, the natural combination of Spanish and Welsh, the Welsh Patagonian choirs singing in Welsh, and the chair and crown being presented to the best Welsh poem and prose in Argentina were crucial in creating a surreal and spellbinding experience. As one couple from north Wales told me during the eisteddfod, they had '*Wastad 'di bod isho ymweld â Phatagonia* ... always wanted to visit Patagonia', had 'always dreamt of visiting Patagonia', and had decided that this year would be the best year to make the journey, with October being a logical choice of month on the basis that, '*Do ni methu colli'r 'Steddfod!* We couldn't miss the Eisteddfod!' Tour companies often took advantage of the 'magical' and 'surreal' elements of the eisteddfod in developing their marketing strategies. Teithiau Tango, a family business in Aberystwyth who had been organising tours of Welsh Patagonia for nearly seven years at the time of the research, described the Chubut Eisteddfod tour in a way that resonated with the comments of tourists visiting the eisteddfod:

> Travel to Welsh Patagonia next autumn and enjoy warm days, a welcoming Welsh heritage and something every Welsh person will recognise – an Eisteddfod! Hosted in the city of Trelew, this is an Eisteddfod with a Latin twist and is *something that has to be seen to believed*. [Emphasis mine]

For many Welsh tourists visiting Welsh Patagonia, the Welsh Patagonian eisteddfod was their first experience of the mixture of Argentine and Welsh culture, and the snapshot of what they saw became their own representation of Welsh Patagonia. In other words, their experience of the eisteddfod influenced their perceptions of what Patagonia was, the image that they took back to their friends, families, colleagues and neighbours in Wales, and their expectations of later trips which were inspired by these images and memories. Whilst there were several elements of the Welsh and Patagonian eisteddfod that could be noted as being similar, such as the structure of competitions, the presence of the Gorsedd ceremonies, and the ceremonies of the chairing and the crown, the Welsh Patagonian eisteddfod had evolved into its own unique institution. Many of my interlocutors from Wales commented on the ways in which the eisteddfodau of Patagonia and Wales were similar but simultaneously radically different, pointing especially to the visual differences (such as the presence of Argentinian flags and traditional Argentinian dance costumes), the linguistic and musical differences (namely the mixture of Spanish and Welsh, and the mixture of Argentinian folk music with traditional Welsh music), and the different ambience (in Welsh Patagonia, despite being a highly regarded, well-organised event, and despite some competitions being highly structured, the eisteddfod was generally a relaxed occasion). Contrastingly, in Wales, the eisteddfod pavilion where the competitions took place was generally a silent and serious environment. Nevertheless, the focus of both eisteddfodau tended to be on the unifying force of the festival. As Ap Aeron Jones notes:

> Every contest constitutes, not a battle for a prize, but an opportunity to learn and enjoy the sharing of an enriching experience. The participation in these competitions is open to every person and group that seeks it, for no one is specifically invited to participate, but all are welcome ... It further contributes to promote mutual understanding and international Peace through the universal language of music, poetry, and dance. As recognised, this minimises the differences between Nations and unites thousands of hearts in a joyful harmony.[45]

Ap Aeron Jones emphasises the sheer force of the eisteddfod here, in its ability to generate international peace and minimise international cultural differences in a 'joyful harmony'. In practice, there were two sides to this joyful harmony. Precisely because the festival represented the culmination of months of hard work and preparation, it was a key context in which emotions were heightened, whether these were emotions of enjoyment and happiness, as Ap Aeron Jones suggests, or other emotions stemming from complex issues of conflict and power dynamics between my interlocutors. Further, in that the Eisteddfod season was one of the busiest times of the year in terms of tourism, it was also a key context in which many of the encounters which will be explored in subsequent chapters were formalised, staged, publicly performed and watched by onlookers. Therefore, the eisteddfod was a key site in which power dynamics were created, performed and navigated for Welsh tourists and Welsh Patagonians.

### 'Is there peace?' Success and potential slippages in the ceremony of the chairing

Keane argues, in *Signs of Recognition*, that a ritual performance is one which has within it an element of creation, whereby it presents relationships as already existing whilst simultaneously creating and consolidating those relationships as 'real'. However, this is not always a simple process. Keane further argues that ritual performance is 'fraught with both logical dilemmas and practical hazards, and it cannot be understood by looking at its efficacy and successes alone'. In this respect, he calls for a focus on the 'potentials for performative infelicities and material misfortunes', arguing that attention to when things go wrong or to the moments in which the performative fails to have its intended effect are equally central to analysis as a typically successful performance.[46]

Whilst Keane's focus is on failure in the context of ritual performance, failure has been a broader theoretical concern in anthropology. Askew notes that in the context of nationalism, there has been too much focus on the effectiveness of state construction. She argues that, instead, we should shift our focus to consider moments at which the state does not come into being, highlighting that 'however unified a nation may appear ... it is always and necessarily ... a work in progress'.[47] Pelkmans makes a similar point in relation to state ideology, arguing that a focus on failure is important in and of itself (rather than only focusing on failure in relation to success), given how often it occurs. He further argues that 'the ideas that are most conspicuously present, that are most aggressively pushed, are also the most likely to collapse under their own weight'.[48] Zigon draws on his fieldwork in Moscow to make a similar argument with regards to moral breakdown. He argues that the move to study morality as a set of shared values reflects more closely an anthropological reflection of morality, in that morality in context is something that is 'normally unquestioned ... and simply done'. Contrastingly, by refocusing on moments of moral breakdown, these being those moments of ethical dilemmas when our interlocutors 'need to consciously consider or reason about what one must do', we can begin to understand better the real significance of ethics and morality to our interlocutors.[49]

In contrast to this anthropological focus on moments in which things did not go to plan, Brooks and Lublin focus largely on the success of the re-establishment of the eisteddfod, on the ways in which it was 'enjoyed by growing audiences composed of both Welsh and non-Welsh descendants', and the ways in which it has contributed to the preservation of language and Welsh culture.[50] They follow Hobsbawm to argue that the Welsh Patagonian eisteddfod represents a reinvention of tradition, whereby the eisteddfod rose 'up from the ashes' as a direct response to the attempts of the Argentine state to 'Argentinise' Welsh culture.[51] Whilst we should not downplay the success of the re-establishment of the eisteddfod, it became clear during the ceremony of the chairing in the Chubut Eisteddfod that the *potentiality* of things going wrong – what Keane refers to as 'slippages' – were just as potent, and just as revealing of power dynamics, as their actual materialisation.[52]

The ceremony of the chairing was perceived to be the most important and prestigious of the eisteddfod. In the ceremony, a poet was awarded a unique, handmade wooden chair, for the best poem written in Welsh in traditional form on a pre-decided theme. Winning the chair would bring with it a great amount of status within the Welsh Patagonian community, as the poems were judged by established poets from both Patagonia and Wales. During the ceremony, the winner would remain anonymous, referred to only by his or her chosen pseudonym, which would be called for the poet to take his or her place on the stage. A trumpet would sound, and to the third sounding of a trumpet, the poet would be asked to stand, with some selected members of the Gorsedd solemnly walking down the aisle to 'collect' the poet and bring them to the chair. A series of celebrations would follow, including traditional Welsh dancing, a speech by the head of the Gorsedd (who would also read out the winning poem), the presentation of gifts – such as flowers – to the winner, and a greeting read out to the poet, usually by a young child who was a member of the group of traditional Welsh dancers.

In the Chubut Eisteddfod in October 2015, the wool barn on the outskirts of Trelew was full for the ceremony. I had been invited to play cello for the ceremony alongside Paula on violin, Alberto on piano and Sofia on flute. Paula was a violin teacher, and the director of the string group, of which I was a member as a cellist, at Gaiman Music School. She was a tall and thin woman, always impeccably dressed, with long brown straight hair, thin-framed silver glasses and an impressive command of the Welsh language. She grew up in Buenos Aires but moved to Gaiman in her twenties. She had no Welsh ancestry, but she became a fluent Welsh speaker, and had spent a year studying in Lampeter in west Wales to perfect her skills. She later married Dafydd, a prominent and wealthy member of the Welsh community in the Andes and moved to live with him for a while in Trevelin. After her mother was tragically murdered in Trevelin by what she suspected were native Indigenous people (though nobody was ever officially convicted), she moved back to Gaiman with her two young children, Emma and Daniel. At the time of the research, Daniel was living with his father in Trevelin, and Paula visited them with Emma for the summer months and for the Christmas holidays. Paula was very committed to her work. During fieldwork, she was juggling two jobs – teaching violin in the Gaiman Music School and teaching music in Escuela 100, a primary school that was also in Gaiman. Towards the end of fieldwork, she accepted another job teaching violin in a small music school in the nearby seaside town of Playa Union.

Aside from the presence of us four musicians at the edge of the stage, and the empty eisteddfod chair, which was lit by a spotlight, the stage was completely bare. We played a solemn introduction in a canon style (with melodies overlapping), each of us taking turns with the main melody, as members of the Gorsedd in their blue cloaks, and the children in their traditional dancing outfits, walked slowly to the stage from the back of the hall. The audience perched forward on their chairs in anticipation. The atmosphere had changed from one of informal fun to one of tense excitement. Once everyone had reached the stage, they stood still and looked straight ahead. The ceremony began with a short introductory song, which was typically sung at the beginning of the ceremony. The male soloist's words were echoed by the Gorsedd and the others on stage. Following this, Ana, the head of the Gorsedd, gave an introductory speech, welcoming everyone to the ceremony, before an academic from Cardiff University read out the judgement of the poetry, and the winning poet, seated in the audience, was asked to stand to the third sounding of a trumpet, which played a simple, piercing melody.

With the first and second sounding of the trumpet, the anticipation built, and the crowd stretched their necks and looked around to see if anyone was standing up. Finally, at the third sound of the trumpet, the poet stood, and the crowd burst into applause, cheering loudly. A spotlight moved across the crowd to find the poet, and once the poet had been located, it followed him as he moved from his seat to the aisle where he waited, smiling nervously. Finally, he was greeted by two children and Awel, a longstanding member of the Gorsedd, who walked slowly to him from the stage. Awel had moved temporarily from north Wales to Gaiman to teach Welsh for the Welsh-language project eleven years ago and had stayed after falling in love with a local Welsh Patagonian dentist. '*Es i ddim nôl* ... I didn't even go back,' she said to me one evening over dinner, '*Neshi i symud popeth drosto, mewn trync* ... I just shipped all my stuff over here in a trunk!' They had since married and had two young boys. Awel was an active and much-loved member of the Welsh Patagonian community. In addition to working at Ysgol Camwy and Ysgol Gymraeg y Gaiman, she taught harp lessons in the music school and did much of the writing and translation work for the community. Awel and the children draped a white shawl across the poet's shoulders and walked in front of him, leading him to the stage, as his eyes glistened. Before being invited to sit on the chair, a member of the Gorsedd raised a sword in a case above the poet's head, and as he pulled the sword out marginally, he asked, '*A oes heddwch?* Is there peace?' to which the audience responded, '*Heddwch.* Peace.' This was repeated three times. At each response, the 'enormous sword' would be pushed with certainty back into the case, never to be fully revealed.[53] The procedures of the ceremony remained like those conveyed by Parry and Cynan:

> Following the chanting of the opening prayer, the Archdruid opens the Gorsedd Session by partially withdrawing the Grand Sword from its sheath thrice with the challenge – 'Is it Peace?' The Bards thrice respond with the cry – 'Peace.' *A*

*similar ceremony is observed at the Closing of the Gorsedd and at the Crowning and Chairing of the Bard on the National Eisteddfod Stage.*

The Grand Sword of the Gorsedd is indeed a Sword of Peace. It is never fully withdrawn from its sheath in any bardic ceremony. It must always be carried by the point and must never be held, borne or bared against any human being. This testifies that the Bards of the Isle of Britain are men of peace and bear no naked weapon against anyone.[54]

The choice of the sword as an object of peace was analytically striking in that it was a contradiction of the violence that it would usually be associated with. The partial revealing of the sword made the tension more powerful, whilst the potential violence became explicit in that the possibility of fully revealing the sword was always underlying. Alongside the Sword of Peace, there were two other key components to the ritual. First, the sounding of the trumpet in an eerily tense and silent eisteddfod hall and, secondly, singing 'Cân y Cadeirio' (Song of the Chairing), which had a similar question and answer structure to the partial revealing of the sword, with a soloist (one of the male members of Gaiman Music School choir) singing the verse and the audience joining in with the chorus:

> Henffych i'n prifardd ar fuddugol hynt,
> Seiniwch ei enw i'r pedwar gwynt.
> Hwn ydyw brenin beirdd yr Ŵyl i gyd,
> Cenwch yr utgorn i bedwar ban y byd.
>
> Henffych Brifardd! Gweiniwyd llafn y cledd,
> Bloeddiodd yr Eisteddfod yn unfryd, Hedd.

The piercing, clear sound of the trumpet cut through the rising tension with its simple melody. As the sound repeated, members of the audience began turning their heads, looking around to see if anyone had stood up. The winning poet already knew what they had to do – rise to standing on the third sounding of the trumpet. This physical act of standing to the sound brought them into being as the poet of the eisteddfod, an identification that was further affirmed in the singing of 'Cân y Cadeirio' that followed, which performatively named the poet as the *prifardd* (chief bard). The audience joining in with the chorus also had a powerful effect, with the roaring sound of an entire hall of people singing in unison invoking solidarity and unity, marking a unanimous agreement with the chairing of the poet. Song and sound here had a similar role to formal speech as defined by Keane, who argues that 'ritual speech ... embodies an unchanging ancestral heritage that transcends the here and now. But if living people are to benefit from this heritage ... they must speak'.[55] In the context of the eisteddfod, the sound of the trumpet and the singing of 'Cân y Cadeirio' consolidated the history, heritage and, critically, the authority of the Welsh in terms of their decision-making capacity about who should be the chief bard, whilst also bringing this to the present, using present-tense language – '*A oes heddwch?* Is there peace?'

The chairing of the chief bard resonates with Althusser's concept of interpellation. For Althusser, the process of becoming a subject – subjectivation – is closely related to ideology. More specifically, he argues that ruling class ideology is embodied in education systems which in turn produce docile, compliant subjects.[56] Althusser's classic metaphor which he used to demonstrate how this works in practice is that of a police officer hailing an individual on the street. The police officer shouts, 'Hey, you!' and at the very moment in which the individual turns around in recognition of and in response to the police officer, he or she is brought into being as a subject of state ideology. Critically, the subject is not equal, but rather is a subordinate subject in relation to the power structures of the state. Althusser argues that this 'Hey, you!' requires repetition to ensure ideological consolidation – to ensure a lasting rather than a fleeting encounter. An effective interpellation might therefore involve being hailed by the same ideological apparatus in different contexts.

In the context of the Welsh Patagonian eisteddfod, much like Althusser's individual on the street, the poet was hailed by the trumpet, causing a relatively immediate bodily reaction in recognition of subjectivation (in this case, standing up). The songs that followed the hailing by the trumpet served to confirm and consolidate the poet's subjectivity in addition to a particular heritage. However, differently to Althusser's case, the poet was smiling (albeit nervously). He had entered the competition knowingly, with the desire for this outcome – he wanted to become the chief bard of the eisteddfod. Furthermore, this subjectivation was not to a subordinate position. Rather, it reflected more closely a complex combination of desire and mastery.

Butler develops Althusser's ideas to introduce the element of desire, arguing that 'turning around is an act that is, as it were, conditioned both by the "voice" of the law, and by the responsiveness of the one hailed by the law'.[57] In other words, we possess some inherent vulnerability to dominant structures, and moreover we desire to be hailed because we want to be constituted as subjects. We want identification, and we performatively pursue it or, as Butler points out, 'to desire the conditions of one's own subordination is ... required to persist as oneself'.[58] By allowing himself to be hailed by the trumpet and the audience, the poet was submitting to the structure of the eisteddfod and the authority of the Welsh. However, this ultimately led the poet to a position of mastery in that he was hailed as the most powerful and prestigious of all.

Given that the ceremony was highly formal, strikingly so in the Argentinian context, there was always scope for things to go wrong and for the performative to fail in some way. In the 2018 National Eisteddfod of Wales, which was held in Cardiff Bay, the underlying potential for what Keane refers to as 'slippages' was made explicit.[59] The winning poet was standing in front of the eisteddfod chair, waiting for the sword to be partially unsheathed, and for the questioning and answering to begin, knowing that the audience must say 'peace' for the third time before he could be seated on his chair. Two members of the Gorsedd moved into position behind the winner, and they slowly and carefully lifted the large sword that they were holding between them above the poet's head. The hall was silent, until the solemnity of the situation was interrupted by the head of the Gorsedd who was leading the ceremony. Addressing the winning poet, he joked, '*Symuda ymlaen ychydig* ... Move forward a little bit there ... just in case ... be careful that this rugby player doesn't get your head ... because the pseudonym was a football player, no?' The audience clapped and the sound of laughter broke through an otherwise tense moment, revealing, albeit momentarily, the creative potential and flexibility of ritual.

However, this joke also revealed the potentiality of slippage in the ceremony. As Parry and Cynan have argued, ritual speech in this context, in combination with the unsheathing of the sword, was a symbol and a means of testifying 'that the Bards of the Isle of Britain are men of peace and bear no naked weapon against anyone'.[60] The potentiality of slippages in a highly formalised, multisensory ritual like the eisteddfod, considered within the context of the imagery and symbolism underlying the ritual, risked revealing the other side of belonging and the power relations that were always underlying in the settler colony. Here, there was always the possibility of the poet not standing to the sound of the trumpet, of the audience not singing back to the soloist singing 'Cân y Cadeirio', of the Gorsedd members dropping the sword or of the audience not answering '*Heddwch*' to the question of '*A oes heddwch?*' Dropping the sword, of course, would be the biggest slippage of all in a context where the Sword of Peace 'must never be held, borne, or bared against any human being'. All these risks had high stakes in Welsh Patagonia, where performing a peaceful, harmonious encounter was critical to the construction, consolidation and maintenance of Welsh Patagonia as a tangible place.

## 'Someone needs to get rid of that awful dog': actual slippages in the 2016 Gorsedd

The potential for slippages did sometimes become a reality. It was a bright and warm morning in late October 2016. The Gorsedd ceremony to mark the official beginning of the eisteddfod and to welcome new members was due to begin at 9.30 a.m. Capel Bethel was about a ten-minute walk from the stone circle in the Welsh settlers' square, where I was waiting with Gaiman girls' choir for the beginning of the ceremony. The members of the Gorsedd had met an hour or so earlier at Capel Bethel to form a procession. Wearing their blue and white robes, they walked slowly and purposefully to the stone circle, alongside three horses ridden by male farmers from Gaiman (who were also carrying Welsh and Argentinian flags) and accompanied by a group of young dancers from Gaiman Music School who would perform traditional Welsh dancing after the new members had been accepted to the Gorsedd.

As the procession solemnly entered the stone circle, each group took their relevant positions. The dancers lined the pathway: the girls stood on one side wearing white dresses, ties around their waists and each holding a small bunch of wildflowers, and the boys faced them from the other side, wearing white shirts, black trousers tucked into long white socks and black shoes. The farmers and their horses trotted gently around the outer circle before coming to a stop at the edge of the ceremony, stoic and poised. They were striking in their traditional gaucho clothing, and wore cowboy hats, checked shirts and thick woollen shawls wrapped around their shoulders. Their Welsh and Argentinian flags moved lightly – but poignantly – in the breeze.

We stood in the Welsh settlers' square and listened to the familiar call of the trumpet which indicated for the Gorsedd members to take their seats. Ana walked up the two steps to stand on the rock, but the trumpet call was followed by an uncomfortably long period of silence. The microphone was broken. Ana was unaware of the technical issue and continued her speech, her words lost to her audience. Many members of the choir became distracted, and I could see audience members shaking their heads and talking amongst themselves. The situation was exacerbated by the entrance of a stray dog to the stone circle, sniffing curiously at the steps of the large rock before making its way around to visit the choir and audience members, oblivious to the formality of the event. Finally, the microphones were changed and the speeches continued, but the stray dog remained. Alberto rolled his eyes, laughed and talked over Ana, '*Pob blwyddyn* ... Every year something goes wrong. My favourite event of the year is the Gorsedd. It is so funny. I could write a book about it.' Paula, to my right, leaned over and said, 'Someone needs to get rid of that awful dog'.

Slippages, potential and real, were often revealing of underlying power dynamics and dependencies within the community. In this case the slippages and their revelations were twofold. First, the broken microphone, and the distracted chatter that followed among the audience as the head of the Gorsedd failed to capture their attention, was an apt reminder of the centrality of the tools and technology required to disseminate formal speech in ritual performance.[61] Ana continued speaking, but the sound of the audience became louder than her singular voice, reminding us of the simultaneous fragility and dependency of creating a unified collective.[62]

Secondly, the stone circle was seen to be a sacred space, in which only Welsh should be spoken. Paula's comment was a pertinent reminder of the exclusive component of the ceremony. The Gorsedd portrayed itself as an inclusive space. This was symbolised, visually, by Argentinian and Welsh flags, and by the presence of tourists from Trevelin, Esquel and Wales. Sonically, inclusivity was portrayed in the singing of both the Welsh and Argentinian national anthems, and in the song sung by the girls' choir. The lyrics to this song depicted the unity of Wales and Patagonia – 'your house and dignified chapels provide shelter just like in the land of song' – but also suggested an image of peace using words such as 'soothing', 'sweet', 'love', imagery which became more explicit in the final line, 'All day and night I think that peace is with you, my sweet colony'. Ultimately, in this context, the unwelcome presence of the stray dog cut through the messages of unity, belonging and harmony, as a clear reminder that there were limitations to who could enter, belong and speak within the stone circle.

### 'Relaxing into the music': enjoyment, flow and subjectivation

Whilst Keane focuses on slippages in the context of ritual performance, in the Welsh Patagonian context, the disjuncture between the smooth running, enjoyment and 'flow' of the eisteddfod, and the potential (and real) slippages expressed itself in a broader sense, as moments of enjoyment or moments of disgruntlement. These moments extended beyond the specific ritual performances, often occurring in situations and conversations in the lead up to the eisteddfod or in its aftermath. As highlighted in the ethnographic vignette with which this chapter opened, the relaxed and informal ambience of the eisteddfodau in Welsh Patagonia was one of its defining factors. Competition was not the key focus. As one instrumental soloist said to me:

> *Por supuesto* ... Of course I like to win ... it feels good to win, just like when you win with the choir you feel good, you get a trophy, and it feels like the hard work is all worth it ... but that is not the main point. *No hay mal sentido* ... There are no bad feelings, we greet each other afterwards and we always leave as friends.

Key to creating this ambience were the same elements of fun, enjoyment and belonging that permeated choir rehearsals and Argentinian social life more broadly.

Enjoyment in the context of rehearsals and the eisteddfod was not viewed as being the antithesis to hard work but was rather seen as an integral component and a central motivating factor. As Alberto said to me one day, shrugging his shoulders and pulling a face, 'If it wasn't fun, then can you imagine attending hours and hours of choir rehearsals!' My interlocutors who were tourists from Wales variously called this enjoyment 'getting into it' or 'getting involved', something which was mirrored in my Welsh Patagonian interlocutors' discussions of *'relajarnos* ... relaxing ... *disfrutarnos* ... enjoying ourselves'. Ultimately, enjoyment was a vital component to the success of the eisteddfod, and was a state that generated feelings of immersion, belonging, inclusion and connection.

One afternoon, Rosario and I were sharing *mate* in her kitchen when she pointed to a similar connection. Rosario looked directly at me, took a long sip of the *mate* and tapped the end of her cigarette out of the window before explaining her recent enjoyment of the event:

> 'A few years ago, even though I taught English at Ysgol yr Hendre, I never really went to the Eisteddfod, *pero* ... but I really enjoyed it this year. Since having a baby and working in the nursery, things have changed. I see every day the hard work that the staff and pupils put into preparing for the Eisteddfod. *Trabajan todo el año* ... They work at it all year, but make sure that it is fun for the kids too, *viste?* Benji [Rosario's son] is a part of it and *ahora puedo ver* ... I can see now how important it is for him to feel like he belongs by participating in the rehearsals and the final Eisteddfod. I mean, you can look around Gaiman and see ... *sabes* ... you know ... the road signs in Welsh, and you can attend some Welsh events, but it is really the Eisteddfod that is the most important. *Creo que realmente es el único momento del año en que podes ver la mescla de Gales y Argentina.* That is the one time in a year where you can really see the mixture of Welsh and Argentinian.

Her eyes were wide as she spoke of her newfound enthusiasm for the eisteddfod. She said, 'It can teach my son a lot ... how to work hard towards a goal, *pero al mismo tiempo* ... at the same time it is good for his mind and brain, as well as giving him a sense of belonging in our culture in Chubut.' Whilst her comments were surprising in the sense that they signalled a radical shift in her own participation in the eisteddfod – and more broadly in terms of her relationship with Welshness – on the other hand they reflected a broader theme, the powerful capacity of music to act on individuals, in doing so generating feelings of belonging, alongside the agency in the manipulation of this power for the benefit of my interlocutors' 'minds' and 'brains'.

Rosario points here to the relationship between work and enjoyment at the eisteddfod. As she emphasised, when we watched the choirs and individuals performing, we were also imagining and remembering the hours of preparation, rehearsal and the series of smaller performances or concerts that were behind the final performance. Gell in *Art and Agency*, argued that a central component of the power and agency of art is that 'art objects are the equivalent of persons, or more precisely, social agents'.[63] Part of our feeling of awe is attributable to conceptualising the human agency behind it – the hours of work, the skill, the preparation and the concentration that become embodied in a work of art. Similarly, behind any polished performance are hours of classes, training, rehearsing, and perfecting, even whilst the goal is to conceal these hours for the audience. What Rosario drew out as being specifically Welsh Patagonian in this process was that the hard work consistently took place within a philosophy of enjoyment. Maria explained the rationale behind this in a conversation that we had one evening following the Chubut Eisteddfod in 2016:

> *Os rydym yn dechrau paratoi yn gynnar ac yn araf* … If we start preparing early and slowly, then in the long run it works better. It takes the pressure off; choir can continue to be fun and more like a social event than hard work … By the time the eisteddfod comes around, we can work harder but it is less pressure than it would be if we sang other songs then suddenly started the preparation for the eisteddfod. *Da' ni'n gwybod y caneuon* … We already know all the songs without trying.

Paula nodded in agreement, saying, 'It's much better, *da ni'n gallu mynd mewn i'r ffolderi yn yr ymennydd* … we can just dip into our choir folders that we keep in our brains and sing … that helps us to relax and enjoy the concert more.' The feeling of enjoyment that was so encouraged during choir rehearsals was also present during the eisteddfod. Just a couple of days after the Gorsedd in 2015, we were in the converted wool barn on the outskirts of Trelew waiting for the Welsh traditional dancing competitions to begin. The eisteddfod was running late, night had fallen, and the building – made of tin – was getting bitterly cold. However, with several more competitions to get through, there was a while yet before the day would end. Alberto, dressed in black dancing shoes, long white socks, balloon style shorts and a white shirt was gearing himself up to perform in the traditional Welsh dancing competition with his wife and the other dancers. Nearing his fifties, he stood out amongst the other younger dancers, and he knew it. '*Tria hwn* ... Try a bit of this,' he said to me with a wink, handing me a large thermos flask. I took a swig and was surprised at the strength of the whiskey. He roared with laughter at my reaction, and his friends joined in. 'This is what you need to be able to eisteddfod with energy until three in the morning. How do you think I dance so well? *Tisho mwy?* Do you want more? *Ti fydd yn dawnsio nesaf!* You'll be dancing next!' I laughed. Judging by the ratio of whiskey to mixer, he was probably right.

Around fifteen minutes later, the introductory music began to play for the traditional Welsh dancing competitions. I watched from the back of the room, holding the flask containing the remainder of the whiskey, grateful for its warmth. As the men and women walked in pairs up to the stage, the music increased in volume and their walk developed into a skip before the dancing begun. The long skirts of the women blew out as they moved, their heeled shoes tapped and clicked on the floor, and the audience clapped and cheered as the pairs of dancers gracefully swirled around one another. I shook my head to myself as I saw Alberto, grinning widely as he whirled around the other dancers. The music, which played from large speakers, moved quickly, without pausing, but the rhythms were steady, with string instruments, recorders and an accordion playing in cheerful unison. Those on stage were clearly enjoying themselves, and the audience was clapping to the beat. As they finished performing, the dancers stood in a row, held hands and bowed together.

Music and sound had a specific role in generating the enjoyment of the eisteddfod. Much of the music that was performed in the eisteddfod was uplifting; it had a harmonious and feel-good nature. This was especially so in the case of the music performed by the choirs, such as 'Croeso Patagonia' and 'Cân y Wladfa'. These two songs (which are explored in depth in chapter 6) both emphasised, through their lyrics and through their upbeat nature, the positive influence that music had in terms of bringing people together, as we sung of *'brodyr Cymry a'r Wladfa yn uno mewn cân* ... brothers of Wales and the colony uniting in song'. These ideas were reflected in a structural sense in the eisteddfod, in its combination of Welsh and Argentinian performances. When I asked Rosario how she had found that she had been able to enjoy the eisteddfod this year in contrast to the previous years, she elaborated:

> I found that what I needed to do was relax into the situation, listen to the music, *disfrutarme con amigos y relajarme con la musica* ... enjoy with friends and relax into the music. Once I did that, then I found that I could enjoy it so much more and then I felt better. Before, I was *muy tensa y estresada* ... too tense and stressed.

Through this process of 'relaxing into the music' Rosario had found a deeper sense of belonging in the eisteddfod. Reaching a state of flow, enjoyment and full engagement was a state in which, at its height, enabled feelings of belonging in the eisteddfod. As Diaz argues, 'intense enjoyment resulting from engagement in intrinsically rewarding tasks is due in some part to an individual's degree of absorption or immersion in relationship to said activity'.[64] Turino further notes that flow is a state in which 'one is so intent on the activity at hand that all other thoughts, concerns, and distractions disappear, and the actor is fully present in the moment'.[65] Cohen and Bodner define this as a 'subjective psychological state often associated with optimal functioning'.[66] The state of flow in music was therefore not characterised by recognition, but was rather one characterised by a 'lack of self-consciousness'. However, this is not to say that my interlocutors were unaware of the impact that music was having on them. Contrastingly, the element of *desiring* identification was central.[67] In the context of the eisteddfod, my interlocutors wanted to belong, and they worked hard to move past other feelings such as feeling 'tense' or 'stressed' to reach enjoyment. Working towards full engagement and flow was one way in which they could move towards identification and the feeling of belonging to the Welsh Patagonian community.

## The politics of inclusion and space at the Chubut Eisteddfod

Rosario's experience highlighted the transformative and creative potential of the eisteddfod, in terms of its capacity to bring people together. Key to this were the feelings of enjoyment and fun that the atmosphere invoked for its participants. However, it was also a context that exacerbated and created internal community politics and was sometimes perceived as a source of pressure and stress. Several moments related to the eisteddfod during fieldwork did not fit clearly into Keane's category of slippages, but rather represented 'moments of disgruntlement' that referred to other kinds of tensions stemming from, for example, the financial implications of hosting visitors, or from the politics of converting a large wool barn. Whilst Keane calls for a focus on both ritual performance and its relationship to what he calls the 'mundane activities', his argument is that the focus on tensions, hazards, risks and slippages in the ritual performance will ultimately reveal tensions that can be explored further in more mundane contexts.[68] Contrastingly, in the Welsh Patagonian context, the moments of failure and conflict that occurred beyond the eisteddfod made explicit new tensions and power dynamics.

Just as Rosario was telling me about her renewed interest and feeling of belonging in the eisteddfod, there was a knock on the front door, and it was Bauti, Rosario's good friend. He worked in Trelew for a textiles company as a clothing designer, and I often saw him on the bus to Trelew. He was tall, thin and outspoken, with a diamond ring in his ear. I had briefly seen him at the eisteddfod on the previous Saturday and I asked him whether he had enjoyed it. He laughed, and said, 'No.' Expertly, he flicked a cigarette out of a box and tucked it behind his ear. With a shrug and a grin, he elaborated on what he viewed as being the problematic elements of the eisteddfod:

> Instead of trying so hard to make it like Wales, *necessitamos aceptar* ... we should accept that we are in Argentina and take the idea of the festival but have it adapt to the cultural context. If they were to include more types of arts ... photography, dressmaking and cooking instead of only having limited competitions in which people who can speak Welsh can participate, *el Eisteddfod se puede crecer* ... then

the eisteddfod could grow, *y quizás vamos mejorando los relaciones generales en Gaiman también* ... and it would maybe have a good influence on the relationships in Gaiman more broadly as well.

Bauti's comment suggests that the eisteddfod was an exclusive space, and points to a direct link between the improved accessibility of the competitions and the relationships that could be formed in the village on that basis. Issues of inclusion and exclusion were particularly relevant in 2015, with the celebrations of 150 years since the establishment of the settler colony leading to the increased presence of media, tourists and other visitors including film-makers, artists, academics, students and musicians from Wales. Whilst the influx of tourists was broadly described in positive terms, the increase in visitors also brought with it a necessity to host them, in addition to a pressure to perform a particular type of Welsh Patagonia.

The complexity of this was explained most succinctly to me by Elena.[69] Locally referred to as '*brenhines Gaiman* ... the queen of Gaiman', Elena was in her eighties with long grey hair, which she usually wore clipped up at the back of her head. She was a direct descendant of Michael D. Jones (the key instigator of the settler colony in Patagonia) and throughout her life had worked as the headmistress for the bilingual Welsh and Spanish secondary school in Gaiman, Ysgol Camwy. Now retired, she continued to work for the community as the administrative coordinator for the Menter Patagonia Welsh teacher scheme. She was highly respected not least for her fierce personality, wisdom, welcoming nature and directness, but also as a source of knowledge, especially of informal information with regards to the personal politics of Welsh community, and the ongoing or upcoming social events within it. Despite the age difference between us, she became a good friend during fieldwork and one whom I admired, respected and appreciated the company of greatly.

As Elena said:

*Mae'n anodd* ... It is difficult, because every year, we know that beyond the audience of people from Chubut, there are people from Wales ... *pobl pwysig* ... important people. That brings its own challenges, and sometimes adds ... you know ... stress because we want to be good hosts to them and for them to have a *profiad da* ... good experience here.

She further explained that she herself felt personal pressure to 'be a good host', despite being in her eighties and being too tired to engage in all the activities (such as showing tourists around the village). During one choir rehearsal in the weeks before the arrival of a large group of visitors from Wales, Maria, the choir director, expressed concern that a group arriving from Wales wanted an asado. '*Un asado?* An asado? They never said how many people they wanted for an asado. *Wythdeg?* Will it be eighty?' The choir members laughed: it went without saying that it would be next to impossible for them to cater for eighty people. Later, as I travelled in the car home with a fellow choir member, who lived in the same neighbourhood as me, she explained the general anxiety around the visit:

> *No es una problema* ... It is not a problem with the visitors, per se. The problem is that the province has made it appear like we have lots of money, like we can afford to invite people and pay for them, but *no podemos* ... we can't. We are the third world, we haven't got that kind of money. There is this idea that people in Wales are so organised. When we go to Wales, we think, wow, *acá funciona todo* ... this is a country that works. But now nothing has been organised, so it's a mess.

Similar sentiments emerged in the conversion of a large wool barn on the outskirts of Trelew in 2015. The wool barn had been converted into a concert hall for the visit of a large orchestra from Wales in 2015 and was used later that year to host the eisteddfod. The newly converted building was huge. It had the capacity to hold 1,500 people seated and 5,000 people standing, and was fitted with toilets, air conditioning and heating. Rumours quickly began to circulate in the village that the orchestra had made it a condition of their visit to have a concert space large enough to host a symphonic orchestra, and that the local government in Chubut had obliged and had justified funding the conversion of the wool barn on the basis that the hall would be used for many other concerts within the community. Many of my interlocutors felt angry about the conversion of the wool barn, as they saw it as an example of both the irresponsible spending of government money in a context where there was visible poverty, and of the privileging of the Welsh community. In a phone conversation with one of my local Argentinian interlocutors who lived in Trelew, two years after fieldwork ended, I asked her what had come of the wool barn, and she said:

> That barn ... *no te vas a creer che* ... you won't believe it ... they used for one book fair ... you know the one usually in Trelew. Nobody went because nobody could reach it and now it's just standing there *vacío* ... empty ...! *Y al mismo tiempo hay chicos sin comida* ... And at the same time there are children going without food in the other *barrios* ... *yo te dije* ... I told you didn't I ... how it would turn out. It was to make an impression, I think ... to the visitors. *Más o menos nos prendemos fuego a la plata* ... More or less we set fire to the money because we never use [the barn].

In the field, when I asked my interlocutors what they thought about the wool barn conversion, I was often met with shrugged shoulders or, once, a blunt response, 'There is no space to host a symphonic orchestra in Chubut because there *isn't* a symphonic orchestra in Chubut.' Given that even the largest of concerts could easily be accommodated in the local gymnasium, it was very rare for the province to require such a large space. Furthermore, the wool barn was cold, especially at night, as it was made of tin, and it was also not easily accessible by foot from Trelew. Ironically, then, despite its size, the new space was not as inclusive as previous sites. In the run-up to the 2015 eisteddfod, many of my interlocutors, especially those in charge of organising the eisteddfod, became concerned about filling the hall. Would it be possible to attract a large enough audience? Would it look empty in comparison to the tightly packed hall that the festival was usually held in? What impact would an empty hall have for the future of the Chubut Eisteddfod? As the headteacher of the Welsh-medium nursery school in Gaiman told me, in the days leading up to the eisteddfod, '*Dwi isho teimlo'n gyffrous* ... I want to feel excited, but I can't ... not yet [...] When I know we have an audience, and everything is ok ... *wedyn bydda i'n ymlacio* ... then I will relax and enjoy.'

Following the eisteddfod, many of my interlocutors who said that they had 'enjoyed' it followed their comment up with a remark that they felt as though they 'belonged' or that they felt a sense of 'community'. One couple who were visiting from Wales said to me, 'We were talking last night, in our hotel, about how *weird* it is, that we have only been here for three days, *ond da ni'n teimlo fel da ni'n perthyn* ... but we already feel like we belong!' Allowing themselves to get into the flow of the eisteddfod was, for many of my interlocutors, not a difficult thing to do. The general anticipation of the event generated an air of excitement, there was the consistent sound of chatter and laughter in the hall, and much of the music performed, with its upbeat nature, lifted the mood of the crowd. However, being in the flow of the eisteddfod was a privileged position to be in. Not all my interlocutors found that this engagement and enjoyment was so effortless, and consequently they did not feel the same sense of identification and belonging. Bauti felt alienated, for example, by what he perceived as being the lack of opportunities for local Argentinians to participate. Some of my other local Argentinian interlocutors thought that the conversion of the wool barn was a waste of money and were consequently unable to identify positively with the project. Rosario 'changed her mind' and allowed herself to get into the flow of the eisteddfod for the benefit of her son – she knew that enjoyment and 'relaxing' were key to the feeling of belonging within the community. Critically, she also had the option of doing that, given her Welsh descent.

## Conclusions: The other side of belonging

The 2022 National Eisteddfod in Wales was held in Tregaron, a small town in rural Ceredigion, mid Wales. Following a two-year respite due to the 2020 Covid-19 pandemic, it was an eagerly anticipated and well-documented event. Shortly after the week-long event, BBC News released a video of a series of interviews with individuals visiting or working at the eisteddfod, in doing so focusing on the inclusivity of the Welsh-language festival.[70] Whilst the video drew out some key challenges about connecting the festival more closely with communities, the overall tone was positive in terms of the progress made with generating an inclusive and diverse eisteddfod. Later, however, one of the interviewees took to X to state that her comments had been decontextualised in the final video. She tweeted 'It's horrid to see people struggle on the *maes* and the lack of diversity in the stallholders and competitors ... There was no presence from Racial Equality Organisations ... there were major issues with access for those in wheelchairs and mobility scooters.' These tweets started an online debate, with others noting 'In the eisteddfod if you start a conversation with me in English, I will assume it is because I am brown.' Whilst the social media dialogue also emphasised the elements of belonging, with comments that 'this is the most inclusive eisteddfod I've experienced', they highlighted the work that remains to be done, and in doing so emphasised the way in which, no matter how much we may try to paint the picture in a different light, in the context of large ritual performances, power and exclusion is never far from belonging.

As the culmination of the musical year in the Chubut Province, the eisteddfod embodied many of the key themes which will be explored in different contexts in subsequent chapters, such as the philosophy of enjoyment and informality, the connected ideas of belonging and solidarity, and the simultaneous creation and performance of identity, with all the complexities that these themes entailed. When my interlocutors 'relaxed into the [harmonious, upbeat] music' in the context of the eisteddfod, or when they allowed the performance to mobilise them, the interpellation of the ideology of belonging, peace and inclusion was at its most effective. Contrastingly, however, this chapter has also focused on moments of failure. In doing so, it has analysed potential and real slippages in the highly ritualised and formalised ceremony of the chairing. The potential for slippages in this ceremony reflected real issues, and arguably underlying fears. The ceremony of the chairing, and presence of the sword, were representative of peace, an image that was key to the continuation of Welsh Patagonia. The Welsh Patagonian audience knew that dropping the sword in the ceremony of the chairing could not happen. The stakes were too high – it would reveal the violence underlying the construction of Welsh Patagonia. In other words, it was a threat to the process of creating the relations of harmony and belonging that were so central to the eisteddfod. Potential slippages could also become real slippages, as in the case of the Gorsedd of 2016.

In exploring the concepts of failure and slippage, this chapter has addressed one of the key flaws of Althusser's[71] model of interpellation, which is that his account does not allow for failure. In his analysis, there is no hesitation or doubt that the individual being interpellated *will* turn around. For Althusser, this is not necessarily about desire to turn around, but rather it is more to do with our inevitable compliance with ideological apparatuses that shape who we are as subjects. Contrastingly, in the Welsh Patagonian context, there were concrete moments in which the performative did not work as intended, and even in contexts where the slippages did not necessarily materialise, the potentiality for failure was always implicit. When the performative did work, it was not as simple as an act of submission to dominant structures. In the case of the chairing of the poet, for example, subjectivation was desired and not entirely concerned with subordination in that being hailed as the *prifardd* was to become a respected and powerful subject.

Ultimately, integrating the concept of flow and enjoyment, or lack thereof, into the analysis of ritual performance has two key outcomes. First, it enables us to develop a theoretical understanding of what 'moments of disgruntlement' might mean in terms of power dynamics. In this respect, the chapter has moved beyond Keane[72] who focuses on slippages in the specific context of ritual performance, to argue for a focus on the subjective disjuncture between the moments of enjoyment or flow and the 'moments of disgruntlement' that my interlocutors expressed. In this context, this focus revealed new tensions specifically related to the financing and organising of the eisteddfod; tensions that would not have been revealed through a focus on the slippages that occurred in the ritual performance alone. This has further implications for our analysis of performance and performativity. Working towards an analysis that considers not only the concept of ritual performance being performative, as Keane does, but rather which takes practical account of both performance (for example, the eisteddfod) and performativity (for example, the rehearsals leading up to it, and the aftermath) can reveal new power dynamics that are not visible when looking at slippages in the actual performance alone.

Secondly, an ethnographic focus on the concept of slippages also begs the question: who chooses what a slippage is? Whilst we are analysing ritual performance, how are we to know whether our own definitions of slippages are relevant to our interlocutors and fully reflect their concerns? This is a pertinent question both in terms of locating slippages, and in terms of analysing them. The term, to an extent, implies an outsider looking in, defining what he or she views as errors, which arguably cannot work in a context where there can be disjuncture between what an audience member and performer might view as a slippage. For example, subjective experiences of minor musical performance anxiety, if well managed, are also not always visible to the audience. On the other hand, a highly musically skilled audience member might notice a more-or-less irrelevant slippage in a piece of music that the performers could be unaware of.

However, this is not to suggest that we should do away with the concept of slippages. Alternatively, as this chapter has demonstrated, a consideration of points of potential and real slippage can be useful in that they are revealing of subtle contradictions and tensions within ritual performance. This chapter has argued that these should be considered in combination with the expressions of enjoyment and 'moments of disgruntlement' expressed to us by our interlocutors, which may occur long before the ritual performance begins or long after it is over, and which may reveal new tensions. The focus on both slippages and 'moments of disgruntlement' paves the way for the remainder of the book, which argues for a broader consideration of both the objectifying acts of looking, watching or gazing in addition to the lesser studied processes of listening, hearing and engaging, which were so key in the Welsh Patagonian context. Ultimately, the attention to slippages, flow, enjoyment and moments of disgruntlement highlights the contradictions between agency and control, between order and risks of failure, between objectivity and subjectivity, and between belonging and exclusivity embedded within the eisteddfod.

# 4

# Performing Patagonia under the gaze of the Welsh other

> The tourist gaze is constructed through signs, and tourism involves the collection of signs. When tourists see two people kissing in Paris what they capture in the gaze is timeless romantic Paris.[1]

## Introduction: 'Cân y Wladfa'

It was a Monday evening in October 2015, and we had two evening choir rehearsals scheduled in the music school: the girls' choir rehearsal followed by a mixed choir rehearsal. It was rumoured that members of the BBC National Orchestra of Wales (BBC NOW) were to be present at both. I was one of the first to arrive, as I had already been in the music school all afternoon assisting with violin lessons. I began to pull out some chairs for the girls' choir rehearsal, and shortly afterwards Alberto arrived clutching a thermos flask of hot water in one hand and *mate* in the other, with Eleanor (his mother and the girls' choir conductor) at his side. Behind them was an unfamiliar man, whom I assumed to be the man referred to a few days ago by Paula as the 'important person' from Wales. 'I have been trying to get through to Eleanor, but she's busy with an *important person* from Wales,' she had told me, her eyes wide. He was tall, broad and at a guess around thirty years old, but unintimidating in jeans and a casual striped t-shirt. He seemed friendly, but shy, and his head was slightly lowered as he entered the room, his eyes rising to greet us and his mouth breaking into a restrained smile a few moments later. When Alberto greeted me, I took the opportunity to ask who the newcomer was. It emerged that he was a choir inspector from Wales who was going to assist with the girls' choir rehearsal.

The first song that we sung was 'Hwiangerdd Mabon' ('Mabon's lullaby'), a lullaby for soprano and alto accompanied by soft chords on the piano. The music was composed by Alberto and the lyrics were written by Awel. The lyrics evoked quite effectively the spectacular Patagonian sunsets, which were a splashing of red, orange, pink and purple, in addition to the broader Patagonian landscape – *'Mae'r haul yn machlud heibio Gaiman* ... the sun sets beyond Gaiman, and Camwy drags lazily to the sea'. When we had finished, Eleanor looked at us with sparkling eyes. 'Is there anything in particular you girls would like to go over?' she asked. I suggested a song called 'Cân y Wladfa' ('Song of the settler colony'). It was an emotive, romantic song composed by Alberto that the girls' choir had been singing for a few years. Eleanor, who was quite a frail woman, stood up from her usual seated conducting position and marked the beat with great force. Her dangling earrings were swinging vigorously, and we were singing with far more energy than usual. I felt completely engaged in the act of singing the song, and in that moment truly meant the words that I was singing. I could see, and feel, that the other choir members were similarly energised. Dylan, the choir inspector was grinning, filming on his smartphone, with tears in his eyes. At the end of the song, Eleanor asked Dylan what could be improved, to which he responded, 'I don't know what to say, I feel quite emotional. The hairs on my arm are standing on end. I can sense the passion.' I had goosebumps too. The excitement and energy in the room was palpable, unusually so.

The side door opened, and people started trickling in for mixed choir rehearsal, which was due to start a few minutes later. Choir was busier than usual, and the room was full and stuffy. The news had spread quickly in the weeks before that members of the BBC NOW (National Orchestra of Wales) would be present at this rehearsal. We began by singing 'Croeso Patagonia' ('Welcome Patagonia'), an acapella piece written for four-part choir, accompanied by the beat of the *bombo* (a traditional Latin American drum). The lyrics combined Wales and Argentina, 'sleeping a siesta before having a cup of tea', and melodically parts of 'Calon Lân' were recognisable within the Argentinian rhythms. Following this, the conductor of the BBC NOW took over. He had boundless energy and an eccentric spark. He confidently led the choir with what he himself referred to as the 'little Spanish' that he had picked up from his holidays in Spain. With great enthusiasm, he led the choir through the songs that we were going to sing with the orchestra in the concert: 'Ar Hyd y Nos' ('All through the night') and 'Hafan gobaith' ('Another Day'). Despite the short amount of time that we had to rehearse these two long, harmonically difficult pieces that we had never seen before, the choir improved significantly. The rehearsal finished later than usual, at 23:00, but nobody seemed tired.

⁂

What do Welsh tourists see when they attend the rehearsal or performance of a Welsh choir in Patagonia? What happens to the members of the Welsh choir when they are being watched by a tourist? This scenario did not seem to be simply a case of performing with more energy than usual for an audience. This chapter argues that when under the recognition and gaze of the Welsh other, Welsh Patagonia came into being as a concrete entity. In making this argument, it seeks to bring the role of the imagination, shame and power to the forefront of an analysis of the tourist gaze.[2] Imagination was key to this encounter, both in the sense of the capacity of the Welsh Patagonians to imagine how the tourists wanted to see them, and in the capacity of the tourists to imagine Welsh Patagonia from home before their visit. In the moment of being – or *potentially* being – observed, Welsh Patagonia was at its most self-conscious, and subjectivity as Welsh Patagonian – along with identity or membership within the 'group' – was at its most secure. The chapter focuses on the dynamic encounter between imagination, performance and the gaze – the gaze of tourists and officials in the making of Welsh Patagonia.

This chapter first considers Gaiman Music School and its relationship to tourism. The role of the imagination (imagining Patagonia from Wales and imagining Wales from Patagonia) and its connection to subjectivity is then discussed, through an exploration of singing the Welsh national anthem out of context. It argues that the ways in which Patagonia was imagined in Wales and the ways in which Wales was imagined in Patagonia represented something social and creative that was re-defined in every social interaction. The chapter then considers the performance of Welsh Patagonia in two key contexts, providing an ethnographic analysis of tourist interactions in Gaiman Music School and in more official contexts, such as during concerts and the annual celebrations on 28 July to mark the arrival of the first settlers in Patagonia, formally known as 'Diwrnod y Glaniad' ('Day of the Landing'). Finally, following Bianchi's argument that a critical analysis of tourism requires a sustained engagement with relations of power that shape tourist interactions, it considers the ways in which joking was used by my interlocutors to comment on the differences between themselves and the tourists.[3] This highlights the agency in these interactions, and the ways in which imagining others was predicated upon a range of practices which maintained group boundaries.[4]

### Tourism in Chubut: 'If you're going to visit, it has to be this year!'

During fieldwork, Welsh tourism and the subsequent connections, exchanges and communication via social media platforms, such as Facebook, Instagram and X, between Wales and Patagonia were a huge part of the economy of the Chubut Province. As Gibson notes, 'social media has further amplified and refracted what we once understood as the tourist gaze: fuelling the search for the perfect Instagram photo'.[5] In Welsh Patagonia, this was closely connected to Gaiman Music School, which operated as a hub of Welsh activity in Gaiman. In Gaiman, word of mouth quickly spread to tourists that Gaiman Music School was operating an open-door policy for visitors from Wales and, in 2015 especially, it became common for tourists to turn up at choir rehearsals, slipping through the side door and waving enthusiastically at the choir members before watching the choir rehearsal. Visitors from Wales sometimes chose to take an observational role, whilst others joined in with the singing. After the rehearsal there would be an opportunity for choir members to chat with the visitors, and as such Gaiman Music School became central to tourist interaction.

2015 was a particularly significant year for tourism in the Chubut Province. It marked 150 years since the establishment of the settler colony in Patagonia, which inspired several individuals and groups to visit. A group of fifty prominent individuals from Wales including the comedian Rhod Gilbert, Welsh weatherman Derek Broadway and former Welsh rugby international Shane Williams completed a six-day trek in Patagonia to raise money for Velindre Cancer Centre in Cardiff. The National Youth Choir of Wales also completed a Patagonia tour which consisted of singing in several concerts around the province, and the BBC National Orchestra of Wales hosted concerts and workshops in Gaiman Music School. Alongside these large group visits, several key individuals also visited, including the Welsh harpist, Gwenan Gibbard, the Welsh textiles artist Cefyn Burgess and the Welsh singer Casi Wyn, and many other tourists decided to make the once-in-a-lifetime trip too: as one couple enthusiastically declared to me during their visit to the eisteddfod, 'If you're going to visit, it *has* to be this year!'

Accompanying the excitement and nostalgia for the original journey of the Welsh settlers was increased publicity and UK media coverage for Welsh Patagonia. From 2015, BBC Radio Wales began to host various programmes, including a three-part series on the Welsh settler colony and the reasons why the Welsh settlers left Wales, a programme following the six-day charity trek in Patagonia, and a programme focusing on the invisibility of Welsh women of Patagonia in the historical narrative, hosted by Welsh comedian Sian Harries.[6] BBC Radio Cymru also broadcasted a programme called 'Remembering Patagonia'.[7] Several news articles were also published at around the same time, with headlines such as 'Patagonia 150 years on: a little Wales beyond Wales', '150th anniversary of Welsh emigration to Patagonia', 'Welsh settlers' "path of friendship" in Patagonia', 'Can the Welsh language survive in Patagonia?', 'How is the Welsh language being preserved in Patagonia?', 'Welsh connection important boost for Patagonia's economy', 'BBC National Orchestra of Wales first for Patagonia', and 'Record number of Welsh learners in Patagonia, Argentina'.[8]

Alongside this, there were several Facebook, X and Instagram pages in which people from Wales and Argentina communicated regularly with each other, by sharing photos and memories with each other, by sending each other messages and by commenting on each other's posts. Menter Patagonia had an ongoing Facebook, Instagram and X page. Of the 150 celebrations, the hashtag #patagonia150 was tagged in 668 photo posts on Instagram, and in hundreds more posts on X. There were several pages dedicated to the settler colony on X, including a 'Patagonia 150 page' (@Patagonia150), a page for Welsh people in Patagonia called 'Galeses en Patagonia' (@galespatagonia), and a page for a social project initiative of the BBC National Orchestra of Wales, which grew out of their 2015 visit, to send instruments to the music schools and groups in Patagonia, which was called 'Patagonia Instrument Project' (@pataginsproject). The social media pages were used at the time of fieldwork and beyond by those in both Wales and Patagonia to upload photos from past related events, to advertise future events, to find contacts in terms of accommodation, to find host organisations or individuals in both places, to outline volunteering or community-work plans and to keep in touch with – or find the contact details of – friends met in either place.

The tourism industry was supported by travel companies: Teithiau Tango ('Tango Travels'), Welsh Patagonia (based in Esquel in the Andes) and Latin Routes (based in the UK) all organised annual tours. Most of the customers who travelled on these 'all-in-one' tours were from Wales. Angharad, the sales and marketing executive for Teithiau Tango, who herself had visited Patagonia with Teithiau Tango prior to taking up a full-time role in their Aberystwyth offices, explained to me that she felt that many of her customers 'were ticking Patagonia off their *rhestr bwced* ... bucket list' as it was '*rhywle ma' nhw wedi breuddwydio mynd* ... somewhere they had always wanted to go for the Welsh connection'.

In this sense, travel companies, the broader Welsh Chubut economy and members of the Welsh Patagonian community all benefited in their own ways from the circulation of the 'empty landscape' narrative, which came with ideas of untouched Welshness. The empty land trope fed into the ways in which the formal memory of the province had been constructed to hold the establishment of the Welsh settler colony as the most significant event. Berg argues that what she has termed 'the Welsh-national community':

> envision tourism to the Welsh colony in Argentina as a way to experience *pure* and *untouched* Welsh heritage, with heavy emphasis placed on hearing the Welsh language spoken in a region that has not been *contaminated* by English ... many Welsh tourists come to Patagonia with the expectation of hearing an unadulterated form of Welsh.[9]

Benson draws on her fieldwork with British migrants in rural France to make a similar argument. She notes that 'rural France is imagined as the rural idyll', whereby many of the migrants who live there had initially visited as tourists, with their permanent move partly being determined by the desire to develop meaningful social relationships in a small community. Analogously to the nostalgic ideas of Welsh Patagonia being a place where it was possible to encounter a pure, harmonious, English-free Welshness, Benson argues that 'underpinning such perceptions [of rural France as being a more authentic way of life] ... is a nostalgic understanding of village life as a close-knit community where "everybody knows everybody"'.[10]

Similarly, Novoa (2021) draws on her fieldwork in Lota, a former coal-mining town in southern Chile, arguing that nostalgia is mobilised 'as a driving force to organise and challenge official historical narratives, planning modes, and [exclusionary] heritage tourism practices'. In Lota, the nostalgic tourist narratives that Novoa researched focused on the histories of women and Indigenous people, which tended to be marginalised in the 'official' narrative in favour of a masculine, privileged narrative. For example, one of Novoa's interlocutors, Paulina, the daughter of an urban Indigenous woman, organises guided tours for visitors in which she 'tells stories about ships, sailors, and prostitutes and highlights the life of the cabarets in the lower sector of the city'.[11] Whilst the focus on narrative and imagination in both these cases resonates with the Patagonian case, there is a key difference in the case of Novoa, in that the narratives and stories told in Welsh Patagonia tended to reinforce – rather than challenge – the dominant historical narratives.

Ultimately, tourism, media coverage, social media and the circulation of key narratives were inseparable – they worked together to promote Welsh Patagonia to visitors, with news coverage and social media sparking new interest in Patagonia. To take one example, in response to a Facebook post by the BBC NOW during their visit, one viewer commented, 'Amazing! Welsh is still spoken in Patagonia!'. Ultimately, choir rehearsals and the interactions they generated between choir members and tourists created spaces in which ideas and imaginations about the other were defined, articulated, complicated and performed.

## Imagining Wales

> Music both defines and transcends the borders of destinations, while it emphasises and challenges notions of tradition, provides opportunities for liminal play, transgression, and

resistance, and helps define the identities of visitors and the visited.[12]

Whilst the numerous Welsh events held in the Chubut Province were varied, they all held one thing in common: they began with the audience standing and singing the national anthem of Wales, and ended with the singing of the national anthem of Argentina. The Gaiman string group also regularly rehearsed the national anthem of Wales, and the mixed choir would end rehearsals by singing it if they were in the presence of visitors. Singing or playing the Welsh national anthem was significant in this respect, in that it often became a key moment in inspiring the imagination of Wales or Patagonia.

The first time I took part in the collective singing of the national anthem of Wales was one day after arriving in the field, on 28 July 2015, in a ceremony to commemorate the arrival of the Welsh to Patagonia. The main purpose of the ceremony was to unveil a plaque outside the chapel where forty-three of the original Welsh settlers were buried. There was a buzzing chatter as we waited for the pianist to drum out the introduction to the anthem on the keyboard. I listened to the mixture of Spanish and Welsh, enjoying the way in which the two different languages and accents intertwined into each other. A pause in the introduction and an enthusiastic yet casual anticipatory wave from the pianist signalled the gap for us to take a collective deep breath. We obliged, and filled our lungs, before singing the first verse in Welsh, '*Mae hen wlad fy nhadau yn annwyl i mi ... gwlad beirdd a chantorion ...*' I glanced around the crowd. Some were reading the words from the sheet handed to us at the beginning of the ceremony, but others knew the words by heart. Standing among a crowd of locals and tourists outside Capel Moriah in Trelew, huddled in our winter coats, it was strange to consider that we were 8,000 miles away from the country that we were singing for and to.

When the BBC NOW visited Gaiman Music School in 2015, we were asked if we could end the rehearsal by singing the national anthem of Wales. Later, a video of Gaiman choir singing the anthem was published on the orchestra's Facebook page, with the post, written by one of the visitors, stating, 'Very few of the Argentines in this video have ever been to Wales, and not all of them speak Welsh ... but last week they belted out the anthem as if they were on the pitch at the

Millennium Stadium.' The video shows the rehearsal of the mixed choir singing the anthem, directed by the conductor of the BBC NOW. The anthem was accompanied by Alberto on the piano. In the video, the main hall of Gaiman Music School is brimming with choir members, some having to stand with the lack of available chairs. The anthem is sung with passion: 'belted' out indeed. The piano accompaniment is exaggerated with heavy chords hammered out in the left hand, using trills to generate a dramatic drum-roll effect, and the director shouts words of encouragement where rests in the singing allow. At the end of the second chorus, several choir members harmonise spontaneously, and the choir split into two octaves, with some of the sopranos singing an octave (eight notes) higher than the rest, and everyone laughs and claps.

With the added self-consciousness of singing in front of a camera, singing about Welsh Patagonia suddenly became a much more passionate, engaged event. Tourists would inevitably film and photograph parts of the choir rehearsals, and this filming and photographing was a two-way process, invoking enthusiasm from the singers but inspiring changes in the viewer too. As Gillespie argues, 'it is not only the photographee who is influenced by the interaction, so too is the photographer'.[13] Tourists filmed a selection of things to show to family and friends back home, and their choice of what to film and photograph largely depended on their own ideas about what they came to see – for example, Welsh Patagonians singing the Welsh national anthem. The pre-conceptualisations of Welsh Patagonia held by the visiting tourists and of the social media users at home became affirmed, challenged and re-articulated at the boundary between them and the other. The imagination of the tourists, about what Welsh Patagonia should look and sound like informed the reality that played out in front of them (quite literally so, in that the choir were explicitly asked to perform the Welsh national anthem for their visitors). Simultaneously, it was at this point that Welsh Patagonia 'became itself'; in other words, we appeared to the tourists at our most coherent, as a tangible, bounded, identifiable group of Welsh Patagonians. This performance of Welsh Patagonia therefore in turn informed the imagination of its viewers.

Later in fieldwork, during a rehearsal of the music school's string group one October evening, we played the Welsh national anthem twice, and afterwards, Juan, one of the violin teachers, who lived in the province of Rio Negro where he worked as a violinist in a philharmonic orchestra, turned to me, frowning. He pointed to the chorus with his bow on my sheet music and said, '*Sabes* ...You know, in Argentina we sing this part twice when we sing the Welsh national anthem, *creo que ustedes lo cantan una vez* ... I think you only sing it once.' I nodded, and Paula responded to his remark, '*Mae e ar gyfer cadarnhau'r iaith* ... It is to affirm the language.' Juan responded, '*Sí* ... Yes, it is almost that when we sing the Welsh national anthem here it must be sung with *más entusiasmo* ... more enthusiasm and conviction.'

Whilst Paula's comment could be taken to suggest that people in Patagonia needed to practise their Welsh or make it more present in an Argentine context, Juan's response points to the relationship between music, the imagination and creation. The suggestion here is that at least some imagination about other places may come from the musical piece. In this case, the imagination came from the structure of music or the musical style, whereby singing the Welsh national anthem in the Patagonian context, and the repetition of the chorus, was imbued with intentionality and purpose, and imagined to be connected to the affirmation or consolidation of the connection between place and person. Singing, in this context, must be enthusiastic and convincing – it is a declaration of commitment to, and a creation of a tie of belonging to, a specific place.

The discussion in the music school resonates, in part, with Butler and Spivak's argument that singing the national anthem is an act of becoming. They argue that illegal Latin American immigrants in the United States sing the American national anthem in Spanish (a language not officially recognised by a very nationalist state) to declare their right to belong. It is a performative act – to sing it is to become it – and the 'counter-nationalist' act of singing in Spanish leads to the possibility of the recognition of diversity and multiplicity by the state.[14] Similarly, as my interlocutors pointed out, the act of singing the Welsh national anthem in Welsh, in the context of Argentina where the majority language is Spanish, served to reinforce the presence of Welshness as well as to consolidate the links between those singing and Wales. As Butler and Spivak note:

> The US national anthem was sung in Spanish as was the Mexican anthem. The emergence of '*nuestro hymno*' introduced

the interesting problem of the plurality of the nation, of the 'we' and 'our': to whom does this anthem belong? ... It's not just that many people sang together – which is true – but also that singing is a plural act, an articulation of plurality. If, as Bush claimed at the time, the national anthem can only be sung in English, then the nation is clearly restricted to a linguistic majority, and language becomes one way of asserting critical control over who belongs and who does not.[15]

However, there is a significant difference between the two examples. Beyond the fact that the Welsh were not singing the Argentinian national anthem in Welsh, but rather singing the Welsh national anthem in Welsh, the power relations of what Butler and Spivak describe are quite different to the dynamics in the Welsh Patagonian context. The Welsh Patagonians were a powerful group, both economically and politically. They were not illegal immigrants; by contrast Argentina had invited them to live there as part of its broader civilising mission in the late 1800s, and they were drawn into this mission. Due to the influx of money that the Welsh community received from tourism, as a social group they were much better off financially than many of the local Argentinians with whom they shared the Chubut Province. The implication here is that, differently to Butler and Spivak's argument, singing the Welsh national anthem in Welsh in Argentina could be about asserting power or authority rather than about asserting their subordinate rights to belong.

In addition to affirming the connection between Wales and Argentina, singing the Welsh national anthem in Chubut created a disjuncture between context and music, and it is within this disjuncture that we find scope for imaginative and creative ideas concerning place and personhood, something especially significant for those who had never visited Wales or who did not view themselves as having a Welsh connection by descent. Shortly after the string group rehearsal finished, I walked home. There was a warm breeze, indicating the very welcome emergence of spring after a bitterly cold winter. My hands were in my pockets, my headphones over my ears and my mind was far away, reflecting on the day's events. I was walking across the bridge above the Chubut River to the other side of the village, where I lived, when I bumped into two of the girls who both played first violin in the string group, Martina and Valentina, who were walking home in the same direction. They were good friends with each other, both being around 14 years old, and living close to each other in Gaiman. Both girls were local Argentinians, without Welsh descent, but regularly played Welsh music as members of the Gaiman string group. I greeted them by giving them each a kiss on the cheek, the typical Argentinian way, and we walked the rest of the way home together. As we turned a sharp right into our neighbourhood, Martina looked up at me with her big brown eyes full of curiosity and asked me, somewhat shyly, *'Cómo es Gales?* What's Wales like?' I was thrown by her simple question.

When I realised that Martina and Valentina were waiting patiently for a coherent explanation, I tentatively explained that it was pretty, with lots of green space, an abundance of hills and winding roads, but that just like any place, it had its problems: political, economic, structural and social. I told them that I grew up in Aberystwyth, and that it was quite a bohemian, arty, seaside university town, but that many young people tended to leave as there were not enough opportunities for jobs locally. They looked intrigued, and I began to gain a better understanding of how it must feel to not have any trace of Welsh descent, nor to have ever visited Wales, but to play the national anthem of Wales weekly in their violin lessons, and to be admired and photographed by Welsh tourists for doing so. Martina later elaborated during an interview, 'Yes, when I think about it, I think … wow … *que loco* … but we are used to it … *no sabemos Gales* … we don't know Wales, but we don't know anything different to what it is like here with a mixture of Wales and Argentina.'

Whilst some of my interlocutors did have quite fixed ideas about what Wales was like, many of my interlocutors, like Martina and Valentina, were open to new imaginings of Wales. Fixed ideas about the types of people who lived in Wales or about the quality of life there were often based on my interlocutors' own subjective experiences of Wales or Welshness, inevitably coloured by a myriad of factors such as their social environment, economic circumstances, personality and the geographical location of the part of Wales that they had visited. Paula often spoke about Wales in terms of it being better than Argentina. She often described it as being cleaner, more organised, with better education and fewer social problems like poverty or social inequalities, problems which she frequently described as existing in Argentina, a country she described as being '*yn y trydydd byd* ... in the third world'. Alberto focused less on material aspects, but always emphasised the beauty of the green landscape, an emphasis that was in line with his own personal interest in nature. A friend of Paula's who had not visited Wales would get a completely different image of Wales from a friend of Alberto's, and Martina and Valentina's image of Wales would undoubtedly be coloured by their experiences in the string group as well as by my own descriptions. The theme of imagining Wales was complex and multi-layered. Images were constructed from personal experience, from music, from conversations with peers, friends and tourists, from watching television or reading, and these images were not necessarily fixed – it was possible for people to play Welsh music, to listen to or sing lyrics invoking specific imagery, and to remain unsure about what Wales was like or to be open to different representations or interpretations of the country.

## The dynamics of seeing and being seen

In theorising these dynamics of seeing and being seen, Whitfield suggests that it is possible to speak of 'lenses' in this context.[16] She argues that Patagonia is viewed both in Wales and in current fiction through a lens combining the exotic and familiar, whereby a common language ultimately overrides differences of geographical, social, political and economic context. Such an image is sometimes prominent in fiction: consider this extract from a children's book with a bear named Alun as its protagonist, who travels from Wales to Patagonia on the back of a whale to re-experience the journey of his ancestors:

> Everyone was listening carefully to the teacher, as she spoke of a distant land, far, far away. A long time ago, many from Wales travelled to Patagonia on a large ship, called the Mimosa, in search of a new life. Patagonia is very far from Wales, but *despite the long distance between the two countries, they are very similar.*[17]

The message of this children's book is clear: it is a long way to travel, but ultimately you arrive in a place not too dissimilar to home. Welsh Patagonia is often represented, especially in Wales, as being a 'little-Wales-away-from-Wales'; a hub of Welshness that can flourish, so long as it receives the right developmental support from Wales. As one of my neighbours in Aberystwyth, who had never visited Patagonia herself, put it, 'we [meaning, the Welsh] have ownership of the place'. It is in this context, where Patagonia is seen as being 'a place in progress', that schemes like the Welsh Language Patagonia Project (which sends Welsh teachers to the Chubut Province annually to deliver Welsh lessons) and the Patagonia Instrument Project (which collects old, unwanted and unused instruments in Wales and sends them to schools in Patagonia) can flourish.

Even in the context of re-emerging themes like 'exotic', 'familiar' and a 'hub of Welshness', lyrics to songs and fiction books, whilst powerful in their own ways, cannot be taken as stand-alone examples of how Wales or Patagonia were imagined by various individuals. In that music, poetry or art cannot be taken as being 'the lens' through which Patagonia or Wales were imagined, the word 'lens' is not analytically useful in a context of constant cultural exchange between Wales and Patagonia and where Welsh ideas about Patagonia and Patagonian ideas about Wales were heterogeneous and complexly interrelated. The concept of viewing Patagonia through a lens implies distanced observation and does not seem to require an awareness on the behalf of the one being watched.

Sartre's concept of the gaze, which he developed in *Being and Nothingness*, is useful here. To be watched or gazed upon implies in many ways a physical presence of another person, even if this is not always literal (it could, for example, be a virtual presence). We all know, or can imagine, the feeling of being lost in thought whilst reading a book in a library, looking out a train window or painting a picture. Sartre argues that this individual, lost in his or her own activity, is not yet aware of him or herself as a subject. For Sartre, we become aware of ourselves as subjects when we are confronted with the gaze of the other:

> Let us imagine that moved by jealousy, curiosity, or vice I have just glued my ear to the door and looked through a keyhole. I am alone and on the level of a non-thetic self-consciousness. This means first of all that there is no self to inhabit my consciousness, nothing therefore to which I can refer my acts in

order to qualify them. They are in no way known; I am my acts and hence they carry in themselves their whole justification ... My attitude, for example, has no 'outside'; it is my pure process of relating the instrument (the keyhole) to the end to be attained (the spectacle to be seen), a pure mode of losing myself in the world.[18]

It is only when Sartre's subject is caught looking through a keyhole by someone approaching him from behind that he becomes profoundly, embarrassingly aware of his own subjectivity and presence in that moment. This is closely linked to the imagination. The feeling of shame at being caught peering through a keyhole and the possibility of seeing the other as a subject comes from our capacity to imagine how you are seen by another. As Sartre puts it, 'my fundamental connection with the other-as-subject must be able to be referred back to my permanent possibility of being seen by the other'.[19]

Whilst Sartre's focus is on individual human identity, his interest in the creative capacity of the gaze and the role of the imagination and shame is what makes his allegory especially relevant here. Urry was the first to theorise what he called the 'tourist gaze', initially arguing that it objectifies residents and in doing so has the ultimate power and authority over them.[20] He later revised his ideas to account for the 'large increases in the growth of tourists emanating from many very different countries ... that once were places visited and consumed by those from the West'.[21] Others following him have argued variously that gazing cannot account for the active and involved tourist as it implies a certain objectivity and passivity, and that tourism is not only about how tourists view locals, but also about how locals view them.[22] Following this, it has been posited that during the tourist encounter, there is a process of meaning and identity construction for the tourist too,[23] that this is different for domestic and international tourists,[24] and the submission to the tourist gaze can also be considered a form of 'staged ethnicity' whereby traditional heritage is capitalised,[25] that the tourist gaze as Urry saw it necessitated a level of hospitality that is currently declining, making way for a new concept – the 'wicked gaze'[26] – and that a consideration of the representations generated by travel writing are also paramount to the creation of imaginaries.[27] With the rise of technology, scholars have also argued for a recognition of documentary film, photography, social media and other means of producing – and reproducing – images of people, animals and landscape, which are key to the maintenance of the tourism industry.[28]

Ultimately, Sartre's concept of the 'gaze', when considered in the context of more recent studies in critical tourism, allows analytical space for recognition on the part of the one being gazed upon, for an exploration of the dynamics of seeing and being seen and, crucially, space for exploring the contestable power relations between the looked upon and onlooker and how they relate to broader power structures.[29] In this, it is concerned with a social relationship and interaction with implications for subjectivity and self-awareness.

## Performing Patagonia under the gaze of the Welsh other

> *Dim ond calon lân all ganu,*
> *Canu'r dydd a chanu'r nos.*
> ('Calon Lân', traditional Welsh song)

It was late October in 2015, and we were edging towards the hotter months, yet on this Saturday it was raining relentlessly, leaving the typically dry mud streets of Gaiman awash with rainwater. We had arranged to have an extra rehearsal in preparation for the arrival of the BBC NOW, who were due to arrive in the valley a couple of days later, to spend a week there. The full orchestra had arranged a concert and some members of the orchestra had also arranged to do some community work, which involved travelling around the various music schools in the valley to teach, to conduct workshops and to perform smaller concerts.

There was a huge amount of media coverage surrounding the visit, especially given that Catrin Finch – a famous, world-renowned harpist from Wales – was part of the tour. The BBC News website provided detailed coverage of the journey before it had even begun. The motivations behind the trip were described by Suzanne Hay, the head of partnerships and learning of the orchestra in a BBC News interview as a desire for the community to experience new forms of music.[30] As she put it, 'To have a professional full-sized symphony orchestra for them [i.e. people living in Chubut] is going to be a once in a lifetime experience, and hopefully really inject a new energy into music-making in Patagonia.' Michael Gary, the director, described the tour as a unique opportunity, stating that, 'To feel the passion and hear the noise coming to them off the concert hall stage is a wonderful experience for them.' Further emphasis was placed on the practicalities, such as the fact that 260 instruments would be accompanying the players, adding up to 3.5 tonnes of cargo which would travel more than 17,000 miles.[31] This anticipation in the media surrounding the event was felt in Patagonia too as everyone eagerly and nervously awaited the visit.

Paula had arranged an additional rehearsal over the weekend in light of this, emphasising that the children must be sufficiently prepared to be able to play the relevant pieces with the members of the BBC NOW, who were professional musicians. Arriving at the music school, I let myself in through the narrow, wooden side door, knowing that this would be the door that Graciela (the head of the music school) would leave open for weekend rehearsals. The familiar, high-pitched sound of violins tuning grew louder as I neared the rehearsal room. There were seven of us altogether including myself, Paula, Emma (Paula's daughter), Martina and Valentina (first violins), and Gabriel and Zoe (second violins).

'Can you start off by doing some scales with them? *Dwi angen ysgrifennu rhan i'r anthem ar gyfer Zoe* ... I need to write out a part for the Welsh national anthem for Zoe', Paula asked me. I smiled, nodding. We started with an A minor melodic scale, and then moved on to play a major scale, Eb. I asked the children to play one note per bow, then two per bow, then to play in triplets (three notes per beat), then to play faster and faster until it became impossible. The children and I laughed, and Paula told us to stop. She asked if we could play 'Calon Lân' followed by the national anthem of Wales, and then she turned to me and said, 'You're from Wales ... you must hear these two pieces all the time and know them so ... well, have you any advice on how to play them, musically?' I laughed and replied, 'I'm not sure ... just always play with *amor*... love.' It was a half-joke, albeit not one of my best, but Paula took my comment seriously. Her voice lowered, softened and the children listened intently.

> *Escuchen* ... Listen, children ... when the BBC NOW comes, it is important for you to show, visually, by being happy and

by smiling, that you *want* to be here, and that you are *happy* to be here. Think about Lucy, and how happy she usually looks.

Paula's comment and her emphasis on the visual and on 'showing' points to the self-conscious core of performance. As a self-conscious act it is, to a certain extent, flexible and open to manipulation, based on the type of impression you want or need to give in a particular context, an impression which in turn is influenced by ideas of the expectations and desires of the 'audience' to which you will perform. The rehearsal was not happening in a void, but rather had as its reference point the arrival of the BBC NOW. In other words, the children's performance was taking place under the gaze of the Welsh other at anticipatory distance. Ultimately, what these varied situations held in common was the coherence of Welsh Patagonia when it was performed, either in practice or in an expectant sense, as a tangible and homogenous whole to outsiders, especially to tourists and visitors from Wales. As a group, we appeared united and, crucially, we felt united, sharing the same vision and goals. Sartre's argument touched upon earlier in this chapter emphasises that the reason that we are most acutely aware of ourselves when confronted with the gaze of another is due to our capacity for imagination and, in particular, our capacity to imagine what we must look like from the onlooker's perspective.[32] In this context, we knew which image we needed to perform, and we were aware of the 'emotive power of music to communicate and (re)confirm a shared collective identity'.[33] There was a clear collective understanding that we needed to sing about the Wladfa with conviction, happiness and enthusiasm.

Another concept central to Sartre's argument is shame – the shame felt in imagining how we must appear, having been caught looking through a keyhole. He notes, 'I am this being ... my shame is a confession'.[34] Sartre's concept of shame is pertinent here in that it emphasises the social qualities of shame as something which arises in relation to others.[35] Dolezal notes that this account of shame 'reveal[s] something essential to the structure of human existence; the vulnerability at the core of our existence and the concomitant human need for connection to others, or belonging'.[36] Anderson takes a more pessimistic view, arguing that feelings of shame are not neutral, noting that 'shame in particular is the feeling of being judged by the other'.[37] In the Welsh

Patagonian context, shame was both these things; in other words, it was simultaneously concerned with belonging and judgement. It was explicit in the anticipatory rehearsal, in which we discussed the desired image that the musicians of the BBC NOW would be looking for and considered how we could create this image – by appearing happy as we played our instruments, for example. In this performance, our enthusiasm and sense of belonging was implicitly related to our capacity to imagine what the audience wanted and what would happen if we did not perform as expected.

## 'Tut, tut, we aren't being very Welsh': performing Patagonia for officials

A similar process could be seen during official celebrations and more formal meetings, especially during the annual celebrations marking the arrival of the original settlers to Patagonia, which took place in the week at the end of July. These celebrations usually started with an early morning meeting in Puerto Madryn where tourists and locals gathered around a statue on the seafront to commemorate the arrival of the original settlers, whilst locals re-enacted the arrival by rowing boats, lifting Welsh and Argentinian flags, and listening to speeches alongside attending concerts and teas in the following days, organised by the committees of the chapels in the valley.[38] As Geraldine Lublin described in an interview with the BBC:

> The festival of the landing is the most significant festival for the Welsh in Patagonia, and 2015 will mark 150 years since the first settlers from Wales established themselves in Patagonia. Investigating the history of the festival on the turn of its birthday has been eye-opening, as I have discovered just how early the festival won an official acknowledgement by Argentinian officials. I saw in the Drafod [a local newspaper] that the viceroy of Chubut, Alejandro Conesa, had given a speech in the celebrations of the festival of the landing by saying 'we must remember that we owe everything that is in Chubut today to that group of 153 people who landed in Puerto Madryn 35 years ago'.[39]

This day – 28 July 2015 – was full of celebrations to commemorate the arrival of the first Welsh settlers to Argentina, with the added excitement of it being 150 years since they had landed. In the morning, a group of local actors dressed in traditional Welsh clothing depicted the landing, arriving at the harbour at Puerto Madryn in what Elena jokingly referred to as the 'Mimosa *newydd* ... new *Mimosa*', which was adorned with large Welsh and Argentinian flags. When the speeches welcoming the groups of tourists and emphasising the importance of Welsh cultural continuity were over, it was time to travel to Trelew, to Capel Moriah, for a ceremony that was to take place before most of the chapels in the valley opened their doors to serve a Welsh afternoon tea. The chapel was significant for its cemetery, which was the rest place of forty-three of the original Welsh settlers, including Lewis Jones, the founder of Trelew.

There were already several people there when I arrived and, looking around, I recognised a few familiar faces from my first fieldwork trip in 2013. We were surrounded by Welsh and Argentinian flags. The ceremony started late with the singing of both the Argentinian and Welsh national anthems. Tourists and locals clicked their cameras and clapped, as formal speeches were given by the first minister of Wales, and the British ambassador. Speaking Welsh, the first minister of Wales, Carwyn Jones, pointed to the significance of the Welsh settlers in their creation of the settler colony, acknowledged the importance of the Welsh-language teaching projects and the sending of teachers from Wales in terms of generating cultural continuity, and finally emphasised the desire to strengthen links between Patagonia and Wales. He later reiterated his speech in an official statement from the Welsh government in which he wrote:

> I was warmly welcomed at every event and the strong *links between Wales and the Welsh communities in Patagonia were firmly cemented* during my visit. I concluded my official programme by hosting a reception to thank the Welsh of Chubut for their hospitality and *continued commitment to keeping the Welsh culture alive* for future generations.[40]

That we were in Argentina, that there were fewer people singing the Welsh national anthem than the Argentinian one, and that the faint whisperings of conversations in Spanish were audible amongst the crowds whilst Carwyn Jones spoke into a crackling microphone felt like minor details in relation to the all-encompassing evocative speeches, powerful national imagery, clicking cameras and emphasis on the 'Welsh community', continuity and identity that was surrounding us. '*Anhygoel i feddwl ein bod ni ym Mhatagonia* ... It is incredible to think that we are in Patagonia, but it is just like Wales,' one tourist remarked to me, astonishment in her low voice, 'There really is a feeling of being Welsh here.' Elena similarly emphasised in a later interview with BBC Radio Wales that alongside paying respect to the ancestors, the day was about acknowledging and supporting the continuity of Welsh language and custom that was visible in the valley.

Following the speeches, a plaque was unveiled by Carwyn Jones outside the chapel, and a wreath was placed on the grave of Lewis Jones. After listening to a solemn Welsh song sung by Casi Wyn, who had travelled from north Wales, the ceremony came to a close and the crowds slowly began to disperse to make their way to Gaiman to a chapel of their choice for a 'Welsh tea', which was a selection of cakes and sandwiches served with tea, usually costing around 150 pesos a head, which at the time of the research was around £7. I accepted the offer of a lift back to Gaiman with Elena and two distant relatives of hers from the United States who were visiting the area. I assumed that we would be going to Capel Bethel for tea, given that it was where Elena could be found every Sunday as an active participant in the regular chapel service. When we were about halfway to Gaiman, Elena admitted that she '*wir eisiau* mate ... really just fancied some *mate*' instead of having tea, especially as the queues to the teahouses would be long. Back at her house, we sat around the table in the kitchen, and Elena tutted and laughed as the conversation slipped into English, 'We aren't being very Welsh.'

The obvious contradiction between Elena's emphasis on the continuity of language and Welsh cultural traditions being followed by her almost immediate flexibility was not referred to by Elena herself, which made clear that, for her, there was no contradiction between the automatic performance of a homogenous Welshness when it was necessary and the swift change into a more flexible identity that followed. Once away from the gaze of tourists, the presence of officials and the questioning of news reporters, the homogeneity of Welshness slipped in favour of the more typical, relaxed daily experience of a specific type of Welshness within Argentina, whereby the mixture of languages, including English at times, and cultural preferences were a natural given. In the official meetings, however, speeches tended to refer to the Welsh community as a concrete whole without considering the specific Argentineness of their situation. The emphasis on the continuity of Welsh culture and the links between Wales and Patagonia, along with the more striking visual elements, such as the presence of Welsh and Argentinian flags, helped to reproduce these feelings of belonging to a particular 'community' amongst participants in the audiences. Locals often performed back to news reporters the same homogenous image that was evoked in official speeches, demonstrating the efficacy with which a particular version of Welsh Patagonia was brought into being in certain contexts: under the gaze of officials and when surrounded by nationalistic items such as flags. These moments, even if some were somewhat fleeting, had huge significance, as they were the site at which key ideas were created, ideas which later became attractive to potential tourists.

Figure 11: Welsh and Argentinian Flags

Figure 12: Welsh and Argentinian bunting

## 'Why have they dressed like elephant hunters?' Laughter and power

> Humour can be an important tool for overcoming or levelling various hierarchies and inequalities, yet it can simultaneously also reproduce and reaffirm them.[41]

These encounters between tourists and locals, and the dynamics of seeing and being seen embedded within them, were saturated with structural power relations, and my interlocutors were acutely aware of the specificities of these unequal dynamics. On the first day of the eisteddfod in 2015, several busloads of Welsh tourists arrived at the Predio Ferial (a large wool barn that had recently been converted into a concert hall on the outskirts of Trelew). They stared at, photographed and filmed local Welsh Patagonians who were dressed in Welsh traditional costumes in preparation for the Welsh traditional dancing competition: the children in their green and red outfits, and the choirs singing in Welsh. I was watching the tourists, from my seat, and Paula must have been doing the same, as she commented, '*Mae'r pobl yma, sy'n dod ar y bws* ... These people who come on buses, in a week they will see more of Patagonia and Argentina than I have seen in my life.' I nodded quietly, uncomfortably aware of the truth to her statement.

In this context, joking was often 'utilised to demarcate difference, [to] express and negotiate power relations', and as a social tool to comment on difference and formality in a 'light' way.[42] One example of how this was navigated through laughter came from the eisteddfod in 2015. I was with my interlocutors at the Gorsedd ceremony which was about to begin. The audience was growing rapidly. I could see my fellow choir members arriving, and I waved to them, smiling. They were easy to spot, in their black shirts, black trousers, black shoes and characteristic bright blue scarfs. I could see some others from Gaiman, Trelew and a few from Esquel. However, most of the audience were tourists. They stood out clearly, in part because in a small village like Gaiman, you very quickly come to identify a new face, but also due to the constant clicking of smart phones and cameras, and even more so for their summer clothes. They were all wearing white or cream cargo-style or linen shorts with white or lightly coloured shirts, or long trousers with light shirts, practical walking sandals and large sun hats.

For the locals, however, for whom 'summer' was 45 degrees, the mild October temperatures of 20–5 degrees were not yet enough to warrant even contemplating getting out of long-sleeved clothes or coats. The general attire for the Gorsedd was no different from winter clothes, albeit with the addition of sunglasses. The contrast was strikingly clear. As I scanned the crowd, my thoughts were interrupted by Sebastian. Sebastian was a tall, witty Argentinian historian with Welsh Patagonian connections. He lived in Comodoro but travelled often to the Chubut valley for research and to the UK to present his work at conferences. He nudged me, and with a huge grin, asked in English, 'Why have they dressed like elephant hunters?' He pinched his fingers and thumbs together and shook his hand up and down – the typical Argentinian gesture to express a mixture of lack of understanding and bemusement. He laughed then, a snickering-out-of-control laugh. I laughed too, relieved to not be the only one who had picked up on the curious contrast in outfit choice.

Alberto played a flowery introduction to the Argentina's anthem, and the choir led the singing, which was followed by the enthusiastic applauding of the members of the Gorsedd, who were still waiting at the side of the circle, and of the other attendees of the ceremony who were standing opposite us. A solo trumpet broke through the crowd to indicate that it was time for the Gorsedd to take their seats in their allocated chairs, which were lined in rows within the stone circle. In pairs, they walked slowly, majestically and proudly. Most members of the Gorsedd were older individuals, and most of them were bards, wearing suits and formal clothing underneath their long blue robes. The druids were wearing white robes and headwear, and amongst them was the archdruid of the Welsh Gorsedd. The archdruid of the Patagonian Gorsedd, Ana, was wearing a blue robe, with a gold and red crown.

Gorsedd members were such due to their contribution to Welsh culture in Chubut, whether this was through their work (many were teachers of the Welsh language in the nursery and secondary schools in the area, and some ran the Welsh teahouses in Gaiman) or through their personal lives (by learning the Welsh language, teaching Welsh to their children, dancing Welsh traditional dances, or supporting cultural activities such as the eisteddfod and other festivals such as the 'Gŵyl y Glaniad' or 'Festival of the Landing'). Most members of the Gorsedd were nominated to this position after demonstrating a committed contribution to the continuation of Welsh culture through a combination of the two. Ana, the archdruid, climbed up two steps to the top of a large rock in the middle of the stone circle and when the singing had finished, spoke into a microphone, in Welsh, to welcome those present to the ceremony (especially the visitors from Wales and beyond) with a short speech:

> *Mae'n bleser o'r mwyaf croesawu chi yma heddiw* ... It is a great pleasure to welcome you here, and especially to the many friends that have come from Wales to join us in our special celebrations this year with the Wladfa being century and a half. It is an extreme honour to welcome the archdruid of Wales, Mrs Christine James ... the archdruid of Cornwall ... and a representative from Brittany. *Mae'n anrhydedd arbennig i ni eleni* ... This is a special honour for us this year ... also the gorseddau of Ireland and Scotland have sent us their greetings as they cannot be present. It is an honour to us ... *yn ein Gorsedd bach ni* ... in our little Gorsedd ... the representation is so important. A big welcome here to all of you.

Towards the end of the ceremony, the three archdruids began to walk around the outer circle, where the audience members and choirs were seated, to greet them individually. They walked profoundly slowly and solemnly, their long white robes almost reaching the ground. Just before they reached the girls' choir, Alberto turned to me, grinning, and said, '*Nes i ddim sylweddoli bod y tri gŵr doeth yn dod* ... I didn't realise that the three wise men were coming.' I laughed, as did most of the other sopranos within earshot. The altos further down the choir, noticing the ripples of laughter travelling through the choir, began to ask each other, '*Que dijo?* What did he say?' then shared in the laughter as the joke was repeated. The archdruids thanked us for the 'lovely singing'. We greeted them politely and thanked them for coming, before exchanging one final giggle as they moved on to the next crowd.

In the Welsh Patagonian situation, the teasing was asymmetrical, in that whilst the Welsh Patagonians joked about the visible differences between them and the tourists, I never heard tourists joking about the Welsh Patagonians. The laughter in the eisteddfod ultimately reflected deeper inequalities and power structures between Welsh tourists and Welsh Patagonians. This resonates with much of the literature on the topic. Carty and Musharbash[43] argue that an ethnographic focus on laughter is significant precisely because it provides a perspective on how people manage social inequalities. McCullough draws on fieldwork in north Queensland to further argue that 'joking and humour performances ... are enmeshed in the daily structuring of race, nation and alterity in Australia'.[44] Alexeyeff notes that in the Cook Islands, 'humour is a product of global economic forces and accompanying race and sexual politics', arguing that in a context of 'asymmetrical power relations, relative wealth and poverty, jokes ... reflect this asymmetry'.[45] Goldstein draws on her fieldwork in the shanty towns of Rio de Janeiro in Brazil to argue that laughter provided a commentary on the political and economic structures within which her interlocutors were embedded, revealing 'both the cracks in the system and the masked or more subtle ways that power is challenged'.[46] Yoshida makes a similar argument, arguing that female workers in a Japanese inn joke about their experiences at work in a way that both affirms their identity and resists the conditions of their employment.[47] These ideas are reminiscent of a Butlerian concept of agency, whereby submission to, and laughter within, dominant structures can be perceived as a form of agency in its own right.

The Welsh Patagonian context similarly demonstrated that jokes can act as both a light social commentary on social situations – a social diffuser – as well as revealing and relating to more serious social distinctions and structural inequalities.[48] The joking by the Welsh Patagonians in this context acknowledged and negotiated the underlying existence of a form of inequality which emerged from their positionality in a context in which the tourists, as Welsh, were viewed from many of their perspectives as being 'better' than them, both economically and culturally. Humour here was used as 'everyday tactics' to 'manage or diffuse potentially problematic situations'.[49] This laughter directly contrasts with the ways in which it has typically been treated by thinkers such as Aristotle, Plato and Hobbes, who each viewed laughter as being directed towards someone who we perceive as inferior to ourselves.[50] Joking about the inappropriate clothing choices of tourists and laughing at the archdruids robes in their solemnity and formality was not only a 'light' way to subvert situations of global inequality, but also a way to recognise and challenge social hierarchies.

However, there was a critical difference here. My interlocutors occupied a curious position of power and subordination. They were powerful in relation to the local Argentinians with whom they lived, but they also acknowledged the relative economic position of tourists over themselves. Being interpellated by, and submitting to, the tourist gaze and performing a certain image of Welsh Patagonia was necessary for my interlocutors to maintain their identity, sense of community and their relative position of power and prestige in the Chubut Province. Therefore, submitting to the tourist gaze could be an eventual means to gain prestige and power (through increased publicity, or in a financial sense, for example). Here, laughter complicated the idea of jokes being a commentary on, or a reflection of social inequalities, in addition to shedding new light on Butler's concept of having the agency to act within dominant structures as a form of self-mastery.[51] Ultimately, my interlocutors were making a joke out of their own positionality vis-à-vis the Welsh tourists (arguably demonstrating agency within dominant structures), but this laughter simultaneously came from its own relative position of prestige (in relation to their local

Argentinian neighbours), a position that was closely connected to the tourist encounters that they were engaged in.

## Conclusions: the potentiality of the gaze

In the days and weeks after events in the village, several albums of photographs would be uploaded online. At Paula's house one afternoon, we were sitting at the kitchen table drinking tea when she put her glasses on, opened her laptop, opened Facebook and started flicking through a set of recently uploaded photographs. She squinted, frowning at the screen, '*Ni wedi gwneud lot o bethau gyda'r grŵp llinynnol* ... We do loads of things with the string group and never put anything online, so I guess people in Wales just think we do *nada* ... nothing.' In this case, Paula was imagining the scenario of tourists at home looking for Welsh performances in Patagonia, and being met with nothing, and her comment reflected the shame that she associated with that situation. What this points to is the possibility of a 'potential tourist gaze', one which works from a distance. Whilst Sartre's emphasis is largely on the gaze as a literal and physical presence, he does point towards the possibility of being made a subject in the absence of presence:

> The fact remains that I can discover that I have been mistaken. Here I am bent over the keyhole: suddenly I hear a footstep. I shudder as a wave of shame sweeps over me. Somebody has seen me. I straighten up. My eyes run over the deserted corridor. It was a false alarm ... What then is absence?[52]

The notion of an absent yet present gaze has been developed more precisely by Foucault, in *Governmentality*, in his notion of panopticon – the idea that in a prison situation, where the prison officer is located in a tall tower in the middle of cells laid out in a circle, the prisoners behave accordingly not because they are always physically under the gaze of the prison officer, but rather because of the notion of possibility: they feel the possible gaze of the prison officer from afar.[53] The uncertainty around whether the prison officer is watching them because they cannot see him or her leads to the possibility of being watched all the time.

The gaze of the other, as demonstrated by the simple anecdote from Paula, could be felt at a distance, as a *possibility* rather than a reality. A string-group rehearsal organised in anticipation of the arrival of the BBC NOW, or a reflection on how the string group could be perceived by social media users 8,000 miles away, are two examples of the ways in which the gaze of the Welsh other worked in a more imaginary way, with individuals discussing the ways they could and could not, should and should not act during the concert. Similarly, social media performances from Welsh Patagonia were self-conscious, invoking a coming into being at a distance whereby a version of Welsh Patagonia was performed on social media platforms under the possible gaze of the Welsh other. This was closely connected to possible feelings of shame – shame at not living up to the imagined standards or the online presence that the tourists were looking for.

In conclusion, Welsh Patagonians created an image of Welsh Patagonia which influenced what other tourists could expect to find, and these expectations in turn influenced the image that locals sought to generate. This chapter has argued that it was a two-way process: in the performance of a song with increased energy or in the performance of a specific kind of nostalgic Welshness at official events, Welsh Patagonia performed itself, and in doing so came into being as coherent under the gaze of the audience: the Welsh other. This chapter has further argued that the presence of joking demonstrated that the awareness of the tourist gaze was not simplistic. In making this argument, the chapter has outlined the ways in which the gaze and the imagination were intrinsically connected in the Welsh Patagonian context. The empty land trope of Patagonia had resonance in Wales and fed into the creation of an imagined Welsh Patagonia, which in turn fuelled the booming tourist economy. Tourists often arrived in Welsh Patagonia with their own ideas about what it would be like, what they had come to look for, and what they would see. The performance of Welsh Patagonia to tourists took place with reference to imagining the kind of Patagonia that tourists were coming to see: a heightened or exaggerated Welshness. During these encounters, both Welsh Patagonians and tourists found their imaginations being articulated, re-articulated and challenged. The following chapter seeks to explore the role of the tourist gaze in more detail, by considering the role of the 'local gaze' in terms of representation, reflection and the place of documentary film in the tourist encounter.[54]

Finally, to realise that the core of Welsh Patagonia and the feeling and appearance of the community as a concrete whole came from its performance to tourists, visitors and officials is to emphasise the centrality of tourism and cultural exchange between Wales and Patagonia in this context; most importantly, to realise the complex role that the Welsh Patagonian community played in performing and producing the image that they needed to project, and demonstrates quite how fleeting, how constructed and how performative the concept of cultural coherence or wholeness is.

# 5

# Mirror, mirror on the wall, who is the most Welsh of them all?

> Like translation, ethnography is also a somewhat provisional way of coming to terms with the foreignness of languages – of cultures and societies. The ethnographer does not, however, translate texts the way the translator does. He must first *produce* them [...] The ethnographer ... *presents* languages, cultures, and societies in all their opacity, their foreignness, their meaninglessness; then ... he clarifies the opaque, renders the foreign familiar, and gives meaning to the meaningless. He *decodes* the message. He *interprets*. The ethnographer conventionally acknowledges the provisional nature of his interpretations. Yet he assumes a final interpretation – a definitive reading. 'I have finally cracked the Kariera section system,' we hear him say. 'I finally got to the root of all their fuss about the *mudyi* tree'.[1]

## Introduction: two awkward moments

It was a Sunday evening in December. At Elena's suggestion, a few of us were sitting around a table in Siop Bara, Gaiman's local coffee shop and bakery, as a way of welcoming a young couple who were visiting Chubut for a couple of days. We had come from Capel Bethel, at the other side of the village, where we had taken part in a *cymanfa ganu*. The waiter came to take our order and we made small talk as we waited for our drinks to arrive. The couple were travelling around South America on their honeymoon and had decided to pass through Gaiman as they were learning Welsh. As we listened to them recounting all the incredible places they had visited, they suddenly turned to me and asked, almost in unison, what I was doing in Patagonia. Elena swiftly put her arm around me, squeezed my shoulder, winked at me and answered on my behalf, with a wicked laugh, 'Lucy is studying the *local people* ... she follows us around and looks at what we do, that's all she does!' She indulged in their look of surprise and continued, 'No, *really*, she doesn't do anything else, well apart from a bit of cello in chapel ... and then she's going to write a *LIBRO* ... a BOOK! A book about the real Welsh Patagonians.' She laughed, and I could not help but laugh too, amused by her unusual burst of childishness. The visiting couple glanced at each other, slightly bemused and laughed nervously. I nudged Elena and responded jokingly, 'You'll miss me when I'm gone!'

The sun was setting by the time we began to think about leaving. The others left quickly, in time to catch a bus to Trelew, where they were living. Elena offered me a lift part of the way home. '*Dwi'n flinedig* ... I'm tired,' she said, 'but I'll be kind and take you to the bridge.' We trundled along the stony road in her little white car in companionable silence. I was looking out of the passenger seat window when Elena said, '*Mae sawl person wedi dod yma* ... Several people have come here and written horrible things about the Welsh community, *sabes* ... you know.' I turned to look at her, but she was looking straight ahead at the road. I explained that my work would offer an anthropological insight into the community. She smiled briefly, nodding in response, but her eyes remained fixed on the road. I hoped that she felt somewhat reassured, but her concern cut like ice through the carefree laughter of earlier, and the sound of the stones flicking up from the road hitting the bottom of the car seemed louder.

Almost exactly a year later, a doctoral student in linguistics visited Gaiman for a month. She was documenting and analysing different forms of Welsh as part of her research on language change, and she wanted to find Welsh speakers in the valley who would read out lists of Welsh words on tape, to be analysed upon her return to the US for their accents and different use of mutations. In the car on the way home from choir one evening, I asked Paula whether she was going to take part in the research project, as the researcher had recently called for participants via an online post in the Menter Patagonia Facebook group. She hesitated. Presuming that she had not heard of it, I responded quickly, '*Sai'n meddwl bod rhaid i chi 'neud lot* ... I don't think you have to do much, just read out lists of Welsh words.' Paula's body tensed slightly, and her lips tightened. Her response was snappy, 'No. *Dwi ddim am gymryd rhan.* I won't participate. I don't know who they think they are, coming here for two days and studying us *como si fueron* ... as if we are ... *dinosaurs.*' Taken aback by her response, I blushed, but did not respond.

⛰

Crapanzano, with whom this chapter opens, argues that ethnography is never neutral: it is always a form of interpretation.[2] Lichterman likewise highlights that the knowledge of the ethnographer can only be partial, related to the ways in which ethnographers are 'situated in one or more identity positions in social-structural hierarchies'.[3] Schindler and Schäfer argue that ethnographic writing practices, such as writing scratch-notes, developing these into fieldnotes, writing drafts and revising papers are also in themselves a form of interpretation and representation.[4] Ruby considers these ideas in relation to film more explicitly, expanding the idea of an 'anthropology of visual communication', which he defines as being an anthropological analysis concerned with the communication and representation of visual media.[5] Arguments relating to interpretation are relevant to many other forms of representation beyond ethnographic research or writing: journalism, film-making, theatre, photography and radio recordings. In Welsh Patagonia, several films, radio programmes and online articles about the Welsh Patagonian community and Welshness have been written by various visitors to the province. Furthermore, news reporters and other journalists, in pursuit of data and evidence, have often invited the local community to take part, by participating in interviews, featuring in recordings or acting in films.

One of the key criticisms of Urry's early work on the tourist gaze is also a key issue of Sartre's concept of the gaze.[6] Both these thinkers allowed little room for the agency of the individuals being observed in their analyses, and in doing so 'extend mythologised (colonial) visions of Otherness'.[7] In the Welsh Patagonian context, their work does not allow room for the ways in which the gaze of tourists and the gaze of the locals (or the gaze of the onlooker and the gaze of the individual being watched) could work both ways in that 'the locals construct their gaze upon previous and numerous encounters with tourists'.[8] In the context of performance, it has been argued that 'performance and audience feed each other in a process of mutual becoming'.[9] Geiger has further pointed to the ways in which cinema, and the production of images, has become a central component of selling the concept of travel, arguing that 'motion picture technology – like tourism, a growing leisure pursuit – kept pace with modern travel developments, mirroring and often exploiting them. The tourist and image-making industries are mutually dependent'.[10] This chapter considers these issues – performance, tourism, representation, film and the mutual gaze – through an ethnographic exploration of the moment at which the Welsh Patagonian community came face-to-face with the representation of their performance in films during film nights held in the Casa de Cultura in Gaiman whereby the 'subject rediscovers him – or herself within cinema'.[11]

This chapter draws on Lacan's theory of the mirror stage to consider 'film as mirror', arguing that film in this context makes explicit the performance of the self.[12] Much like Sartre, Lacan's theory is based on looking, gazing and recognition, but at the same time it enables a more in-depth consideration of issues like desire, self-awareness, the mutual gaze of tourists and locals, and the role of documentary films in the valley in this process of subjectivation. This chapter follows others who have drawn on Lacanian psychoanalytic theory in the context of film analysis,[13] and on Gabbard's argument that 'cinema and psychoanalysis have a natural affinity'.[14] Lacan argues that when infants view themselves in the mirror, they objectify themselves, and in doing so, they encounter a gap between the self as experienced and the self as reflected. Metz argues that 'the spectator is absent from the screen: contrary to the child in the mirror, he cannot identify with himself as an object'.[15] Lacan's theory is a useful starting point to consider encounters in which my Welsh Patagonian interlocuters viewed their performance on screen, as differently, the spectators were present in the screen, and were confronted with the gap between the self as objectified and the self as experienced. This gap not only pushed the viewer and actor to a level of self-awareness, but also created space for individuals to reflect critically on their own roles in bringing Welsh Patagonia into being as a coherent community through representation in films, theatre radio programmes, music or research articles.

The chapter first contextualises the discussion within the broader politics of representation in Welsh Patagonia, with a focus on theatre, film, television, cameras and the scholarly gaze. It then considers the viewing of the film *Galesa* through a metaphorical reading of Lacan's mirror stage, arguing that when local actors in the film were confronted with their own performance, they were confronted with a gap between their own self-image and the image that was represented. This 'gap', or the difference between the self as experienced and the self as performed, pushed them to reflect critically on many issues relevant to their lives, such as mobility between Wales and Argentina, feeling torn between Wales and Argentina, and the use of the Welsh language. In making this argument, it addresses Gabbard's criticism of Lacanian film theory, which is that it is tends to be too heavily focused on the processes of creating meaning through film, rather than the content. Contrastingly, Schneider[16] argues that participatory cinema cannot be separated from its social context, as it is embedded both in the social events surrounding the films (such as film nights), in addition to within the local, informal commentary on locals' appearances in the films. Therefore, process and content are treated as inseparable in this chapter. Finally, the chapter draws on contexts in which friends dressed up in traditional Welsh costumes to introduce the concept of 'peers as mirrors', arguing that peers too can act as a mirror: a mirror made up of other individuals rather than a mirror offering a direct reflection of their ego.

## The politics of representation and the scholarly gaze in Welsh Patagonia

Fieldwork was a haze of interviewers, film-makers, researchers, photographers, musicians, librarians, journalists and artists passing through the village. This was especially the case in 2015, a significant year which marked 150 years since the establishment of the settler colony in Chubut. 'New arrivals' in the village were weekly and at peak times, such as during the annual eisteddfod, daily occurrences. Against the background of daily routine in the valley, the circulating news that a 'new investigator' was in the village to collect data for so-and-so-a-project, the intermittent calls on Facebook and WhatsApp for 'interview-participants' and the sudden appearances of newcomers observing, taking photos or recording in choir rehearsals were consistent features of fieldwork.

The purpose of visiting varied widely amongst what were locally subsumed under the umbrella of '*investigadores* ... investigators' – from conducting feminist studies of the settler colony, to anthropological work looking at the ways in which all the institutions in the settler colony cooperated, to researching for the British Council in order to write reports on the Welsh education programmes, to photographing the landscape to knit Patagonian-inspired blankets, to photography projects,[17] to doctoral research investigating the linguistic specificity of Patagonian Welsh, to undergraduate dissertation research, and to artists searching for personal musical or poetic inspiration. Amid this diversity of documentation and research, several elements remained consistent. Cameras documenting even routine events were omnipresent, and all the projects shared the same subject – the Welsh Patagonian community. These projects all became significant in terms of their contribution to the varied ways in which Welsh Patagonia was represented and ultimately imagined in Wales.

One example of how tourist interactions were closely connected to representation came from regular 'musical cycles', whereby tourists to the settler colony viewed performances in Welsh Patagonia, and engaged in musical practice by attending choir rehearsals, playing in musical groups, teaching, conducting workshops or performing concerts. When tourists were musicians, they were often inspired by the performance of Welsh Patagonia to create their own musical compositions depicting images of the settler colony and to share these compositions, both at home and in the settler colony during any subsequent visits. These pieces and poems generally conveyed a positive and harmonious portrayal of the settler colony. One example of the creation of this musical cycle could be seen in the work of Gwenan Gibbard, who visited in 2015 during the celebrations and who later returned in October 2016. In an interview with Wales Arts International after her 2015 visit, she said:

> Nothing could have prepared me for the thrilling experience of being there myself, on South American soil, further away from home than ever before, while *at the same time feeling safe and completely at home among friends and kindred spirits* ...

> I had tried on a number of occasions to imagine what kind of a place the 'paith' would be [...] I gazed at *this remarkable, magical landscape* for ages, just as if I were watching a film ... *the Welsh language and Welsh culture – these were absolutely central to the lives of the early settlers in Patagonia, and I see that they're still incredibly important in the lives of Welsh Patagonians today*. I felt the enthusiasm of the old and the young alike, and a desire to sustain the language and our traditions [...] I have been inspired by my journey and am keen to try to sing about the experience – we'll see what happens![18]

Gwenan kept her word, and by her visit in 2016, she had composed and recorded a CD titled *Y Gorwel Porffor* ('The Purple Horizon'), inspired by her experiences in the settler colony. In the tracks of her CD, Gibbard plays the harp and sings poetic lyrics, in a variety of folk Welsh styles, most notably 'cerdd dant'. The CD is comprised of a series of six songs, all written in Welsh, and all inspired by various encounters that she had experienced in the settler colony. The themes of the songs include depictions of the landscape as '*perffaith, y gorwel porffor* ... perfect, the purple horizon', explorations of religion – 'when a man is measured, he is asked by God, not how he died but how he lived'; light-hearted songs about celebrating a birthday through the medium of Welsh in a nursery school – '*Mae Lisa fach yn dair mlwydd oed* ... little Lisa is three years old'; and more solemn songs about origin and heritage – 'old language before the birth of other languages ... she is our nation through all nations and she will lead our *hiraeth*'.

One song called 'Ddoi di draw?' ('Will you come over?') is written about Puerto Madryn, and in late October 2016, Gwenan played it in a concert that she performed in Capel Bethel in Gaiman. Written in a folk style, the harp played an underlying melody with bouncing chords, both on and off the beat, in a major key. A repeated little melody intermittently broke through, tinkling down through a scale which connected the verses. Above this was the sound of Gwenan singing skilfully in a mezzo-alto voice, and each verse followed the same chirpy melody, overall making it a memorable and uplifting piece of music. Madryn was a relatively large town, and its main feature was its large, expansive beach, which was especially busy during the hot summer months. It was typically viewed as being a wealthier area in comparison to Trelew and Gaiman, and this was reflected in the higher house and rental prices, and in the luxurious and expensive shoe, clothing and homeware shops in the area. Madryn had further significance for the Welsh community, as it was the first place where the Welsh settlers had landed before travelling by foot to Gaiman. On the promenade in Madryn, there was a large stone monument of 'La Mujer Galesa', or 'The Welsh Woman', which represented the arrival of the first Welsh settlers, and on 28 July each year, there would be an early morning gathering at that spot to mark the annual celebration of the arrival. Madryn was therefore a popular tourist destination for Welsh visitors, despite having relatively few Welsh speakers in comparison to Gaiman or Trelew.

The piece was an easy listen. It had a cheerful, upbeat feeling to it, and several members of the audience were happily tapping their feet whilst listening before applauding for a very long time afterwards. The lyrics repeated the question, '*Ddoi di am dro i draeth Porth Madryn? Will you come for a stroll to Puerto Madryn beach?*', reminiscent of a childlike persistent questioning, adding to the feeling of adventure and excitement that the song invoked. The lyrics describing '*yr iaith yn sŵn y cregyn ... the language in the sound of the shells*' and the '*ogofâu yn llawn atgofion ... caves full of memories*' subtly depicted the omnipresence and embeddedness of the Welsh language. Ultimately, the song depicted an image which likely reflected the reality of the typical tourist experience of Welsh Patagonia, for whom it was ordinary to spend a week or so in the village, without much contact with locals beyond the Welsh Patagonian community.

Whilst the issues of documentation and representation were exacerbated in 2015 due to the influx of visitors, they were not new issues. In 2014, René Griffiths, a songwriter, singer and guitarist from Patagonia, who lived for a long time in Cardiff before eventually returning to the valley, published an autobiographical-style book called *Ramblings of a Patagonian*, in which he wrote:

> Back in Wales, a few years ago *I found out by accident that I was in another interesting feature film and had no idea that I had been involved in its production*. As it seems that I was the inspiration for the film, I would normally think that I had been more inattentive than usual, but on this occasion, I need to share the

blame with a distant relative (who I was also unaware of, so I was possibly doubly inattentive). This distant relative turned out to be quite famous, and I didn't know that either, so *all in all the experience was quite a revelation.*[19]

This passage aptly summarises the power structures between an unequal encounter of those representing and those represented.[20] René is talking here about the film *Separado*. The protagonist of the drama was the Welsh musician and composer, Gruff Rhys. The film is based on Rhys's search in Patagonia for René, following his discovery that René is a distant uncle of his. Alongside the search for René, Gruff Rhys also finds himself embedded in Welsh Patagonian daily life, performing music and meeting many people. From the passage above, we can conclude that René does not appear to be offended by his representation in the film, but it is important to note that he also had the possibility of responding critically to the ways in which he was represented. He is trilingual, having lived in Cardiff where he learnt English alongside Welsh (his first language) and Spanish (his second language) and was in a position – economically, socially and politically – to be able to write and publish a book which addresses some of his concerns, albeit in a humorous tone. As Ruby puts it, 'cultures that once were the passive subjects of ethnographic and documentary work are now imagining themselves, and critiquing the images made by others'.[21] Ultimately, however, it remains implicit that in some way Gruff Rhys, as a powerful outsider, felt that he had a right to the data that he sought to collect.

At the time of my research, the broader relationship between my interlocutors and the visiting 'investigators' was based on the co-existence of suspicion and necessity. With time, my interlocutors began to tentatively express occasional feelings of mistrust regarding the constant flow of researchers and people passing through who wanted to document the village, but much like René, they recognised the social importance of providing the data. As one of my interlocutors from Gaiman said, '*Mae'n bwysig ein bod yn croesawu* ... It is important that we welcome people to the community, involve them in what we are doing, as well as getting involved in what *they* are doing to keep the relationships between Wales and Patagonia alive.' In many ways, then, the scholarly gaze co-existed alongside – and overlapped with – the tourist gaze. Despite occasional feelings of ambivalence and mistrust towards researchers or new arrivals to the valley, often, locals would take part in interviews, focus groups, fill in surveys and in practice performed a similar image of Welshness to that presented to tourists – something that became increasingly clear as I spent longer living in Gaiman.

News about potential new arrivals would travel long before each data-collector, teacher, workshop-coordinator, artist, film crew, anthropologist, orchestra or radio presenter would arrive in the village. My interlocutors would often conduct research of their own, by asking around and by searching for individuals on social media. '*Wyt ti'n nabod y ferch sy'n dod dydd Mawrth?* Do you know that girl that is going to be coming on Tuesday?' people would ask me. 'She doesn't live far from you in Wales, do you know her? *Cómo es?* What is she like?' With time, people became even more open about their ambivalence, such as when the choir director announced that some people would be visiting '*y côr lleol* ... the local choir', holding two fingers up as speech marks, and rolling her eyes to indicate the irritation induced by the phrase. Others were sceptical about whether the increased attention, connections and opportunities were beneficial to the whole village. One of my interlocutors suggested that the publicity was only beneficial to a select few individuals, stating that, 'I don't know if it is too good ... some people are becoming world famous ... and the rest of us stay behind.' She explained that journalists and film-makers came with their own ideas about what – or who – would capture the attention of an audience back home, and tended to focus on 'key' individuals from within the Welsh community. Consequently, other potential protagonists were 'left out', despite being fluent Welsh speakers with high levels of involvement in the Welsh community.

However, alongside these critiques, the documentation of Welsh cultural activities was viewed by many as central and necessary to the continuation of Welsh culture in the valley. During fieldwork, the recording of the activities of the Welsh community via photography carried with it a certain element of prestige. October 2015 was significant in this respect, in that it marked the public recognition of the work of a local photographer, Jonathan, who lived in Trelew. With a considerable amount of dedication and for several years he had systematically attended, documented and uploaded to Facebook vast quantities of photos of the Welsh Patagonian community events, thus disseminating the activities and, crucially, the existence and continuation of the Welsh community to a far wider online audience. In 2015 Jonathan was accepted to the Gorsedd at the Chubut Eisteddfod. In the speech preluding his admittance to the Gorsedd, his work was hailed as 'essential' and 'central' to the Welsh community.

## Self-awareness of the performance of Welshness

What might seem to be a contradictory co-existence, of the suspicion surrounding 'investigators' with the view that investigation and representation was a necessary part of keeping the settler colony alive, made sense in its broader context, a context in which my interlocutors repeatedly performed a homogenous and harmonious Welshness alongside a self-awareness that the Welshness performed to tourists and others was in some ways different to the reality which informed it.

In 2015, the National Youth Theatre Company of Wales collaborated with Clwyd Theatre Wales to create a theatre project called 'Mimosa', based on a drama written by Tim Baker in 2011. The purpose of the musical theatre production was to depict the journey of one family of original Welsh settlers on board the *Mimosa*. It focused especially on the challenging journey, the arrival to the barren land – and the inevitable disappointment and heartache that came with that, the search for fertile land and the importance of Welshness and the Welsh language. It followed the story of 31-year-old William Jones, his wife Catherine (also thirty-one) and their two daughters, 3-year-old Mary Ann and 16-month-old Jane, who had left their home in Bala, north Wales, for Patagonia. Their voyage was fraught with tragedy and grief as both daughters died on board the *Mimosa*. However, it ended on a note of hope, with the birth of two babies on board, and the discovery of the Chubut River and nearby fertile land. Baker described the show as 'a magical, amazing story but one that is also full of disappointment, anger, and hardship'.

The play was initially performed on a tour of Wales in July 2015 with a cast of four professional Welsh actors (Dylan Williams, Hanna Jarman, Tom Blumberg and Bethany Gwyn). They were later joined by sixteen young actors in association with the Urdd and two young actors from Patagonia to perform in the National Eisteddfod in Wales in August 2015 before beginning their Patagonian tour shortly after, with performances in Gaiman, Puerto Madryn, Trelew and finally in Trevelin in the Andes.

In August 2015, I attended the play, which was performed in the gym in Gaiman, with two friends, Sebastian and Katy. Katy, Sebastian's partner at the time, was an American anthropologist who was living in Trelew, and was in the final months of her fieldwork. We shared *mate* as the lights dimmed. The play provided an interesting interpretation of the historical events, particularly with respect to the tense relationship between English and Welsh, which was a large part of the motivation to leave Wales. The ship's captain was English, and there were several arguments throughout between him and those on board. Throughout the play, the captain shouted orders, especially at women, which would be swiftly followed by the male Welsh settlers on board acting to defend themselves in a morally righteous way: a father, for example, stepped up to defend his young daughter. Given that the various characters were played by the same group of actors, the actors changed the tone of voice and stance to differentiate between roles and to create a clear dichotomy between the English and the Welsh. The English speakers spoke with exaggerated Queen's English and the way in which their bodies occupied the space on stage was significant. They swaggered with their shoulders back with an air of arrogance that was indicative of wealth and upper classness, which was contrasted with the Welsh settlers who consistently made themselves smaller by pulling their shoulders forward, shuffling in their old clothes and huddling together in a way which portrayed them as subordinate, loving, caring, poor and humble.[22]

At the end of the show, as Sebastian, Katy and I were leaving, we were approached by the door by a teenage boy with a microphone. He asked us eagerly, '*A oes modd i chi recordio rhywbeth* ... Would it be possible for you to record something on tape, saying what you thought of the show?' We looked at each other and it was clear that we all felt reluctant to contribute. I said in Welsh that I thought the show was excellent. Katy stayed silent, and Sebastian responded, in English, 'I am originally from Patagonia, and so it was very close to home. For me, it was very emotional.' The boy with the microphone grinned widely, clearly pleased by his answer, and prompted further, 'Was it good to see lots of people speaking Welsh on stage?' 'Yes,' Sebastian performatively constitute it ourselves.[28] Both Lacan and Butler have moved beyond Sartre to consider the role of desire in the process of subjectivation. As the remainder of this chapter will demonstrate, in the context of Welsh Patagonia, this can help to explain the continuation of the performance of Welshness alongside the joking and laughter that indicated a self-awareness of the differences between two realities.

### Viewing the performance of the self: S4C's Galesa

The self-awareness of the performance of Welshness was especially heightened in a context where members of the Welsh Patagonian community gathered for film nights to watch their own performances of Welshness. Abu-Lughod's seminal article on television draws on her fieldwork with women in an Egyptian village to argue for increased ethnographic attention to encounters with media, in contrast to a focus on ethnographic film, defined broadly as 'any documentary film about non-Western culture'.[29] She states that we must begin to consider the 'significance of television's [and by extension, film's] existence as a ubiquitous presence in the lives and imaginaries of people in the contemporary world'. The messages of television, film and the media, though they may be imbued with intentionality by producers, are modified both by the ways in which people frame, interpret or reflect on these experiences, as well as by the everyday realities and power structures within which these messages are inevitably embedded. She points to the gap between the villagers' ideas of what the series represented for them (in that it opened up a discursive space for them to comment on the differences between their lives vis-à-vis the wealthy women on the screen), and the intentions of the director (who had intended it to have a feminist message), arguing that 'the same cultural texts have different imports in different contexts'.[30] Schneider makes a similar argument in the context of Saladillo, Argentina. In his analysis of participatory cinema (community cinema which draws on local non-professional actors and resources), he argues that the films are 'not primarily about the screen but about what people do in front of and behind the camera', highlighting throughout the importance of 'agency, participation, and sociality', or in other words, the broader context in which the film is created.[31]

In the Patagonian context, one example of a similar film was *Galesa*, directed by S4C (a Welsh-medium television and broadcasting company). *Galesa* was filmed in Gaiman over eighteen days in April 2015. Its cast was made up of one professional actor (the protagonist, Elizabeth Fernandez, who at the time of the research was living in Cardiff but who was originally from Gaiman) and local Welsh Patagonians in other roles, thereby 'blur[ring] the boundaries between amateur and professional'.[32] The film was created using structured reality techniques, which meant that the actors were not given specific scripts to follow, but rather were provided with a broad storyline and encouraged to improvise their lines within the structure. This is an important element to consider in a context where we have moved away from viewing documentary films as representative of 'authentic embodiments of culture' to consider the role of 'the strategies of dramatic enactment', such as the use of structured reality techniques to create a specific plot.[33] Whilst watching the films, self-awareness of the disjuncture between performance and reality often manifested as critical self-reflection, of the gaps between the representation and reality of Welsh Patagonia, and in terms of my interlocutors' awareness of their own roles in the homogenous representation of the settler colony. The storyline of the film also encouraged my interlocutors to consider other subtle – and arguably more current – themes, such as the relationship between mobility and status, the feeling of being torn between Wales and Argentina, and the ways in which Welsh language use was represented.

In August 2015, a few weeks into fieldwork, Menter Patagonia had arranged the debut film viewing of the film *Galesa* in Casa de Cultura. I felt a growing sense of curiosity as I walked from my house, over the bridge and up the road. Upon my arrival, I was greeted at the door by two young boys. They were both wearing red Welsh football shirts and offering small squares of *torta negra Galesa* as people arrived. Holding a piece of *torta* wrapped in a white napkin, I walked down the corridor and pushed open another door which led to the room where the film was to be shown. I was surprised to see the large room nearly full. I sat next to Emily, a Welsh undergraduate student who was studying Spanish in Scotland, and who had been living in Gaiman for a few months as part of the exchange programme for her degree, and leaned forward to greet Awel, who was sitting in front of us with her two children. There was a large square projector screen hanging from the ceiling at the front of the room, with two black speakers placed on chairs either side of the screen. Within the space of ten minutes, the room was full, and before long, Rhiannon motioned from the front for someone at the back of the room to flick the lights off. Rhiannon was a Welsh teacher from Wales, who was working for the Menter Patagonia project for 2015 and 2016. Her husband, Tomas, originally from Dolavon, was of Welsh descent, and was also working for the project that year. Since meeting in Patagonia several years previously, when Rhiannon had been working as a Welsh teacher in the valley for the first time, they had married and normally lived with their two young children in Wales. The whole family were living in Patagonia during the time of my fieldwork. Rhiannon and Tomas were working as Welsh teachers, and their two children were attending local schools. As the lights dimmed, a loud ripple of 'shhh' ran through the audience, and the opening music began to play.

The film follows the true story of Elizabeth Fernandez who plays herself in the film. She was originally from Gaiman and had moved to live in Cardiff to act in the popular Welsh soap opera *Pobol y Cwm*. It is an exploration of her struggle to accommodate different personal and societal pressures as she returns to Argentina to visit her hometown, Gaiman, after several years away. Her time in Wales had been spent working at a prestigious and highly paid job with several famous Welsh actors, and consequently she returns to Gaiman with a new status of village-celebrity. However, this new-found fame turns out to be somewhat of a burden, and throughout the film she is presented with several demands that she feels uncomfortable with. Her old friends, family and acquaintances are represented throughout the film as having been 'left behind' by her in Gaiman and have new ideas to share with her concerning the ways in which she can 'help' them – not only in an individual sense, but also, more broadly, in terms of the Welsh community.

The film begins with Elizabeth arriving in Gaiman, and a meeting between Elena and Elizabeth in Elena's home, during which Elena provides her with a long list of people that she must contact whilst she is in the area. In real life, Elena acted as a kind of 'grandmother' figure to many local young people and visitors in the village, which is the role that she appeared to have in the film too. It slowly emerges throughout the film that all the listed people want something from

Elizabeth, such as a role for themselves on *Pobol y Cwm*, a trip to Wales or money. Consequently, the questions posed to Elizabeth by her family and friends during her visit to Patagonia are big ones. Will she stay in Chubut? How can she improve their lives and give back to the community with her newfound contacts, fame and wealth? Throughout the film, Elena's character comes across as manipulative, and she puts a huge amount of pressure on Elizabeth to stay in Chubut, by outwardly complaining that many people, especially young people, often leave Patagonia for Wales. She explains to Elizabeth that although people pass through regularly from Wales, with some staying to help with Welsh culture and language in the valley, it is not sufficient. She tells her, convincingly and sincerely, '*Ni angen pobl* ... We need people, we need you, Elizabeth.' Several people, me included, could not hide their amusement. The bluntness and directness of Elena's character were amusingly accurate, and in many ways, represented an exaggeration of her normal self.

Ultimately, what is supposed to be a relaxed return to her hometown, to her family and friends, and to her old choir rehearsals, leaves Elizabeth feeling torn – between staying in Gaiman with her family and old friends to support the community or continuing with her new glamorous life as a television star in Wales. It is within this context that the storyline of the film turns on the question of whether Elizabeth should stay in Argentina or whether she should return to Wales. Throughout the film, Elizabeth is haunted by a dramatic ghost-like woman dressed in a pink dress and blue bonnet, intended by the directors to represent the presence of the original pioneers. Patagonia is depicted as vast and deserted, with several panoramic shots of Elizabeth walking across empty land carrying only a red suitcase, as she tries to come to a decision about her future. The explicit message of the film is that the spirit of the original Welsh settlers still exists as a haunting presence within the descendants, structuring many of their actions and influencing their decisions.

Jain argues that Indian films are an exact reflection of the patterns of mobility, whereby the protagonists of the films created before 1990 always leave India for short career breaks then return, and the protagonists of films after 1990 reflect the reality of increased global travel.[34] Karush makes a similar argument in the context of Argentine films during the Peronist era.[35] According to his analysis, radio and cinema during that time were a direct reflection of political discourse, with storylines embodying the idea that 'Argentina [was] a nation irreconcilably divided between rich and poor' and invoking imagery of humble poor people and wealthy villains. However, *Galesa* depicted a simplistic ideal of mobility from Argentina to Wales in comparison to the reality. Emily, sitting to my right, shook her head and murmured, 'It's not that simple', as the actors on the screen asked Elizabeth if they too could live in Wales. Mobility was related to many factors, including free time, personal motivations to travel, job or project opportunities, family dependants and health concerns, but the consistent theme during conversations about mobility was economic status, given the expense of travelling such a far distance. On the one hand, some of my interlocutors, whilst speaking Welsh fluently and being highly committed to Welsh cultural activity in the valley, had not had the opportunity to visit Wales for many years (if ever) at the time of fieldwork. On the other hand, some of my interlocutors spoke less Welsh or participated in fewer Welsh cultural activities but due to their younger age had access to scholarship opportunities to go to Wales to participate in Welsh courses, or they simply had the economic means to travel. Mobility from Wales to Argentina was therefore accessible to a much larger group of people, with far more Welsh people visiting Argentina than Argentinian people visiting Wales.

Feeling torn between Wales and Argentina was also a running broader concern in the settler colony and was often closely connected to marriage between Welsh Patagonians and Welsh people (which was relatively common). Some couples who moved to Wales stayed there permanently, whilst others decided to return to Argentina in later life, and vice versa. Whilst every marriage had its own unique history, it became apparent that couples faced similar difficulties. One half of the couple had to leave behind family, friends, home and their career in Wales or Argentina to reconstruct their life in a new place, a pressure which many couples admitted produced new challenges to the relationship, with worries about being unable to visit family members and friends regularly (especially those who were ageing or unwell), finding appropriate work in their new homes, persisting language barriers, bringing up their children in different cultural contexts or education systems than to the ones which they were accustomed to, and about adjusting to the radically different climates.

In her analysis of transnational family relationships in the context of Italian migrants in Australia, Baldassar argues that the emotions of 'missing' and 'longing' and a wish that 'they [the family members] could be physically closer to each other' are central to the maintenance of transnational relationships.[36] Baldock also points to the feeling of 'being torn' as a common component of transnational relationships.[37] Several of my interlocutors referred to this as feeling stretched, at least at times, between the two places. As one interlocutor who had moved with her (Welsh Patagonian) husband to Wales confided in me, long after fieldwork had ended, over a cup of coffee in Wales, 'I feel like Elizabeth sometimes ... *ti'n cofio'r ffilm 'na?* Do you remember that film? Like half of me is in Argentina and half of me in Wales.' This comment resonates with Schneider's argument that 'filming became an ethnographic meta-discourse, being embedded in and reflecting upon the ethnographic reality of the town, but also making evident and exposing specific social norms and relations'.[38]

Throughout the film, Welsh is presented as being the language of daily life, with the actors greeting each other in Welsh on the streets and speaking Welsh in their homes. However, the knowing giggles in the room as we were watching these scenes were indicative of the shared knowledge that everyday conversation was usually conducted in (or at least quite quickly slipped into) Spanish, especially when not in the presence of Welsh tourists or other visitors. During fieldwork, some of my older interlocutors from the Welsh Patagonian community did speak Welsh to each other regularly, and some families seemed to be more committed to bringing their children up bilingually. Amongst these were a small but significant number of families who had moved from Wales more recently, and who only spoke Welsh at home. However, in general, conversations tended to slip back into Spanish, especially when topics became more complicated, as was often the case when discussing politics or economics, for example. As Rosario put it to me, one day:

> Someone asked me once whether I thought the Welsh colonisation had been successful, and I think, it hasn't, in that it hasn't been successful in the way the Welsh colonisers wanted it to be, but in another way, it has been, because here we are, *en el culo del mundo* ... in the arsehole of the world, and we speak a few words of Welsh.

The laughter during the film's showing indicated that, to the viewers, the exaggerated performance of speaking Welsh was obvious.

The film ends with a portrayal of Elizabeth's uncertainty, as she stands in the middle of a deserted *paith* with her long hair blowing in the Patagonian wind, clutching a bright red suitcase, and looking wistfully out at the expansive land around her. Several audience members could not contain their laughter at the depiction. The credits of the film began to roll, and the audience clapped and cheered enthusiastically, with some standing. Rhiannon and Tomas ended the evening by thanking everyone for attending. They joked, '*Bydd angen sesiwn ffilm arall i ddeall y ffilm* ... Deciphering the film would require another film session in itself.' Some audience members laughed, and Elena called out from the audience, '*No entiendí nada* ... I did not understand what was happening in the film, I couldn't follow the storyline.'

### Face to face with representation

The following day I had promised Elena that I would go to her house in the morning to help her make Welshcakes for an upcoming annual Welsh tea that was organised by the Gaiman mixed choir. At around mid-morning, I pulled my coat tightly around myself against the bitter cold as I knocked on the front door. I smiled to myself as I heard her shouting, '*Cer rownd* ... Go round, to the back, to *porch y cathod* ... the cat's porch.' The 'cat's porch' had been named to honour a cat and her numerous kittens which Elena had (somewhat reluctantly) allowed to live there in a cardboard box. I walked around the side of the house to let myself in through the glass door. We sat around the kitchen table with mugs of hot tea, and as I was grating nutmeg with a tiny grater into a bowl to add to the mixture, I asked her what she had thought of the film that we had watched the previous evening. She paused mixing the dough, leaving one hand in the bowl but lifting the other to push her hair out of her face using the back of her wrist, and looked up at me. She shrugged and explained that it had felt strange to view, and that she had not understood much of it, despite being one of the main characters.

Discussing the scenes, she said, 'It was odd to me, the ways in which the film-makers made it seem so natural, when actually we had been directed.' She paused again, shook her head, waved her arms towards the kettle, and laughed, remembering, 'I had to film one bit about five times, the scene with the *mate*.' She laughed again remembering the scenes depicting the *paith*, before saying, 'Poor Patagonia, looking like the end of the earth ... That bit with poor Elizabeth looking across the *paith* with her suitcase ... well, *que loco che* ... how crazy!' I smiled, remembering the scene. Elena pushed the bowl of dough over to me and as I began rolling the dough and cutting the Welshcakes into small circles she shrugged, 'I still don't quite understand the film.'

Later that week, I had a chance to catch up with Paula after the string group rehearsal. She had arrived at the film night characteristically early and had been sitting at the other end of the room to me. As we were packing away the instruments at the end of the rehearsal, I asked her what she had thought of it. She paused whilst piling up the chairs and explained:

> Well ... I didn't have a main part in the film. *Nes i fwynhau'r noson* ... I enjoyed the film night ... not a lot goes on in Gaiman so it is a good thing when Menter Patagonia hold different evenings. It was funny to me because I know everyone who acts in the film. But ... I do feel like some things were slightly misrepresented ... like that scene with the *asado* ... everyone from Gaiman eating together – *dyw e ddim felna bob dydd* ... that is not an everyday occurrence. But I suppose we could have said that to the film-makers!'

Much like Sebastian's and Lucas's comments revealing their self-awareness of these gaps, both Elena and Paula demonstrated a critical understanding of their own roles in perpetuating the film's depiction of Welsh Patagonia, in addition to touching on the power structures between themselves and the visitors. Both Paula's comment, 'I suppose we could have said that to the film-makers', and Elena's comment, 'It was odd to me, the ways in which the film-makers made it seem so natural', subtly suggested that they had not voiced their critiques to the film-makers themselves. Furthermore, Paula's and Elena's comments, when taken in the context of earlier discussions on the themes of mobility, feeling torn between Wales and Argentina, and the Welsh language, point to the viewing of *Galesa* as being first and foremost an encounter that brought together the social reality for Welsh

Patagonians with the reality depicted in the film. Through viewing themselves externally, the encounter ultimately generated reflection and debate through the exposure of the gaps between the two.

### Film: the metaphorical mirror stage?

Lacan argued, in his mirror stage theory, that typically developing human infants, when they are around 18 months of age, pass through a developmental stage in which they are confronted with the external image of their own body, reflected in a mirror.[39] This could be either a literal mirror or a metaphorical one, if presented to them through the mother or other primary caregiver. The infant, according to this mirror stage theory, identifies with the image, at least on a basic level, and this is when the infant begins to have a sense of self, but in that the image in the mirror is of a complete, unified body which does not correspond with the infant's physical vulnerability and dependence on others, it more concretely represents an ideal 'I' towards which the subject will strive throughout his or her life. Gallop notes that the 'mirror stage is a turning point. After it the subject's relation to himself is always mediated through a totalising image which has come from outside.'[40] What is of significance in the Welsh Patagonian context is the 'gap' between the objectified reflection and internal self-image that is theorised by Lacan. Looking in the mirror – or at yourself on film – therefore means to confront the gap between the performed self as presented in front of you and the self that you thought yourself to be.[41]

Lacan's theorisation of the mirror stage is complicated by Rubenstein, who, taking Lacan as 'referring to an actual mirror', argues that the obsession with mirrors and self-reflection is bourgeois, noting that 'this reading reflects the ways that actual mirrors are taken for granted in bourgeois society; it effaces bourgeois dependence on mirrors'.[42] Rubenstein draws on his work with the Shuar who live in Ecuador, in the easternmost foothills of the Andes and the uppermost fringe of the Amazonian rainforest, to argue that the Shuar do not experience their image as received and reflected in the reactions of another 'me' ('ego's') but alternatively, that their subjectivity is constituted through visions – or encounters – in relation to other separate beings ('I's').

Rubenstein's argument enables a consideration of how subjectivity can be constituted through encounters with others rather than self-reflecting beings. However, arguably, the mirror can be both actual and metaphorical. Films in the Welsh Patagonian context fit exactly with the concept of an 'actual mirror' as described by Lacan, because the viewers are faced with their own accurate yet delusory performance. The performances in this context are accurate in the sense that they are 'real', but equally they are delusory in their presentation of a modified version of the daily life of Welsh Patagonia. *Galesa* challenges both our perceptions of what a mirror is or *needs* to be, and in the process of doing so illuminates an important aspect of performance – that whilst it is a performance, it can be both accurate (or real) and a modified version of reality at the same time. As Mulvey notes in her seminal essay on the centrality of the mirror stage to analysis of film:

> It is an image that constitutes the matrix of the imaginary, of recognition/misrecognition and identification, and hence of the first articulation of the I, of subjectivity … Hence it is the birth of a long love affair/despair between image and self-image which has found such intensity of expression in film and such joyous recognition in the cinema audience … The cinema has structures of fascination strong enough to allow temporary loss of ego whilst simultaneously reinforcing it.[43]

In the Patagonian context, film nights help to shed light on the ways in which Lacan's mirror stage can be analytically useful for anthropology, especially in terms of thinking about the subjectivation of individuals, communities and the relationship between this subjectivation and performance. Lacan emphasises that the image mirrored to the infant is that of a unified and somehow independent body in contrast to the reality, which is a body that is entangled in a web of dependency relations. As explored in the previous chapter, the performance of Welsh Patagonia similarly tends towards a representation of it as a unified or homogenous community, yet when this image is mirrored to its viewers (who are also its actors), they are confronted with the perhaps slightly uncomfortable gap between the self and community as presented and their lived reality. Like Lacan's infants, those living in Welsh Patagonia are entangled in webs of dependency, but differently to Lacan's infant, their webs of dependence are intrinsically related to – if not contingent on – the maintenance of the performance of homogeneity. In this context, the economic and cultural dependence on tourism fuels and is fuelled by the maintenance of Welsh Patagonia as a tangible entity, rather than the performance of homogeneity or the unity in the mirror existing as contrasting to the reality of dependence, as Lacan has it.

### Peers as mirrors – 'I can't see how I look but looking at you ... we must all look so strange!'

Rubenstein, in his critique of Lacan, argues that subjectivity for the Amazonian Shuar is constituted in relation to other separate beings (I's).[44] Whilst he does not deny that individuals experience their actions reflected in the reactions of another (whereby the other is another 'me'), for the Shuar this is not the primary mode of the making of subjectivity. In this respect, his argument is reminiscent of Goffman and others who consider the encounter with the other as central to their theories of performance and subjectivation.[45] However, in the Welsh Patagonian context, the constitution of subjectivity through the mirrored image of another 'me' (in films) was in co-existence with the creation of subjectivity through encounters with other 'I's'. Beyond coming face to face with their own performance in films, there were also situations in which individuals were confronted with the performance of the self through the mirror image of other individuals.

Recognising the self through others in Welsh Patagonia was most prominent in contexts in which individuals dressed up in traditional Welsh costumes for various events. Individuals tended to reflect on their own performance and subjectivity not at the moment in which they were dressing up, but rather when they saw other individuals dressed in the same outfits as them, engaging in the same performances and mirroring their performance, yet with the crucial difference of being another 'I'. In other words, dressing in Welsh traditional costumes in the field created yet another type of mirror, whereby peers – other 'I's (separate individuals), rather than other 'me's' (actual reflections of their ego, as in the case of a literal mirror or the performance of the self on film) – reacted to each other's costume in a way that also demonstrated a reflexivity about their own performance. A few months into fieldwork, I received a message from Paula asking me whether I was free the following morning, to perform in a concert in a small chapel a few miles away from Gaiman. I agreed, and she phoned me to explain a little further:

> A teacher from another school is arranging a school trip for her pupils, and they are travelling to every chapel in the valley in the morning, something to do with Welsh heritage. *Bueno* ... Anyway, I was talking with her yesterday after the girls' choir rehearsal had finished and she was asking whether I would be able to get together a small group of musicians – say me on keyboard, you on cello, and Emma on harp, and whether we would be able to be in Capel Glan Alaw set up with our instruments at around 11 a.m., so that when they pass by the chapel, they can come in and find us playing Welsh music. *Byddwn ni'n gwisgo gwisgiau Cymreig* ... We are going to wear Welsh outfits. *Te voy buscar a las 10?* Shall I pick you up at 10?

The following morning, we braced the Patagonian wind and trundled along the stone road from Gaiman to Capel Glan Alaw. Glan Alaw was one of the smallest chapels out of the twenty-four in the valley, and one which quickly became a firm favourite of mine. It was quite rurally located, made of red bricks and was about the size of a small, single-storey house. Emma was sitting in the back seat of the car, with a small harp balanced across her knee, wearing a traditional Welsh outfit – a red and black checked dress. Paula and I were in the front seats, and the sound of Welsh folk music playing from the CD player filled the car. After a few months in the field, I was starting to become more accustomed to these types of situations. 'Oooh Emma, you put your outfit on already,' I grinned at her, and Paula laughed. 'Don't worry,' she replied, 'We have more outfits for us in the boot.' I laughed. A few moments later, having collected the key from the caretaker who lived in a nearby farmhouse, we arrived at the small chapel and parked the car outside. I took the cello out of the car and Paula reached into the boot to pull out Welsh traditional outfits – a hat and scarf each for us to wear. Diligently, we put them on.

Mirror, mirror on the wall, who is the most Welsh of them all?

Figure 13: Capel Glan Alaw

Figure 14: Arriving at Capel Glan Alaw

As we waited for the school students to arrive, Emma and I sat in the open boot of the car, sharing *mate*. Paula, dressed in a Welsh hat and long skirt with a shawl over her outfit, took the keyboard into the chapel, and returning a few minutes later could not contain her laughter. 'Seeing you two there, in your outfits ... it makes me laugh ... I can't see how I look but looking at you ... we must all look so strange!' Emma and I turned to look at each other, and we laughed too, as for the first time I began to properly reflect on how we must be about to come across to the viewers of our performance, dressed in Welsh outfits clutching our *mate* flasks for warmth. 'They must think that we dress like this all the time,' Paula remarked.

The idea of peer relations as being a key element in the construction of behaviour and subjectivity is a common thread in the literature on the influence of peer relations.[46] Winkler-Reid, in her ethnography with girls in a London high school, argues that the dynamics of seeing and being seen are key to creating peer relations and female subjectivity in this context.[47] In the school context, the girls' interactions with each other and much of their understanding of who they are and who they want to be comes from commenting on others and striving to be like – or not be like – others. Similarly, in the Patagonian context, with no mirrors to hand and with no films to watch with hindsight, my interlocutors' understanding of – and reflection on – their performances came from another type of mirror, that of their peers, much like the girls in Winkler-Reid's school.

The reactions of laughter to the gap between our performance of Welshness in Capel Glan Alaw and the reality of our daily lives was reminiscent of the laughter heard whilst watching the performance of Welshness in hindsight on the screen. However, whilst the component of laughter remained consistent in its signalling of the recognition of the gap between the performance and the reality of day-to-day life, what differed was who was to be seen in the mirror. Paula, for example, reflected on her own reality by viewing mine and Emma's performances, rather than upon viewing her own performance with hindsight. Subjectivity, then, was constituted both in relation to a mirror of the self (as in the film) and in relation to other beings (through the mirror imaging of peers).

## Conclusions: feeling Welsh, feeling Argentinian

'*Wyt ti'n teimlo'n Gymraeg?* Do you feel Welsh?' I asked Paula one afternoon, as we travelled in the car to Trelew to perform in a choir concert. '*Sí, wrth gwrs* ... Yes, of course I feel Welsh, why do you ask?' she responded, without hesitation. She sighed, and said, 'I know my surname is not Welsh, and some people think that is important ... but being Welsh or not being Welsh is so much more than that. It is also a feeling ... a connection.' She elaborated, 'I feel Argentinian too, of course, I am Argentinian ... I was born here, and I have lived here all my life, I have all the Argentinian habits and gestures ... you know that ... but I was so happy when I was visiting Wales, I speak the language to my children, I sing in Welsh, I drink tea not *mate* ...'. She continued, speaking passionately about the sense of identity and community she felt from attending the choir, and of her enjoyment of singing Welsh songs and playing Welsh pieces. 'I would be lost without choir and the music group,' she stated, simply. I nodded – I knew she meant it. The answers of my other interlocutors were similar. Some were surprised that I had even asked the question, with one of my interlocutors asking me, in a typically Argentinian manner, '*Qué te pasa ... tomaste algo?* What's happened to you, are you drunk?' and others explaining that they felt like a mixture of Welsh and Argentinian, or remarking that they had never thought about it.

For my interlocutors, there was no conflict between laughing at their own performances of Welshness on a screen or at their traditional Welsh costumes and what they experienced as the embodied simplicity of being – and feeling – both Welsh and Argentinian at the same time. In this context, self-awareness, and being able to laugh at yourself, in doing so recognising the gap between performance and reality, was important, and co-existed unproblematically with feelings of belonging. Arguably, this makes sense when considered within the broader context of Argentina, where joking regularly stemmed from a particular type of humour especially focused on physical appearance, individual differences or laughing at a situation. Joking, in this context, could be two things at once. It was used to feel good, and in this respect, my interlocutors would also regularly say that 'Argentinians love joking and laughing', but it was also used to demarcate difference, comment on inequalities and express the positionality of my interlocutors in relation to the power structures within which they were embedded.

This laughter is quite different, then, to the centrality of shame in Sartre's theorisation of the self-awareness that occurs when coming into being as a subject in relation to the gaze of an onlooker.[48] Contrastingly, what this chapter has demonstrated is that there were other elements in the self-awareness of subjectivation, such as the elements of desire or belonging, or striving towards a particular performance, which co-existed unproblematically with a critical reflection of the performance. Similarly, joking was simultaneously about belonging and power. That my interlocutors and I 'got into character', were aware of doing so and reflected explicitly on the implications and consequences of this whilst laughing at ourselves suggests that the performance under the gaze of the other was not something that happened in a reflexive void. In this respect, the Welsh Patagonian context demonstrates how Lacan's mirror stage theory, with its focus on the self-awareness of the gap between performance and reality, and with its focus on seeing an ideal reflection in a mirror, can enrich Sartre's concept of the gaze by enabling discussion of issues such as desire, self-awareness, the mutual gaze (between locals and tourists) and the role of documentary films.

This chapter has built on the concept of the gaze of the Welsh other developed in the previous chapter, to consider the politics of representation in Welsh Patagonia and their relevance to the creation of Welshness, the portrayal of a homogenous community, and the viewing of the performance of the self through film and peers. In a context like Welsh Patagonia with a thriving tourist market and a boom in international exchange, where researchers and film-makers often visited with narratives pre-imbued with meaning for their media to speak, an exploration of encounters of representation has great significance for understanding the power dynamics at play. In the focus on film and representation, this chapter has followed Messier who has argued that 'considering cameras as participants helps us to focus ... on the technical conditions ... and on the representations they produce'.[49] Ultimately, this chapter has focused largely on the film *Galesa*, to argue that when the local actors in the film were confronted with the external image of their own body, rather like Lacan's infant in his mirror, they were confronted with the gap between their own self-perception and the image that had been represented. This gap between the self as performed and internal self-image provided my interlocutors with a productive locus from which to explore and critically reflect on many thematic issues relevant to their lives, such as mobility between Wales and Argentina, feeling torn between two places and the use of the Welsh language. Further, encounters between peers in the field whilst dressing in traditional Welsh costumes provided another context in which individuals reflected on their own positionality vis-à-vis others and on these themes, through viewing a mirror image that was made up not of a reflection of their ego but of other individuals.

Finally, this chapter and the chapter preceding it have focused on the dynamics of seeing and being seen, whether through the gaze of a tourist, through watching films at a film night or through seeing peers dressed in traditional Welsh costumes. The remainder of the book moves from the visual subjectivation to focus more specifically on the dynamics of hearing and being heard in Gaiman Music School, and the implications of this in terms of power structures and the subjectivation of individual and community.

# 6

# 'The community is a family and the choir is the glue': Performing Patagonia for the ear of the Welsh other

> Sound has an extraordinary capacity to work on us before consciousness ... to 'yank our chains', to tune us like instruments. It works across bodies, both within and across populations, and offers possibilities that visual materials cannot.[1]

## Introduction: 'It just goes like this ... it's really simple'

In one of the final concerts that I played in as a cellist in Gaiman, we performed a suite that was the joint creation of Alberto and an Argentinian poet, Sergio Pravaz. The suite combined a lyrical exploration of the harmony of the settler colony with a clever, subtle intertwining of Welsh melodies and Argentinian folk rhythms. Together, the lyrics and the music depicted a particular story of the creation of Welsh Patagonia, one which closely followed the dominant narrative of the establishment of the settler colony; that being a narrative in which the Welsh settlers lived in harmony with the Indigenous peoples with whom they shared the land. In practice, of course, the unproblematic combination of different musical forms was not as simple as it appeared on the sheet music. Well, it was simple for some. To many of those around me, it appeared effortless, and most told me that it was. The other musicians often expressed the complicated rhythmical forms of Argentinian folk music as being corporal, embodied or something that they performed out of habit, and did not elaborate much further than that. However, bringing two rhythms or musical styles together did not come naturally to me. Much to the amusement of my fellow musicians, I struggled to 'feel' the syncopated beats of the *zamba* and *chacarera*, finding myself in a constant search for the security of a 4/4 or 3/4 beat. Having been trained in classical orchestral cello playing, I had no ear for improvisation or folk rhythms. I often said, '*No me sale* ... I don't get it,' to which the rest of the orchestra would laugh, 'It just goes like this' or, '*Es muy simple* ... It's really simple' followed by the clicking of the (next to impossible) rhythms or singing of the melody accompanied with clapping, to which I would have to say, again, 'I don't know, I just don't get it, *no está en mi cuerpo* ... it's not in my body.' It was only with Flor, an Argentinian cellist who played a lot of folk music, by my side that I was slowly able to begin to relax into the Argentinian rhythmical forms and reach something akin to that desired state of flow that my interlocutors seemed to experience so effortlessly.

The playfulness of the music was also a reflection of the social structure, and especially of the informality and fun that permeated choir rehearsals. The atmosphere of choir rehearsals was described fondly by my interlocutors as '*prysur dros ben ond hapus* ... chaotic but joyful', as '*muy típico de acá* ... very typical of here' and as '*muy Argentino* ... very Argentinian'. Contrastingly, my own experience of choir rehearsals in Wales were of them being a relatively formal occasion. I grew up in west Wales and attended Welsh-medium primary and secondary schools as a child, an education of which singing was a central component. My own memories of attending lunchtime choir rehearsals, evening choir rehearsals and weekend choir camps regularly from a relatively young age were ones of standing in rows for hours, structured rehearsals with precisely timed breaks, compulsory attendance, evenings spent learning words for pieces in preparation for the concerts, auditions for entrance to county choirs, and another series of auditions to try for solo parts within the choir. This is not to say that choir rehearsals were not enjoyable, but musical standard and perfection were a priority. Alberto, who had also spent time with choirs in Wales, agreed with me. During one particularly rowdy choir rehearsal, he said to me, 'It is completely different, over there [in Wales], no? You stand up, you arrive on time, *chi mor dawel* ... you are so quiet ... incredible!' It was difficult for me to conceptualise walking up the stairs to a concert stage without knowing the words of each piece, the repertoire and the order in which they would appear, let alone to begin to understand not knowing which piece we were about to sing. Therefore, it took me many months to respond with '*No

Performing Patagonia for the ear of the Welsh other

*tengo ni idea* ... I have no idea ... we will have to ask somebody else' to my interlocutors' questions of '*Que cantamos?* What are we singing?' moments before we were due to go on stage.

⁂

What Kassabian emphasises in the quotation with which this chapter opens, and what this anecdote illustrates, is the close relationship between music and social conduct.[2] This has been a broader theme in the ethnographic and ethnomusicological literature. It has been argued that for the Kaluli in Papua New Guinea, there is a close relationship between their social identity and a particular musical structure called 'lift-up-over-sounding';[3] that the male dominance of certain musical instruments reflects gender structures;[4] that understanding Mapuche songs and understanding the Mapuche concept of personhood necessarily imply each other;[5] that standing up (rather than sitting down 'the traditional way') to play the violin in Saraguro, Ecuador reflects a broader societal push towards modernity,[6] and that classical guitar music in Paraguay is a direct reinforcement of national, racial and class identity.[7] Traditional Argentinian music felt like a game. With its syncopated rhythms that appeared 'off the cuff', its quirky melodies and its creative instrumental combinations, it was a perfect reflection of the informality, playfulness and joking with which social life was conducted. Contrastingly, the classical four-part choral Welsh tradition tended to be more formal and structured in nature, whereby the music often moved simultaneously with the vocal parts (rather than working in syncopation). The music, whilst equally creative, in its own way, tended towards stricter rhythms. My own experience of choir rehearsals as a child in Wales reflected this, with their formality and punctuality.

The book, so far, in its focus on how the Welsh community come into being under the gaze of the other, and on how film acts as a Lacanian mirror to present the performed self to its audience, has been subject to the typical biases of subjectivity studies. Within subjectivity studies, especially studies bearing the influence of Foucault's tower, Sartre's gaze, Lacan's mirror or Althusser's police officer, the focus remains overwhelmingly on the subject either being formed through speech or through a visual encounter, whereby the subject, to be formed, must either hear another person calling him or her into being or be aware of him or herself being seen by another.[8] Foucault's prisoners are watched, or at least feel as though they are being watched, by the omnipresent guard. Sartre's subject's feeling of heightened sense of self stems from being seen by an onlooker. Lacan's infant forms a sense of self by seeing an ideal version of him or herself which in turn 'sees' the infant in the mirror. When Althusser's police officer shouts, 'Hey you!', his interjection is heard by a person on the street, causing that individual to turn around and *see* the police officer, in doing so coming into being as a subject of the state. All the performative encounters considered thus far have been focused on the processes of 'looking' and 'seeing', and on the ways in which they manifested themselves in the Welsh Patagonian context.

Whilst recognising the contributions of theories of the gaze, this chapter moves away from the role of the gaze and towards listening, hearing and what Clifford called the 'ethnographic ear', to explore the significance of sound in this context.[9] It draws on choir rehearsals in Gaiman Music School and self-administered musical therapy to argue that, in the Patagonian context, alongside the visual formation of subjectivity, another form of subjectivation took place, through music and aural experiences. It demonstrates that by addressing issues of performance, performativity, desire and subjectivation through different senses, new insights can be revealed about the process of subjectivation and the subject. In doing so, despite the use of the separate terms 'musical structure' and 'lyrics' it considers music and lyrics as a unity in terms of their social experience, following Ingold who argued that their separation is an imposition:

> Speech may be present in the song, in the words that accompany the music – thus the song may be conceived as it is written on paper, in two registers proceeding in parallel: the musical sequence written as a series of notes, and the linguistic sequence as a concurrent of words.[10]

## Soundscapes and subjectivity

When Clifford asked his readers 'what of the ethnographic ear?', his intention was to call attention to other senses aside from sight, and especially to the aural dimension of social life.[11] Beyond the fact that music has been relatively absent in anthropology,[12] Clifford wanted to encourage his readers to move beyond the Western emphasis on observation and from the elevation of writing above other forms of documentation (such as audio recordings). Many following him have since argued for recognition of the musical dimension of social life.[13]

In this respect, it has been argued that the concept of 'soundscape' is productive in working towards an anthropology that can account for sound.[14] A focus on 'soundscape' takes into consideration the ways in which sound connects with place.[15] The sounds constituting a Welsh Patagonian soundscape, for example, would be different to those making up the London soundscape; within the Welsh Patagonian soundscape there would be different individual soundscapes in the shopping centre, the music school and in the bars in Trelew. Ingold argues that on the most literal level, the concept does not make sense, noting that 'when we look around on a fine day, we see a landscape bathed in sunlight, not a lightscape. Likewise, listening to our surroundings, we do not hear a soundscape. For sound, I would argue, is not the object but the medium of our perception'. Sound, for Ingold is more a 'phenomenon of experience – that is, of our immersion in, and commingling with the world in which we find ourselves'.[16]

Ingold elaborates that we do not phenomenologically experience the world divided up into sections in terms of the senses, further highlighting that in the insistence on a connection between sound and space, the concept of soundscape cannot account for sounds that travel, such as sounds that are recorded and then played out of context, as is the case for CDs recorded by Welsh tourists who have visited Patagonia. Connected to this is the issue that the concept of soundscape implies a shared sound, and therefore it cannot account for private sounds as experienced through headphones.[17] Another implication in the idea of soundscape is that it exists independently of individuals, as opposed to the idea that people themselves create the soundscape, and with it the type of image that they seek to portray. Finally, it implies that everyone in a particular space or place experiences the same soundscape, obscuring the fact that different people experience sounds differently due to varying factors such as context, mood, class, race and gender, and crucially, that the soundscape is not necessarily equally audible to everyone.[18]

Whilst many of Ingold's criticisms of the concept of soundscape resonate with the Welsh Patagonian context, his concept of the phenomenological sensory experience as a completely immersive one has implications in terms of understanding the processes of subjectivation through sight and sound. If we cannot separate the concepts of hearing and vision, then the mechanisms of subjectivation through gazing or through sound must be similar. However, how then can we account for what my interlocutors saw as being the unique relationship between music and feeling, the conceptualisation of their musical instrument as an extension of their body, or the sheer power of sound to act on individuals?[19] Music was unique in terms of the experience it induced, and in terms of what Hofman[20] has described as the 'reaction manifested in the skin, on the surface of the body and in the heartbeat ... something that goes beyond the body, a passage from one experiential state of the body to another'. Thompson and Biddle also refer to 'the mobilising capacity of...music, its capacity to transmit an 'energy' or an 'aura'.[21] Jarman elaborates: 'the fact that the music is additional or even secondary to some other listening ... does not mean that it has no effect on the listener'.[22]

Bloch too, in his analysis of a Merina circumcision ceremony in Madagascar, argues for a focus on the power of music. He describes the ceremonies as being dominated by the repetition of formalised songs, arguing that social control stems from the structure of the song. The formality of the music has two key consequences – it dampens the possibility of creativity on behalf of the singer, and increases the authority of the singer, or as Bloch puts it, 'You cannot argue with a song'.[23] However, Avenburg notes that these types of theories imply 'passive subject[s] who receive and can only accept, reject, or modify offers of musical interpellation' – it is not the case that musical structure and harmony unproblematically imprint themselves on its listeners.[24]

Later scholars have alternatively argued for a focus on social context, or on the human process of formalisation.[25] DeNora argues in her book *Music in Everyday Life* that the process of musical manipulation is a dialectical one, whereby we can be mobilised and influenced by music, but we can also use it to our own advantage in an act of 'self-manipulation'.[26] For example, we might listen to upbeat music to improve our mood or to motivate us during exercise, calming music as a relaxation tool or relaxing music to help us to sleep.[27] This is reminiscent of Butler's concept of subjectivation, whereby submitting to dominant structures can lead to mastery.[28] Consider, for example, Gwenan Gibbard's CD, which was discussed in chapter 5. Paula stated that she would listen to this CD to make her feel happy. In this context, the music on the CD portrayed a romanticised interpretation of Welsh Patagonia, but submitting to this interpretation was also a means of generating happiness or improved well-being.

This chapter argues that subjectivation through music – the enabling of music's powerful effect on us to reflect and create community – was most effective in Welsh Patagonia when my interlocutors and I reached a state of flow: when we immersed and lost ourselves in the music. This was closely connected to the creation of feelings of belonging and enjoyment, with the high levels of absorption and engagement being, in themselves, rewarding.[29] However, being in a state of flow was not a passive act. Flow was a desirable state to reach, and we consciously worked towards it, much like Lacan's image of the ideal self in the mirror.[30] In this context, then, music was a tool, whereby individuals manipulated its powerful qualities to work towards an 'ideal I'. My interlocutors utilised music as a form of self-cultivation – what Kassabian has termed 'management of the self'[31] – through self-administered 'music therapy', which made sense in a cultural context where therapy was extremely widespread in the Argentinian middle classes, with Lacanian psychoanalysis being the most used method. It further argues that musical self-cultivation both reflected and created societal values such as ideals of perfection or improvisation as well as inequalities and issues of accessibility within the community.

In making this argument, the chapter is underpinned by Foucault's understanding of the ethical subject which he developed in the final phase of his work.[32] His conceptualisation of the ethical subject is of a being continuously creating him or herself in a process of self-cultivation, through the ethical principles of caring for the self. This self-cultivation, whilst it takes place within a particular social and cultural framework, is less about compliance with an abstract set of moral rules, and more to do with self-mastery whereby '[the] ethical work that one performs on oneself [is] not only in order to bring one's conduct into compliance with a given rule, but [is an] *attempt to transform oneself* into the ethical subject of one's behaviour'.[33] Musical subjectivation in Welsh Patagonia was not about repression through music, but was a more complex dialogue of power, desire and manipulation.

## 'Que cantamos?': choir rehearsals in Gaiman Music School

Choir rehearsals in Gaiman Music School took place on Monday and Wednesday evenings from 21:00, and though they were scheduled to finish at 22:30, sometimes ran over by an hour with no break. Attendance at choir was not compulsory, and the mixed choir was open to anyone. Once one had 'become a member' by communicating with the choir directors (Maria, for the mixed choir, or Eleanor for the girls' choir) and subsequently attending a rehearsal, attendance was not formally monitored. However, choir members were highly committed, and they attended late-night rehearsals and concerts diligently, in the 45-degree heat of the summer and in the plummeting winter temperatures, on bank holidays and at the weekends. Despite this, I was often nudged by my fellow sopranos, sometimes minutes before we were due to go on stage to perform, and asked, '*Que cantamos? What are we singing?*' This was a blasé question which never showed

Figure 15: Gaiman Music School

Figure 16: The main rehearsal room of Gaiman Music School

any real concern. Despite 'the concert' being seen as 'something to aim towards' by my interlocutors (praised as 'having something to work for'), it was not viewed as the only goal of choir rehearsals in Gaiman.

At the end of one choir rehearsal in September, Elena asked me whether I would be able to go to her house the following day to help her with one of the pieces that we were going to be singing in the eisteddfod in October. '*Dwi methu canu nodyn!* I can't sing a note!' she exclaimed, laughing. The following morning, we sat together in her home sharing a piano stool in front of her slightly out-of-tune upright piano in the study, with the sheet music in front of us, and I played the soprano part with one finger for us both to sing along. After ten minutes, Elena shook her head, 'I still can't. I don't know why I go. I'm too old!' She then elaborated:

> 'It might be the case that I can't sing properly, but the reason I go is really to keep the traditions going, *viste*. It's a good opportunity to socialise with people that I won't see outside of choir. Lots of us are old, and it keeps the old brain going ... it's good having help with you ... taking advantage of you being here ...

*ond dyw e ddim yn ddiwedd y byd* ... but it is not the be all and end all. Choir means more than that to most of the people who sing, well the ones who aren't experts. We try our best, and we have fun, but we are old! *Paned?* Cup of tea?'

Elena emphasised that choir rehearsals were less about perfection and more about being a social opportunity to socialise with people from the community, with whom choir members would otherwise not have an opportunity to see in their daily routines, and a chance to engage mentally in something different. These opportunities were especially significant for those who were retired.[34] For Elena, there was something about singing together that made her feel happy, joyful and connected to other people.

During fieldwork, it became increasingly clear that choir rehearsals were considered to have value in and of themselves in terms of their role in bringing the community together, and that, at their best, were fun and punctuated with continuous commentary, jokes and laughter from the participants. One rehearsal, we were preparing the classic Welsh hymn, 'Pantyfedwen', a solemn hymn in a simple 4/4 rhythm, which we were due to sing in a concert in Gaiman in a week's time alongside the philharmonic orchestra of Rio Negro. We had received a backing track to the singing parts, but this was significantly faster than the speed with which we had been rehearsing, throwing most of us off. The choir was lagging, and Alberto stood up and began to clap a loud beat for us to try and follow. On top of this difficulty with the speed, the soprano part included several top Fs and Gs, which were out of the range of most of the sopranos (me included).

Brenda, a Welsh speaker from Trelew, and Rhiannon, who were sitting in front of me, were giggling; I could see their shoulders shaking. They turned around to include me in their joke. Rhiannon said that they could not reach the notes, and Brenda added that they were going to simply open their mouths and pretend that my voice was theirs. 'I'll do the same thing later in your Welsh lesson, Rhiannon,' she commented, laughing. I could hardly reach the notes, and the laughter was infectious. Brenda winked at me, '*Gwaith tîm* ... teamwork.' Every time we reached – well, tried to reach – a top F or G, I could see them from the corner of my eye miming dramatically, as though singing with great passion. Our laughter and shared experiences followed us out of the rehearsal room and led us to form a close friendship during and beyond fieldwork. Ultimately, the social role of the choir as explained by Elena, and as enacted by Rhiannon and Brenda, was perhaps most explicitly summarised by Alberto, who, following a choir rehearsal one day, put his arm round me and slapped my back enthusiastically, 'Weli di? You see? Mae'r gymuned fel teulu, ac mae'r côr fel y glud. The community is like a family and the choir is the glue.' His comment resonated with MacDonald's statement that 'music is completely woven into the fabric of our lives'.[35]

This idea that music can be mobilised to create feelings of community and belonging is a familiar one in the ethnographic literature. James's ethnography of the songs of women migrants in Johannesburg, South Africa argues that the musical style 'kiba' is entirely within the control of women, used to generate friendship and solidarity.[36] Seeger similarly draws on his work with the Suya, an Amazonian group living in the Xingu National Park in Mato Grosso, Brazil. He argues that music is critical in community coordination, whether concerned with economic activities or with the more personal consolidation of relationships with other humans, with animals and with their cosmology. Music here creates and affirms the 'fabric of social life'.[37] Askew, in her ethnography of musical performance in Tanzania, focuses on the close relationship between music and politics. To take one example, she argues that performances of *Taarab*, which are a type of love song, are a means of managing disputes in Swahili society. These songs provide 'an opportunity for communicating certain messages that cannot be communicated otherwise'.[38] Ultimately, these studies echo what my interlocutors emphasised in the field and what became clear in Gaiman Music School choir rehearsals – the effects of music on self and community and its central role in generating feelings of belonging.

### Singing for the ear of the other

Ideas of music generating ideas of community and belonging were strengthened by the fact that much of the repertoire covered by the choir was created by local composers and poets who wrote about the arrival to the settler colony, about the old Welsh homeland and about the positive relations between the Welsh settlers and Indigenous people. Much of the music composed in Welsh Patagonia was based (both harmonically and lyrically) on the romantic narratives explored in previous chapters. Singing in choir did not occur in a social void but rather choir members sang with a reference point – the ears of their audience, variously other Welsh Patagonians, local Argentinians, and tourists from Wales and elsewhere. By listening to and singing these harmonious compositions during choir rehearsals, concerts and in other situations, in addition to appearing coherent and tangible under the gaze of the other, Welsh Patagonia also sounded coherent and tangible to the ears of the other. At the same time, these concepts of belonging were not simply ideas that remained in the music alone. Playing music together, or singing together, did have an emotional and social impact on the group – it made us feel more connected and had a positive impact on our mood.

Just a few weeks into fieldwork on a cold Monday evening in August 2015, we began learning a Welsh song called 'Croeso Patagonia' ('Welcome Patagonia') with the mixed choir in preparation for the upcoming eisteddfod in October. The piece depicted the arrival of the Welsh in Patagonia and the subsequent establishment of the settler colony. Written for four-part harmony in a major key, it was an acapella piece, to be sung accompanied only by two drums, with swinging, upbeat, dotted rhythms. The piece was written in the style of an Argentinian *chacarera*, meaning that the bombo drum played in 3/4, with the overarching melody in 6/8, resulting in a syncopated rhythm. This was combined with a subtle musical borrowing of the Welsh melody of 'Calon Lân' to mark the end of its phrases. The lyrics creatively intertwined imagery of tea, siestas, *asados*, Welsh traditional songs, *dulce leche* and lemon pie. The final image was one of cultural compatibility and harmony, whereby different musical traditions mixed seamlessly to invoke the cultural mixture. Music, in the structure and lyrics of this piece, was a unifying activity. Musical harmonies overrode any differences between participants, and the four choral sections cooperated without fail and bounced off each other in a complementary way.

The piece opened with an introductory section in which the choir hummed, softly and rhythmically – 'dm dm dm' and 'wwww' – with dotted rhythms. After 8 bars, the choir was joined by a drumbeat, working to set the harmonious, feel-good scene for the first verse. The sopranos and altos took the melody in the first verse, accompanied by the continued humming, slightly quieter now, from the tenors and bases for the first two lines. Then, the four voices joined together to sing of forgetting the 'worries of the old country', the old country being Wales, with a *'tot fach o* mate ... little sip of *mate'*. The chorus was contrasting in its energy, with questions ringing through from the bass, *'Ges di* asado? Did you have an *asado?'* and the sopranos, altos and tenors answering in joyful unison, *'Do, do* ... Yes, yes – a full stomach of beef, two or three chorizos, roasted chicken meat'. The end of the chorus was dramatic, with a change of key to accommodate the Welsh melody of 'Calon Lân', slowing down towards the end. The lyrics read, 'And by the flames of the fire sharing the thrill of Calon Lân, *brodyr Cymru a'r Wladfa yn uno mewn cân* ... the brothers of Wales and the colony uniting in song'. Here, the lyrics explicitly invoked the idea of the Welsh and the Argentinian 'brothers' uniting in song, with singing together taken as a broader metaphor for the good relations between the two.

It quickly became clear that this piece was a favourite for many. The increased energy in the rehearsal room when we sung it was outwardly expressed in the tapping of feet and the exclamations of *'qué lindo'*. One rehearsal, one of my fellow sopranos clapped her hands with delight and said, 'They [the visitors to the eisteddfod] are going to love it.' We worked hard in the rehearsals, each time singing the piece slightly rhythmically and melodically tighter than the previous rendition. Months later, after performing the piece on the stage of the eisteddfod, we sat back in our chairs, awaiting the results of the competition. Shortly afterwards, we heard the news that we had won first prize. Maria grinned widely, visibly thrilled and congratulated the choir members before walking up to the podium to collect the prize. I felt someone tap me on the shoulder, and I turned around. I was greeted by two broad smiles from a man and a woman who were sitting together. *'Ni wedi clywed bo' ti o Gymru* ... We have heard that you are from Wales,' said the woman. The man interjected, 'We are here from Wales for two weeks so we can't see everything but ... well ... that piece gave me a very incredible idea of the Wladfa.'

'Croeso Patagonia' was not the only piece of music that had as its focus the cultural compatibility of the Argentinians and the Welsh in the settler colony. Towards the end of fieldwork, Alberto phoned me. He excitedly told me that he had been commissioned by an Argentine poet called Sergio Pravaz to compose the music for a suite of seven poems about the arrival of the Welsh in Patagonia, and that they were ready to be rehearsed. The poems, written in Spanish, told the story of the creation and consolidation of the settler colony. The first piece was about landing in southern Argentina, and it was followed by the journey at sea, the forming of the four-part choir, the settling of the Welsh settlers in their new home, and finally a song celebrating the success of the settler colony. The rhythms accompanying the poems were catchy and clever and drawn from Argentinian folk music: the *chacarera*, the *zamba*, the *baguala* and the *takirari*. Alberto had composed the music for four-part choir, to be accompanied by a string section (two violins, two cellos and a double bass), a percussion section (with a full drum-kit and traditional Argentine drums), a keyboard and acoustic guitars. I had been asked to play cello rather than sing in the choir.

The first piece of the suite 'Para Llegar al Sur' ('To Arrive in The South') was written in the style of a *baguala*. Originating in the northeast of Argentina, the *baguala* is one of the lesser-known genres of Argentinian folklore, perhaps as it is less 'danceable' than the other, more upbeat – or typically 'faster' – genres, such as the *zamba* or *chacarera*. Its rhythmical form is slow and uniform, and the percussion usually echoes the rhythms of the melody of the singer. After 24 bars of instrumental introduction, the four sections of the choir entered quietly, singing the still melody in unison: 'We will gather together to sing and our verses will be the bread of the land, they will reveal the Psalms and our language will be left in peace'. The singers were then instructed to increase the volume to a *double forte* ('very loud') whilst singing of how the verses will be the bread of the land ('We will gather together to sing and our verses will be the bread of the land') before returning to a quiet and apt dynamic to sing of peace ('*Nuestra lengua estará en paz* ... Our language will be in peace ... in peace').

Lyrically, the focus of the song was like that of 'Croeso Patagonia', drawing on images of people sitting around an open fire, eating and singing together to inspire commensality. The focus on gathering to sing highlighted the uniting force of music in bridging cultural differences. Whilst the musical structures of the other six pieces in the suite differed, the lyrics were similar. The second piece in the suite, 'La Espera en el Mar' ('The Hope in the Sea'), was a *chacarera*. It was louder and stronger, conveying a feeling of increasing hope whilst crossing the sea. The choir sang in unison in the chorus, 'We advance, here and there, together to begin'. The fifth piece in the suite, 'Ya Estamos De Pie' ('We Made It') took the form of a relaxed *zamba*, and the lyrics emphasised the establishment of a village and a community ('we are a village') through sound ('the voice of the whole'). Through the sentiment of the lyrics and the musical style, the suite intended to evoke a positive, hopeful journey and a happy, harmonious arrival at the settler colony, and it was certainly successful in doing so. In describing the suite of compositions to me, Alberto said:

> *Bydd y gyngerdd yn fawr iawn* ... The concert will be very big, I am sure that many people will come. *Mae Pravaz wedi dylunio'r Wladfa yn perfecto* ... Pravaz has illustrated the Wladfa perfectly ... it shows how difficult it was for the first settlers and it shows that they sung to keep the language alive ... and probably to keep them alive in such a difficult situation in the *extreme Sur* ... extreme South! The music I have written is strong ... *llawer o dryms* ... lots of drums ... and the Argentinian rhythms show the mixture of culture and show how easy it is to switch between two cultures for us. The music and the poetry are like a couple ... *maen nhw angen ei gilydd* ... they need each other to show the image we want to portray.

Alberto's emphasis on the calculated portrayal of an image signifies the composition of music in relation to a listening audience, implying an awareness of how it might sound to a listener, the kind of sound a listener might desire and the power to portray a certain message through music. It worked both ways – not only were my interlocutors acutely aware of the ways in which joyous and harmonious group singing might sound to the visiting tourists, but visiting tourists listening to performances by the choir used the imagery and musical harmony portrayed to create and consolidate their own perceptions of the settler colony. These songs, and the stories they told, invoked the dominant popular narrative of the Welsh settlers facing serious difficulties during their journey to Patagonia, struggling initially with the management of the barren land, but overcoming these challenges to establish a successful and harmonious settler colony.

Alongside the lyrics, the music had additional elements to set the scene and tone, such as the use of major and minor keys which were used to invoke joy or sadness, respectively, and the use of drums, which portrayed an element of certainty. Consider, for example, the first piece of the suite, 'Para Llegar al Sur', with its slow, uniform melody. The drum plodding along underneath the singers provided an apt portrayal of the length of the journey to Patagonia, the grief of losing crew members, the fatigue of travelling and the endless search for land on which to settle, whilst emphasising the continuity and perseverance of the settlers. The faster, quirkier rhythms of 'La Espera en el Mar' were a perfect way to convey the hope, excitement and joy of searching for – and eventually finding – fertile land. As a choir and orchestra, we reacted to these rhythmic and melodic choices. A slow, uniform melody made us sing and play quieter, and more solemnly. Contrastingly, the choir and orchestra moved more, smiled more and were more energised during the lively *chacarera*. In other words, the musical components had a profound impact on us, in conjunction with the lyrics. As Alberto said to me, 'You just have to listen to the music, and you will be transported on the journey.'

In the discussion of the tourist gaze in chapter 4, I noted that 'we all know, or can imagine, that curious feeling of being lost in thought whilst reading a book in a library, looking out a train window, or painting a picture'. For Sartre, an individual who is in this state of immersion – lost in an engaging activity – is not yet aware of him or herself as being a subject.[39] He would argue that we become subjects at the exact moment at which we are looking out a train window, painting a picture or reading in the library, and feel the eyes of another person watching us. When we stop what we are doing to look up, or turn around, we become subjects, and in our capacity to imagine how we must look to the individual watching us, we also become aware of the subjectivity of the other.

In the context of music, we all know, or can imagine, that feeling of being lost in music, whilst listening to a piece of music that evokes happy or sad memories, whilst playing a musical instrument that (at our best moments) becomes an extension of ourselves, whilst singing with friends in a choir or whilst attending a gig at a festival. We all know, or can imagine, the feeling of when a particular song becomes 'stuck' in our heads, or when it has a particular impact on us – so much so that we seek it out in moments when we know we need to listen to it. This is where sound demonstrates its differences to the gaze. In Welsh Patagonia, whilst there was an awareness of how sound might sound to a listener, in terms of generating feelings of belonging and community, subjectivation through music was most effective during this state of 'flow'.[40]

Csikszentmihalyi was the first to define the concept of flow in his book *Beyond Boredom and Anxiety*.[41] Since his work, the concept of flow has been researched extensively, with scholars agreeing that the state of flow is characterised by 'total absorption, concentration, action-awareness, distortion of time and intrinsic enjoyment' in the activity at hand.[42] Much of the work on flow has focused on listening to or performing music and, in particular, on individual flow achieved through activities such as sports or music, and on the ways in which entering a flow state improves creativity, enhances performance and increases the levels of enjoyment of the task.[43] Hackert et al. have further explored the concept of a collective group flow, arguing that the presence of others can enable flow. Group flow, according to their analysis, is different to individual flow in that the focus is on the interaction and coherence between group members, rather than on individual absorption, which Hackert et al. argue creates a perception of a whole for an observer, noting that the overlap between self and other 'fosters a collective state of mind, which is particularly relevant for the emergence of group flow'.[44]

During choir rehearsals, or whilst listening to concerts, the moments in which my interlocutors felt most uplifted and most united with their fellow choir participants, or the audience around them, were also the very moments in which they were fully absorbed in the activity. These were the rehearsals when time seemed to fly, when my interlocutors all suddenly realised at the end that hours had passed and that it was night. They would suddenly come back to their senses, saying '*Tengo hambre* ... I'm hungry' or '*Dwi wedi blino nawr!* I'm tired now!', an indication that these fundamental human needs had been forgotten in the moment of absorption in the music. The goosebump or tear-inducing moments, when the music and its meaning was embodied by my interlocutors, were not necessarily the moments in which they were so acutely aware of their subjectivation, but rather they appeared to be the moments in which there was a lack of self-awareness in the activity. In other words, whilst my interlocutors did demonstrate a self-awareness of the power of music, in that they explicitly reflected on it, the actual moment of subjectivation through sound did not occur at the point of recognition, but rather at the point of collective interaction and individual immersion when they were lost in the music.

### 'The reason I play...': musical therapy in Argentina

Laukka argues that although there are studies making the link between music and belonging, there is little work to show why this may be the case, and 'future studies should ... pay more attention to the motives for engaging in various activities'.[45] Many qualitative and quantitative studies since have pointed towards the positive effects of music on overall health and well-being.[46] Research has focused on community music therapy such as the creation of community choirs for older adults,[47] the impact of music lessons (especially within schools) on psychological or social variables and cognitive development,[48] the positive outcomes of music therapy across a range of diagnoses,[49] and the ways in which listening to empowering music has a positive impact on self-esteem.[50]

One evening, despite the plummeting temperatures outside, Paula and I were sitting in the ice-cream parlour in the centre of Gaiman. '*Ti* ... You,' she declared, pausing to lick her vanilla and chocolate cone, '*fel fi* ... are like me'. I looked at her, expectantly.

> Some people play instruments to be the best, you know, musically. For those people, it is easy for them to lose themselves in the music. For others, though, like you and me, the reason we play is to better ourselves, as people, rather than to play perfectly, you know, musically. For people like you and me, I do think you can learn to perform a musical concert with confidence, it's just like you can learn to speak in front of a crowd ... *Dwi'n gallu gwneud hynny nawr ers gweithio fel athrawes* ... I can do that now since starting to work as a teacher, but I think it is so difficult to reach that moment when you are lost.

Paula's comments suggested that she saw practising the violin, playing music and reaching the optimum flow as a path to self-improvement, inner peace or happiness on a deeper level, beyond the simple increase of musical standard or development of community, and this became something which she elaborated on time and time again during fieldwork. This concept of manipulating the powerful qualities of music for one's own benefit also resonates with MacDonald's definition of musical therapy as 'interventions [which] will [not] have musical developments in terms of increasing technical skills as a primary objective'.[51] Paula regularly cited the therapeutic qualities of violin playing as being one of her main motivations to play. As she emphasised one evening, '*Wnaeth cerddoriaeth fy achub i* ... Music saved me ... The musical community here, when I was in my twenties, saved me.' I nodded, and she continued, 'The reason that I play the violin,' she explained to me, 'is that it helps me mentally, and it gives me space to deal with my problems, *yn ogystal â mynd at terepia* ... in addition to seeing my therapist.'

Zhang has argued that 'life stories and personal narratives of feelings are essential in the cultivation of a new therapeutic self and personal growth', and music similarly fitted into a coherent narrative for Paula.[52] She regularly told me the history of her moving from Trevelin where she lived with her family to Gaiman in her late teens, about the death of both her parents when she was relatively young, about her estranged brother, about the difficulties of marriage, and about the struggles and joys of parenthood. All these factors were key points in her narrative which inspired her to begin taking more 'seriously' her musical studies by playing more violin and attending choir. '*Mae'n helpu fi.* It helps me,' she would state, sincerely. Twenty years later, she was a consistent, daily presence at Gaiman Music School and music was a part of her daily self-work. Eleanor had similar ideas about the healing and transformative qualities of music. One scorching summer's day, we were sitting in her living room waiting for the other women to arrive for a girls' choir rehearsal when she said to me:

> You know, I have had cancer twice. And both times, I have been told that the cancer has gone. I think what has saved me, both times, well ... God ... *gweddio i Dduw a credu mewn Fe* ... praying to God and trusting in Him, but also music. Playing music, leading the girls' choir, it helped me to feel better, to feel happier ... *i deimlo gobaith am ddyfodol gwell* ... to feel hope for a better future.

These ideas about the therapeutic benefits of music found concrete expression in Paula's teaching methods. At the beginning of the violin classes that she taught at Gaiman Music School, she devoted fifteen minutes to yoga-style stretching before we began the class, emphasising the importance of finding the connection between mind, body, soul, breath and music. At the end of the stretching, we would reach up to the ceiling and then bring our arms down in front of us, before slowly folding forward, bringing our arms down to the floor. In this final position, Paula would encourage us to think of a moment in which we felt truly at peace with ourselves. 'Try to be back in that space,' she would tell us, in a soft voice. When we eventually played violin, the atmosphere in the room remained still, calming and tranquil. The musical focus during her classes was on an embodied experience of 'enjoying' and 'feeling' the music and allowing ourselves to be moved by it. Throughout, Paula emphasised the importance of good posture and perfect bow-hold in enabling us to be, as she called it, *'uno con el violin* ... at one with the violin'.

My other interlocutors pointed to similar motivations behind their musical activities. One of my fellow violin students was a local Argentinian woman, the mother of one of the young girls from the string group. She was striking with her creative, colourful clothing and jet-black hair. She explained to me that learning the violin, which she had been doing for around a year at the time of my fieldwork, was part of a broader project of self-care, stating that:

> *Baje mucho peso* ... I have lost a lot of weight; I am eating better ... and I come to these classes once a week. I saw Martina coming, and I saw it does her good ... so I thought ... *porque no!* Why not! I am old, but I am not too old to try something new. Since coming I have found that I am feeling less stressed, I am eating better, I smile more, and I am more disciplined in my whole life. Those things ... music ... health ... *van todo juntos* ... all go together for me.

A similar case arose towards the end of fieldwork. I was surprised to see my landlady walking through the doors of the music school with a guitar case. Although she ran her own business selling cakes and food from her home, she was a quiet, family-orientated woman who spent most of her time with her children and grandchildren. She was originally from Chile but had moved to Gaiman when she married her Welsh Patagonian husband, who had since died. Her children were very involved with the Welsh community, and she occasionally attended the mixed choir, but she was a relatively reserved attendee. In the music school, she laughed at my reaction, 'Are you shocked? *Necessito algo para mi* ... I need to do something for me. I am always in the house, cooking, baking, missing my sister in Chile, and cleaning ... well now it's time to do something to better myself.' Ultimately, Paula, Eleanor, Martina's mother and my landlady pointed towards similar motivations to play, in that music was part of a broader project of self-care, serving to – as Foucault puts it – induce 'tranquillity of the mind'.[53]

The concept of musical self-cultivation made sense in the broader context in which it was embedded, where therapy was part of the tapestry of daily life. Zhang draws on her fieldwork in China to argue that the concept of self-improvement through therapy raises the question of how one can become culturally re-embedded following their journey of self-development.[54] She explains how one of her interlocutors, overwhelmed by her responsibilities at home, which included caring for her elderly father and her daughter, had hired a carer to look after her family and left for a journey of self-discovery to Tibet. As Stafford similarly asks, 'exactly whom did they want to make happy? Her parents, their children, or themselves?'[55] Zhang's interlocutor, in leaving for Tibet, ultimately chose to focus on herself, in doing so disentangling herself from her obligations. However, when she returned, she was faced with the new challenge of reconciling her new concept of the self with existing notions of personhood.

Contrastingly, therapy has long been a central component of middle-class Argentinian culture and so ethical self-cultivation was considered the norm.[56] As Koç and Kafa highlight:

> Psychotherapy is generally embraced by the people of Argentina, they are comfortable talking about their therapy experiences, recommend it to others, and seek psychological help not only when they face serious problems, but also to increase the quality of their lives.[57]

In 2018, there were 82,000 (mostly female) psychologists active in Argentina which amounts to 206 psychologists per 100,000 people.[58] Stagnaro has argued that Argentina is 'the country with the most psychologists per inhabitant in the world'.[59] In comparison, there were 46,400 psychologists registered in the UK in 2021, though there are an additional 199,000 individuals employed in therapy settings.[60] Paula's comment about music helping her 'alongside seeing [her] therapist' was a typical one.[61] Many Welsh Patagonians I knew in the field had a therapist whom they saw regularly, or at the very least had received therapy in the past. My adult English students in Trelew would also regularly refer to their therapy in class discussions, as one student commented:

> It is not that you go to therapy when you feel bad and then leave when you feel better. You have to keep going when you feel good, then when things happen in your life that are difficult ... or when you are struggling in your relationships ... maybe with your husband or your children or your friends ... you are already going to therapy once a week or maybe less and you can talk about it with your therapist. I have been going to therapy for nearly 10 years.

Psychoanalysis, at the time of the research, was the most common therapeutic approach in Argentina, in both academia and in clinical practice, with most of the clinical psychologists adopting a Freudian or Lacanian methodology, a psychoanalytical style which focused on narrative construction and childhood experiences.[62] As Dagfal notes, 'Psychoanalysis has acquired such a great scope in [Argentine] academia, in the healthcare system, and in the common understanding of everyday life, that this situation has drawn the attention of the specialised literature and the international press'.[63] Lakoff raises the further possibility that the popularity of Lacanian methodology was rooted in the social and political context of Argentina:

> Others, however, argued that the turn in the mental health community toward Lacan's hermetic philosophical system had been complicit with the military dictatorship's effort to depoliticise the mental health field – that Lacanianism's

detachment from social problems allowed it to survive the 'dirty war' period, while more engaged movements were brutally repressed by the dictatorship following the 1976 coup.[64]

Ultimately, then, this desire for self-improvement was embedded within a broader social context of which psychotherapy was a central component. Koç and Kafa state that 'psychodynamic psychotherapy approaches are predominantly favoured in countries like Argentina'.[65] On a more theoretical level, the concept of self-mastery within dominant structures resonates with Foucault's concept of self-cultivation, and the intrinsic connection he draws between this and the 'principle that says one must take care of oneself. It is this principle of the care of the self that establishes its necessity, presides over its development, and organises its practice'.[66] In other words, to even consider practising self-cultivation, there must be some broader societal framework that is compelling us to look after ourselves, and a broader concept of what that might look like in practice.[67]

For Paula, playing the violin was concerned with the formation of the self in a structured, intentional way. Practising and playing the violin was closely connected with self-improvement, self-discipline and with working towards an 'ideal I', whereby achieving control of breathing before a rehearsal or achieving a full control of the bow by pulling it along the string slowly and methodically led to a level of emotional control which extended beyond the specific context of playing. As she said to me once, at a time when she was too busy to practice the violin daily, '*Y peth gorau i fi yw chwarae bob dydd* ... The ideal for me is to play every day, just a little bit. But right now, life is so busy, and even if I only play once a week, it does help me for the rest of the week.' She explicitly contrasted her reasons for playing with playing to improve musical standards. The primary focus, for her, was on the physical and mental benefits of playing the violin. As DeNora states, 'music is appropriated by individuals as a resource for the ongoing constitution of themselves and their social psychological, physiological, and emotional states'.[68]

Despite Foucault's idea being one of *self*-improvement and *self*-care, 'one of the most important aspects of this activity devoted to oneself: it constituted, not an exercise in solitude, but a true social practice'.[69] White elaborates:

Foucault affirms that caring for others follows naturally from caring for oneself because one cares for oneself as a parent, citizen, friend, or member of the human community ... and in promoting our own individual virtues we are thereby enhancing our connection to the community and to others.[70]

Practising and playing violin, for Paula was an inherently social act. She often organised weekend rehearsals with her daughter, Emma, and me at her home in Gaiman, both in preparation for upcoming concerts and in a more informal sense. During these sessions, we would play various pieces of music, including the usual repertoire of the music school string group alongside additional Welsh folk tunes. Paula would play the violin or would sing, Emma would play the harp or the violin and I would play the cello. This would be a social event, and we would always break for tea and pastries halfway through the session. Paula often emphasised her enjoyment of playing music with other people. In the early days of our friendship, she alluded towards this implicitly, by regularly complaining that her violin teacher continuously set her scales and technical exercises to practise alone. 'Just me, in the house, with my scales,' she would state, wrinkling her nose, in a tone of voice that indicated she was half joking, but half not. Towards the end of fieldwork, she began to confide in me more explicitly and would often say that playing music was better with company. In one of the final weeks of fieldwork, we were walking on the beach in Playa Union together when she said:

> *Un o'r pethau gorau am cael ti yma* ... One of the best things about having you here, is that I have the opportunity to play music with other people ... I mean ... I do have the chance to play with my professors, but they are so focused on improving my standard [...] So that is why it is so nice to be able to play with someone else who understands that it is about *more* than just being a good violinist.

What Paula emphasised was that playing music as a form of therapy, when undertaken within a group, was ultimately more effective as an act of self-cultivation in relation to the alternative of playing alone. This is a common theme in the literature on music therapy. Ahessy argues that for the older adults with whom he conducted research, participation in a music therapy choir reduced symptoms of depression, an intervention that was inseparable from the social interaction generated through participation in the choir.[71] van Rooyen and dos Santos make a similar argument in their article on community music therapy in South Africa.[72] Drawing on their research in weekly choir sessions held for teenagers in a children's home, they argue that the teenagers, through the intrapersonal experience of singing together, improved their social skills and the quality of their relationships, in addition to demonstrating increased self-esteem and better regulation of their emotions. McFerran and Hunt draw on research with an Australian music therapy programme for youth to highlight that focusing on music 'rather than [on] psychological outputs supported significant psychosocial or therapeutic benefits', arguing that connecting through music allowed this particular group of young people to 'solicit the support they needed for coping with adverse life experience'.[73] Ultimately, these examples demonstrate the intrinsic connection between music, therapy and social group.

### The ideal musical 'I'

The musical repertoire chosen by Paula and my other interlocutors on their journey to self-improvement, happiness and inner peace was not banal. As Kavedžija and Walker note in relation to happiness, specifically, 'happiness always involves an evaluation of sorts ... as such, it is intrinsically linked to questions of value'.[74] The same basic premise is relevant for the concepts of peace, tranquillity and self-improvement that were significant to my interlocutors in the process of combining the 'momentary pleasure' or the 'enjoyable and positive experiences' of playing music with having a 'higher purpose [and] a meaningful life'.[75] In this respect, the musical repertoire was chosen not only within a specific social context of which middle-class therapy was a central concept, but also in line with a socially constructed hierarchy of societal and musical value.

    The question here therefore became: who exactly was this better self that my interlocutors were working towards? In other words, what did the ideal 'I' look like in a musical context, and why did it look that way? Graeber has argued that 'insofar as value is social, it is always a comparison; value can only be realised in other people's eyes.[76] Another way to put this is that there must always be an audience'. Graeber's broader argument is that we must consider human beings as existing in a continuous process of creation, with value being the way in which the project of creation becomes meaningful to the individuals involved. This resonates with the Foucauldian idea of self-cultivation that I have elaborated. There is no such thing as a 'better self' that exists in a social void. We create ourselves, in relation to others, based on an underlying value system. My interlocutors' manipulation of the powerful effects of music to become what they saw as being 'better people' took place in relation to certain values of what being a good person entailed, whether this was to do with cultural gendered ideals (such as being thinner, as in the case of Martina's mother), being more sociable, being more disciplined or being more Welsh. Further, there was a clear class component in this kind of self-improvement, not only in that therapy was generally a middle-class pursuit, but also in that being able to even conceptualise improving your position or circumstances is always itself a privilege.

The concept of the 'ideal Welsh I', in Welsh Patagonia was a carefully defined category in a context where my interlocutors were continually performing to a Welsh audience, in addition to viewing their own performances of Welshness in films, where the ideal Welsh 'I' was reflected to them. In these varied contexts, there was an understanding of the ideal Welshness that needed to be performed and projected to an audience of Welsh visitors, who themselves came to the settler colony with their own values and understandings of what Welsh Patagonia was. Much of what was happening in fieldwork was a project of creation, of community and of self, in relation to an imagining of what Welsh Patagonia was, could and should be. Underlying this project of creation was a subtle hierarchical system whereby Welshness was broadly seen to have higher social and economic value than Argentineness.

One conversation with Rosario was particularly illuminating in this respect. Rosario's involvement with the Welsh community changed over the course of our friendship. When I first met her in 2013, she was working in Ysgol yr Hendre in Trelew as an English teacher. In 2016, Rosario became employed in Ysgol Gymraeg y Gaiman. We were drinking *mate* in the kitchen one afternoon, when she suddenly looked up and asked me, in English, 'Could you help me to write a letter, in Welsh?' She explained that she was paid hourly, without holiday or sick pay. 'We are not paid for the hours or preparation or for the hundreds of meetings we have to attend ... you know how it is in Argentina.' She explained that a representative of the Welsh teaching project would be visiting the school that week, and that her colleagues had encouraged her to speak up on behalf of them all. I was not surprised that she had been chosen, given her outspoken, direct and fearless nature. She said, 'I'm going to ask for holiday pay, sick leave, and that we stop being treated like illegal workers, and receive the respect we deserve as trained teachers.' She elaborated, 'Teachers who live here earn around 5,000 pesos a month [around £200 at the time of the research], which is nothing if you are trying to pay rent, maintain a family, and keep up with all the economic changes.'

She explained that the Welsh teachers were offered free accommodation in Trelew in addition to being paid to work at the school. Their wages were modest, but they did not have to pay any rent. Coupled with the relatively low cost of living and non-materialistic culture in Argentina, they had a comfortable quality of life, especially in comparison to many of my local interlocutors. Being Welsh and being able to cultivate and perform Welshness was a privilege. Similar hierarchies were also expressed during a concert that I attended early on in fieldwork. As we were listening to the introduction for the Welsh national anthem, one of my retired Welsh Patagonian interlocutors – who was a regular attendee of Gaiman Music School mixed choir – leaned towards me, and whispered in my ear, *'Dwi'n credu fod yr anthem Gymreig yn well na'r un Archentaidd, wyt ti?* I think the Welsh anthem is just so much better than the Argentinian one, don't you? It just sounds so much better.' I whispered back, 'I think they are both good, *pam ti'n dweud hynny?* Why do you say that?' and she responded, '*No sé* ... I don't know, it's just everything from there [Wales] seems to be better ... a better standard.'

Similarly, Paula would always choose Welsh folk music for the Gaiman string group to perform and said that she preferred this type of music. She would also often listen to traditional Welsh music at home, and often described Welsh music as being 'better' than Argentinian music. She further elaborated: 'I want to play music that makes me feel good and that makes me happy and that is *a part of who I am*.'

Therefore, part of the process of ethical self-cultivation, for these individuals, was to play more Welsh music, and to situate it within their internal hierarchies, even whilst the aim of practice was not to improve one's own standard, musically speaking per se.

### Gaiman Music School: who gets to sing?

The privilege to be able to cultivate an ethical self and an 'ideal I' through music was related to a broader issue of accessibility, both a more abstract accessibility to Welshness, and a practical level of accessibility to the music school. Foucault recognised that the project of self-cultivation is not necessarily open to everyone, and neither is it without its constraints.[77] In Welsh Patagonia, the same musical practice that brought people together was open to some and subtly closed to others. Flood argues that bringing musical skills to a musical fieldwork context can help to facilitate initial immersion. She writes:

> I had done less than three hours of fieldwork at Roy's Opry when I found myself taking an extended fiddle solo in front of a fifty-person audience. My fingers moved automatically through the melody of a fiddle tune called 'Leather Britches' as I contemplated how my plans had gone awry. On my first trip to Roy's, a weekly country music show in eastern Tennessee, I had intentionally left my fiddle in the trunk of the car … the next week I arrived fiddle in hand and was immediately coaxed on stage.[78]

My experience of fieldwork was similar in this respect, as within days of my first trip to the field in 2013 I quickly found a role for myself as a cellist and a singer. However, my access to – and acceptance within – the music school was closely connected to my status as a young white woman from Wales. In other words, having a genuine possibility of working towards the ideal 'I' in a truly 'open' way required some level of engagement with Welshness to begin with. Upon my return to the field in 2015, I was immediately welcomed back to the school and invited to sing in both the mixed choir and the girls' choir, and to play cello in the string ensemble, with the head of the music school, Graciela, saying to me with a smile, 'You'll be one of us by the time you leave.' Later, I was given permissions to attend violin lessons as a pupil, despite it being a few months away from the official date of class registration. Other visitors from Wales had a similar level of accessibility and were regularly invited to join the choirs and music groups in the music school upon their arrival in the valley.

As I slowly began to make friends with other individuals in Gaiman beyond the connections I had developed within the music school, I began to realise that my own experience of accessibility was not reflective of their experiences. One example of this came from Manuela. I met Manuela through Rosario: they had met many years previously through their common interest in languages. Manuela lived in Gaiman with her mother, father and brother. She taught English in Trelew, and she was a kind, clever, articulate and extremely generous young woman. One afternoon, we were sitting in Rosario's kitchen sharing *mate*, when Rosario mentioned to Manuela that I was heading to the music school later that afternoon for the string group rehearsal. Manuela pushed her jet-black hair behind her ears and her glasses higher up her nose. She paused briefly, before saying, 'I enjoy singing, and I used to go the music school all the time ... but then I stopped.' I asked her why, but she did not elaborate much, simply stating that she had not felt comfortable there, and that she preferred to sing at home nowadays. Later, during an interview, she detailed:

> Because Gaiman is a small community, they [meaning, the Welsh community] are considered gossips. I think it is an open community principally because as the years have passed the Welsh descendants have created relationships with people from other cultures and places and to do this it has been necessary to be flexible. *I think that many people who visit from other places can participate in activities like the eisteddfod, choir, and music.* At the same time, for a while now it has been considered *bad or strange if someone who did not have a Welsh surname participated in Welsh activities, but I think that this is something that must be modified and adapted to the multicultural nature of the village* [emphasis mine].

Here, Manuela problematised the notion of accessibility within the music school, pointing out that whilst the community was often open to visitors from other places, internal politics felt more complicated for locals who wished to participate in Welsh musical culture. As White notes of the concept of self-cultivation, 'Foucault is not saying we are free to choose anything we want to do'.[79] What this also exemplifies is the other side of music and belonging – the role of music in establishing communal boundaries. As the relations of belonging are strengthened for those involved, they can be increasingly alienating for those who remain on the outskirts.

## Conclusions: 'Music helps you to live'

> Think of a time when you were involved in singing or playing an instrument, or simply listening to music. You will probably remember that time seemed to stop or accelerate. You were totally concentrated on the music; everything flowed easily, and you felt a sense of joy and fulfilment.[80]

It was a Monday evening in October 2016. I pushed the heavy wooden door of the music school open, and as I breathed in the musty smell of weekend closure, I was greeted with the piercing sound of a single violin tuning, the notes floating from the main rehearsal room. Listening carefully, I could hear a single, high-pitched note, being played softly, methodically and slightly out of key – a sonic indication of the bow being drawn slowly and carefully across the highest string, E. I knew it must be Paula. There was a pause, and then the bow met the string again, this time producing a slightly lower E. Another pause, and this time the E was in tune. Once the highest note had been tuned, the other notes were tuned with it, the violinist feeling for the perfect fifth between the strings. I heard two notes next, an E and a slightly out of key A, which glided up and down in pitch until the perfect space between them was achieved and sonically celebrated with a sustained bowing of a chord – an A and an E in perfect harmony. The tuning continued – a single pitch-perfect A this time, joined by a slightly out-of-tune D. I quietly turned the handle on the door to the rehearsal room and pushed the door open. Paula was standing with her back to the door, tall and poised, holding her violin under her chin, with her right arm bowing the note and the left arm turning the small tuning pegs on the front of the violin as she played. Her arm lifted the bow up again, but just before it touched the string, she turned around abruptly, jumping, before exclaiming hurriedly, embarrassed, 'O, helo ... Oh, hello, I didn't see you there, I was lost in the tuning. I hope it didn't sound too bad!'

For Sartre, despite an acknowledgement of sound and hearing, viewing and seeing are the central principles underlying his elaboration of the gaze: 'All of a sudden I hear footsteps in the hall. *Someone is looking at me.* What does this mean? It means that I am suddenly affected in my being and that essential modifications appear in my structure.'[81] Central to Sartre's idea of the gaze is the possibility of being able to conceptualise how you are viewed by another person in a context like this. However, the above encounter with Paula's tuning demonstrates the possibility, in the Welsh Patagonian context, of considering an aural subjectivation. Paula's focus in the present moment, her full engagement in the flow of the tuning, and the physical, emotional and social impact of music in other contexts such as choir rehearsals or self-induced musical therapy was similar in some ways to the level of concentration of Sartre's individual peering through a keyhole. Yet her comment of 'I hope it didn't sound too bad' indicated less of an awareness of how she might have been viewed by an onlooker, and more of an awareness of how her sound might sound to a listener. The moment of interruption was not the moment in which Paula became a subject in this context, as would be the case for Sartre's individual being caught looking through a keyhole. Rather, the subjectivation through sound would have been occurring before I interrupted, whilst she was fully focused on and engaged in the music, therefore enabling its powerful impact on her.

For Lacan, Sartre and Althusser, though each of these thinkers differ in the precise means by which subjectivation occurs, subjectivation through the gaze requires a certain level of recognition, whereby we become self-aware and recognise the presence of the other.[82] For Sartre, individuals become subjects precisely at the point of recognition. Sartre's individual looking through a keyhole is fully immersed in the activity, and then suddenly feels the eyes of an onlooker. He or she turns around and recognises how he or she might *seem* to the other. There is an element of shame in the moment of subjectivation, whereby the individual is ashamed to have been caught, a shame which indicates that he or she is able to consider the onlooker's perspective.

Lacan and Althusser both differ in relation to Sartre, and in relation to each other. Lacan modified his original mirror stage theory (in which he argued that subjectivation was momentary) to argue that becoming a subject is a continuous process. The concept of the mirror theory, whilst it enables a consideration of subjectivation in terms of it being laced with desire and a certain 'striving' to become a subject, still implicitly retains an element of recognition, in that the infant must continuously see him or herself in the mirror and recognise the gap between the self as reflected and the reality. Althusser takes Lacan's argument (that subjectivation is continuous) a step further to argue that individuals are already *born* subjects. In other words, we are already subjects of the state. However, recognition remains central. In the act of recognition (for example, when we turn around to face a police officer who shouts, 'Hey, you!' at us on the street), we are interpellated, time and time again, by state ideology. Key to this is Althusser's perception of the success of interpellation whereby: 'You and I are *always already* subjects, and as such *constantly practice the rituals of ideological recognition*, which guarantee for us that we are indeed concrete, individual, distinguishable and (naturally) irreplaceable subjects.'[83]

In Welsh Patagonia, the element of recognition, in daily life, whilst under the gaze of the tourist other, or as my interlocutors watched their own performances of Welshness on film, was also paramount. Consider, for example, the moment in the museum, when Lucas and I were laughing about the harp in the corner, the sudden interruption that followed – the sound of the bell chiming to indicate visitors – and the immediate reaction, a spontaneous performance of Welshness. Lucas later told me that it was not a 'performance', but rather part of his identity. At the point of recognition, or interruption, in this context, Lucas immediately came into being as Welsh, recognising what the tourists would be looking for, and aware of how he might seem to them, if he was laughing about the harp and drinking *mate* when they entered. More broadly speaking, my interlocutors felt the gaze of the tourists watching them, recognised the image that the tourists hoped to find in Welsh Patagonia and performed that Welshness to them, both in person and at an anticipatory distance whereby the gaze was felt as a potential subjectivation (for example, in rehearsals prior to the tourists' arrival or on social media). Similarly, in the film nights organised in Gaiman, my interlocutors recognised, laughed at and later reflected on the gap between the self as experienced (in daily life) and the self as performed in the film *Galesa*. Ultimately, in all these performative encounters, there was a certain element of recognition or self-awareness.

Ultimately, this chapter has been interested in the ways in which this subjectivation through sound worked at an intrapersonal community level. In doing so it has explored the role of music in the creation and consolidation of both social relationships and an image of community, through an exploration of music and belonging in Gaiman Music School rehearsals and classes. Across these varied contexts, the fundamental message remained the same in its association of music with positive qualities, be this in bringing people together, or in invoking feelings of happiness. Key to this argument is the idea that the sheet music must 'come to life' as it were or, in other words, it must be played or sung to create feelings of belonging. At the same time, the sheet music does have an element of intrinsic power in that it is created with intentionality, in social and political contexts. This has further pertinence in a context in which the composer lives, works or has travelled within the community. Structure and lyrics are important, and they do help in some way – in this context, the positive and harmonious portrayal of social relationships, and specifically the relationships between Wales and Patagonia, through lyrics and melodies, provided at the very least a platform for these types of sentiments.

Whilst it is important to consider the differences in the process of subjectification as interpellated through vision or through sound, there were similarities too. Analogously to the ways in which under the gaze of the Welsh tourist other, Welsh Patagonia seemed to take shape as a homogenous, graspable entity, the listening to, performing, rehearsing and creation of music which evoked the idea of harmonious relationships between the Welsh and local Argentinians or Indigenous inhabitants of the settler colony, or which portrayed a depiction of a positive and romanticised life in the settler colony, also helped to create this as the perceived reality or subjectivity of the group. This was strengthened by the musical techniques of major keys and bouncy, dotted rhythms (which tended to invoke a more positive and harmonious atmosphere). Musical activities towards the sonic formation of an outwardly homogenous Welsh Patagonia, working in conjunction with the effect of tourism, cameras and the gaze of the other explored in previous chapters. Tourists not only consumed and then reflected the images presented to them through music, but also often, as musicians themselves, later created them based on their experiences in the settler colony.

The lack of recognition required on the part of the subject in the context of subjectification through music implies a subject that is far more porous and more open than the separate subject implied through the concepts of the gaze. However, this is not to imply a compliance with – or lack of knowledge of – subjectivation through sound. If we consider Hofman's argument that 'people experiencing music and sound invest their own affective dispositions, moods, and emotions, and although they are open to the affective environment, they are not just empty vessels for impersonal affect', it is possible to consider the ways in which this subjectivation was more complex than it might seem.[84] Individuals wanted to reach the state of flow, they wanted music to act on them, and some of my interlocutors also had the capacity to manipulate the power of music for their own self-improvement, demonstrating the elements of desire and agency that were present in musical subjectivation.[85] In this respect, this chapter has been underpinned by a similar theoretical concept of music to that of DeNora whereby it can be seen to be both powerful (acting on individuals) and malleable (whereby individuals can manipulate its powerful qualities). Paula's motivation to play, for example, was reminiscent of DeNora's analysis of an aerobics class in England, in which she argued that the women attending the class used music to manipulate their motivation:

> Observing them [the women at the aerobics class] over forty-five minutes shows how music is much more than a mere accompaniment to the aerobic movement, how it is constitutive of aerobic agency ... music may be understood as having active, structuring properties on and for the body [...] Through the creation and *use* of such technologies actors bodies are enabled and empowered, their capacities are enhanced.[86]

Similarly, for Paula and some of my other interlocutors, playing music was about manipulating the self to 'feel' a certain way. In exploring this, the chapter has drawn on Foucault's understanding of the ethical subject and the care of the self, and Graeber's theory of value to consider the dialogue of power, desire (of the ideal 'I') and manipulation that took place when individuals worked to cultivate the musical self in Welsh Patagonia.[87] My interlocutors used music to enable them to feel calmer, happier and to improve their overall sense of physical and mental well-being. Or, as Eleanor said to me gently, later in fieldwork, 'Music helps you to live.' What she implied with this statement was that the powerful qualities of music, in terms of improving mood, inducing emotion or revisiting memories could be helpful during hard times. For her, this was particularly poignant during her treatment for cancer. Engaging in music could therefore also be a means of escapism, whereby my interlocutors could 'forget their worries', as the lyrics to 'Croeso Patagonia' emphasised.

Critically, this self-improvement did not take place in a social void. This chapter has further argued that the use of music as a constitutive tool to make my interlocutors 'feel good' and 'feel happy' took place within a cultural context in which therapy – and specifically psychoanalysis – was a central component, and in which Welsh music was viewed by some of my interlocutors as having a higher value than Argentinian music. That the idea of attending therapy was typically a middle-class concept and pursuit in Argentina meant that the very concept of ethical self-cultivation was grounded in class structures. Furthermore, musical self-cultivation existed within a particular social context which had its own hierarchies of values and taste. As Bourdieu writes, 'to the socially recognised hierarchy of the arts, and within each of them, of genres, schools, or periods, *corresponds a social hierarchy of the consumers*. This predisposes taste to function as markers of class.'[88] His argument is that assumptions regarding taste are ultimately grounded in power structures. In the context of Welsh Patagonia, there was a subtle hierarchy of music for some of my interlocutors and, for them, the act of ethical self-cultivation through music corresponded with reaching the state of flow with specific music – in this case, traditional Welsh music, which was viewed as being associated with qualities such as a clear structure and a high standard.

# 7
## Conclusions: Sound and the subject

> Perffaith, y gorwel porffor
> Heulwen Mai ar lan y môr
> Hwyl ar gwch fel aer a gwin
> Ar y lliw o'r gorllewin
> A daw o sisial y dŵr
> Heriol lais yr arloeswr.
>
> ('Patagonia', *Y Gorwel Porffor*, music and lyrics by Gwenan Gibbard)

### Singing to the sweet colony

It was a bright spring evening in 2016, and the evening light was glinting through the glass-stained windows in Capel Bethel, a welcome change from the dark, uninviting winter nights. 'Patagonia' was one of the songs performed by Gwenan Gibbard as part of her concert to launch her new Patagonia-inspired CD, *Y Gorwel Porffor* ('The Purple Horizon'). The chapel was full, and the members of the audience were all huddled closely together on the wooden benches facing the stage. The familiar sound of chattering and laughter quickly turned to silence as Gwenan pulled the harp towards her, adjusted the pedals and lifted her arms, poised and ready to begin playing. The silent anticipation as we waited for her to play the first note was striking – unusual, even, in the Argentinian context. She sang and played simultaneously with an ease that made the complex tones and rhythms of the traditional Welsh *cerdd dant* appear effortless. Her fingers flew across the strings of the harp, landing in the perfect position each time, and her feet moved naturally on the pedals to change the key for each piece. The instrument was an extension of her. I was sitting near the front of the stage, transfixed by the clarity, sweetness and tonality of Gwenan's voice combined with the dulcet tones of the harp.

Listening to her singing, my mind began to wander through memories from fieldwork. The music reminded me of the joy of watching my interlocutors dance enthusiastically in their Welsh traditional outfits, of the happy moments of rehearsing, performing and competing with the Gaiman mixed choir, Gaiman girls' choir or the Gaiman string group, and of the annual celebrations of the Day of the Landing, when volunteers worked tirelessly in the chapels in the valley to welcome visitors with tea and cakes. The imagery of 'sailing to an adventure' and of arrival was reminiscent of the regular – almost daily – arrival of tourists from Wales to the Chubut Valley and visitors to the museum who had been sold – and were being performed – exactly that image, a once-in-a-lifetime 'adventure', by both the tourist companies, other tourists and the Welsh Patagonian community. Their 'prize for the brave' was their sheer astonishment at being 8,000 miles from home but still hearing the Welsh language. '*Mae fel* ... It's like ... a home away from home', they would declare, with wonder. The tinkling sound of the harp reminded me of the soothing sound of the lapping waves as I spent an afternoon on Puerto Madryn beach with Amy, a tourist from Wales who had visited for a few days. The feeling of being a part of a community, the belonging, group flow that I experienced whilst singing 'Cân y Wladfa', and the genuine meaning whilst singing 'I sing to you my sweet colony, I will always greet you this way ... I love you like another country of my heart' as tourists from Wales filmed, clapped and cried, felt within reach once again. I smiled to myself, remembering the feeling of surprise at the goosebumps on my arms as we sang in that rehearsal and in other concerts, reflecting the development of the understanding that I was being concretely impacted by the music – we all were. Fieldwork was soon coming to an end, and I felt suddenly a wave of nostalgia as I thought about laughing and talking with friends as we shared *mate* or tea and put the world to right at their kitchen tables. As she finished performing, the audience erupted into enthusiastic applause which only lasted for a few seconds before everyone rose to stand. Elena, who was sitting to the left of me, leaned over and said, '*O'n i'n teimlo fel mod i yn Madryn!* ... I really felt as though I was at Madryn, then!'

The lyrics of the song, and the memories that they invoked, reflected closely the romanticised image of Patagonia that was so prominent before, throughout and beyond fieldwork, and the image that has been explored through the various media of interpellation and the performative encounters presented in the book. The romanticised image of Patagonia as a faraway, magical land that circulated in the media, literature and some academic work was what attracted so many tourists to Patagonia, and it was simultaneously the image that was so often performed to the tourists by the Welsh Patagonians before, during and after their visit. It was also, however, a political image that was critical in maintaining a narrative of the establishment of Welsh Patagonia, in which the heroic Welsh settlers arrived at an empty land 'beyond the horizon' and with courage and perseverance built a life for themselves. 'Ynys Afallon' ('Afallon Island') referred to in these song lyrics is significant in this respect, as it is a mythical island that features in Arthurian Welsh legends. It is a magical island often described as being the land of eternal youth, fertility and feasting. Drawing on the mythical island of Ynys Afallon in the song has two outcomes. First, and perhaps the most explicit or intentional outcome, is the comparison of Patagonia with Ynys Afallon in terms of both being places full of promises. In this sense, Ynys Afallon and its associated imagery is like the change that the Welsh settlers sought, away from the influence and oppression of the English. Welsh Patagonia, for those 153 settlers on board the *Mimosa*, was concerned with building a better future, where their language and culture could thrive. Furthermore, both Ynys Afallon and Patagonia can be considered as constructed places – Ynys Afallon quite literally so, in that it is a mythical place, but Welsh Patagonia too in that, as Ortner puts it, 'actors are always at least partially "knowing subjects" ... they have some degree of reflexivity about themselves and their desires'.[1] There was a reflexive awareness on behalf of my interlocutors of the performed image that was so attractive to tourists being exactly that – an image or a performance.

## Multisensory subjectivation, the gaze and flow

Let us return to the ethnographic puzzle originally posed in the introduction to this book: how can we best understand the myriad ways in which subjectivity is constituted in Welsh Patagonia? This book has argued that in Welsh Patagonia, subjectivities of Welshness were constituted through engaging in concrete, performative, multisensory, productive encounters with others. It has argued that the subjectivation that occurred in these encounters was a two-way, multisensory process. For example, encounters between Welsh Patagonians and tourists not only created and affirmed Welshness in the Welsh Patagonian community but also created and affirmed Welshness for visitors too. Coming into being through the gaze and through sound co-existed and intertwined – seen most explicitly in the eisteddfod – but the processes were subtly different. Althusser, Sartre, Lacan and Foucault, each in their own ways, developed theories of subjectivation which centred on looking or gazing and which had an element of recognition as central (even whilst in some cases this recognition was implicit) to their argument.[2] In Welsh Patagonia, key to the heightened performance under the gaze of tourists was the recognition that they were being watched and, more specifically, a recognition of the type of performance that was expected of them. In choir rehearsals that were held in the presence of tourists, for example, the performance of Welshness appeared more engaged, more enthusiastic and the choir appeared united. Further, in the anticipatory rehearsals that were held in the weeks prior to the arrival of visitors, my interlocutors reflected on the kind of image they needed to portray to fit with the expectations of Welsh tourists. Likewise, in the context of watching their own performances as Welsh during film nights organised in the settler colony, my interlocutors recognised their own performances of an idealised Welshness on the screen, and later reflected on the relationship between the images and the reality in the context of key issues like marriage, migration and economy. Finally, when my interlocutors imagined the potential tourist gaze at a distance, for example, when they considered what potential tourists in Wales would think of their images and videos posted on social media, this demonstrated a recognition of the imagined gaze, even if they were unsure when exactly – or if at all – they would be met by it.

However, Welshness in Welsh Patagonia was also about music, with the Welsh choirs, the focus on singing through the medium of Welsh and the annual eisteddfod all being central to the performance of Welshness. The second part of the book has pushed the argument of a visual subjectivation further to argue that differently to subjectivation mediated through the gaze, which required an element of recognition, subjectivation through music worked best when my interlocutors were able to reach a state of flow, taken here to mean a state of complete immersion in, and engagement with, music and sound.[3] Chirico et al. have argued that music, in particular, fosters more experiences of flow than other activities.[4] The state of flow not only led to complete absorption in the activity at hand but was also characterised by 'enhanced skilled performance'.[5] In other words, we perform better when we can reach the embodied state of flow.

Being in a flow state has often been analysed as an individual phenomenon.[6] However, Hackert et al. have argued for a reconceptualisation of the way in which flow is interpreted. They argue that alongside individual flow, 'flow can (and should) be investigated as an emergent state of groups'.[7] In this respect, they highlight that flow can be co-active or achieved as part of a group. Co-active flow is achieved whilst in the presence of other individuals but without any interaction with those individuals, for example in the presence of an audience. Activities such as writing in a library, or working independently in a shared office, would fall under this category. Group flow, contrastingly, could be analysed under the definition of co-active flow and consists of a 'shared experience of a peak group state and a collective state of mind'.[8] This state, according to their analysis, is characterised by joint attention towards a common goal, increased social interaction between the group and a perceived merging between self and others that enables the group to be perceived as a coherent unit to an external observer. As Hackert et al. state:

> Social types of flow such as group flow could induce a shift from self to others and foster an overlap between self and others, which, in turn, fosters a collective state of mind, which is particularly relevant for the emergence of group flow.[9]

Whilst this state was viewed as the optimal state for a musical performance, it was not automatic, and neither was it accessible to everyone. At the point of recognition or heightened self-awareness, such as might occur during moments of musical performance anxiety, or when my interlocutors were unable to engage or enjoy themselves due to being unable to play the piece, it was difficult to reach the state of flow, and the music lost some of its creative power. 'Musical performance anxiety' has been proven to impact on reaching the ideal state of flow required for an optimal performance, as it leads to less enjoyment on the part of the performer and a reduced impact in terms of the affective dimensions of music.[10] Put simply, it is difficult to fully immerse yourself in a performance if you are too nervous or, to push this further, if you simply cannot play the piece, in a technical sense. Reaching the state of flow was therefore not necessarily easily done, but it was possible to work towards it, and upon reaching this state of immersion in the music, whether in public or in private, whether as an individual or with a group, the subjectivation of self and community through music was at its most effective.

One example of the moment of recognition disrupting the flow of musical subjectivation came in August 2013. I had agreed to perform a solo cello piece during a concert that Gaiman choir were organising to mark the end of their annual fundraising tea. The piece that I was going to play was a Welsh folk tune called 'Ar Lan y Môr' ('At the Seaside'). Alberto would accompany me on the piano. We had practised at his house a couple of times in the days leading up to the concert, and had also recorded the piece, just for fun, in his recording studio. The tune was relatively simple, the notes objectively easy and the piece was short. However, when the piano introduction cued me in and we began to play, I could immediately feel myself getting tense. My heart started racing and my palms were sweaty. I had performed in other concerts and contexts without this issue, but I knew exactly what was happening – nerves. I could feel the eyes of the audience on me, and almost all my energy was focused on trying to slow my breathing and control my shaking bow hand, rather than on an enjoyment of – or any real level of engagement with – the piece. I played quietly, nervously and far too quickly – the antithesis to how I had performed during rehearsals, and to how I felt about the piece, which was one of my favourite Welsh folk songs.

Subjectivation during the state of flow is quite different, then, to an individual who is not yet a subject whilst he or she is absorbed in an activity, and who becomes a subject precisely at that moment of recognition or heightened self-awareness. Subjectivation during the state of flow whilst performing or listening to music requires a lack of self-consciousness, being lost in the piece and a deep level of engagement where you might forget that you are being watched by an audience, for example.[11] In a manner comparable to Butler's argument that in every act of subjectivation there is an element of desire, this state of flow was seen as being something to work towards.[12] However, working towards the flow and ultimately manipulating the power of the flow through a self-induced musical therapy was a privilege, as it was embedded within a middle-class culture of which therapy was a central component.

The book has further argued that an analytical focus on these specific moments in which flow was not successful, in which my interlocutors expressed their disgruntlement or lack of enjoyment, and in which interpellation did not work, had implications for considering the broader power dynamics within which the community was embedded. In making this argument, my intention here has, of course, not been to suggest that sound and the gaze did not co-exist as media of interpellation. As evident in the context of the eisteddfod, which was a large multisensory ritual performance, and in the context of choir rehearsals and performances, whereby my interlocutors were simultaneously interpellated by the gaze of tourists and by the sound of music, the two formed a consistent dialogue. Further, the encounters through the gaze and sound presented in the book have demonstrated how, in other ways, the two can have similar outcomes. In this case, subjectivation through sight and sound both shared the construction, performance and maintenance of a coherent, harmonious image of Welsh Patagonia. However, the argument put forward here is that the mechanisms of subjectivation through hearing and gazing are different. The intention here has not been to argue that one is more important or relevant than the other, but rather to demonstrate the ways in which both, in different ways, contribute towards subjectivation and can teach us about what it means to be a subject.

### Flow and the subject

The key question here is, if subjectivation through music occurs in the moment of engagement and flow, what does this mean for Althusser's 'discrete' subject, for whom he argued that recognition was key to subjectivation?[13] Sound as a medium is more fluid and vaguer than the more objectifying and assertive mediums of gazing or looking. We hear sound, but it also acts on the body in ways that do not necessarily require recognition, and we cannot always know where it is coming from, making it difficult to ascertain how exactly it entered. Consider, for example, the moment of realisation that you are humming along to the radio whilst driving, tapping your foot to music as you sit in a cafe or the moment that a song – perhaps one that you only fleetingly heard – becomes stuck in your head days, weeks or even months after you heard it.[14] The physiological effect of music on us is perhaps most concretely evident in research on dementia and music. Scholars have argued that people living with dementia, whilst having a severely reduced memory, can recognise pieces of music that were closely connected to key life events or a particular era,[15] and that this musical identity enables people with dementia to connect more positively with present people and their current place.[16] The impact of music is long-lasting.[17] This image of the subject being interpellated by music blurs the boundary between self and other, and in doing so becomes a subject that is more permeable, porous, flexible and open to change than the subject objectified by the gaze, an image which perfectly reflects the dynamic Welshness of Welsh Patagonia.

This analysis may, at first sight, be reminiscent of the debate between the dividual and the individual in anthropology. This distinction was initially developed by Strathern, who argued that considering the individual as a separate entity is a particularly Western concept which was not consistent with the Melanesian people with whom she worked, who rather saw themselves as dividuals; that is, as persons made up of social relationships.[18] It may also be reminiscent of Taylor's distinction that he developed in *A Secular Age* between what he called 'porous' and 'buffered' selves, which has been directly compared with Strathern's distinction.[19] Taylor argued that for the porous self, there exist few boundaries between the self and other, meaning that the porous self is enchanted – in other words, open to cosmic, religious and spiritual forces that shape him or her. The buffered self, by contrast, is disenchanted – here we have a bounded and modern individual who has a clear distinction between the self and other, stemming from a clear understanding of an independent 'I'. This dichotomy, for Taylor, maps onto a distinction between 'traditional' and 'modern', with the process of change from one to another being a process of disenchantment. However, the Welsh Patagonian context challenges these distinctions in that subjectivation through sound and sight – though the specific means by which they occur differed – co-existed and interplayed, demonstrating that subjects are not either bounded or porous, but both simultaneously. Each element may be prominent at different times, in different contexts and in different encounters, ultimately suggesting that the elements of porosity, boundaries, malleability, agency and desire all intermingle, with this complexity being fundamental to performative encounters.

In making this argument, this book makes two distinctive theoretical contributions, in addition to the practical and ethnographic contribution to the currently limited field of the anthropology of Welshness and Welsh Patagonia.[20] These two key contributions relate to the broader theoretical work on encounters, performance, performativity, subjectivation and sound. Firstly, the book has moved beyond the allegories and metaphors of encounters developed by thinkers like Lacan, Sartre, Foucault and Althusser to consider the specificity of concrete encounters in the field, such as those which occurred between Welsh tourists and Welsh Patagonians, between Welsh Patagonians and their own image on screen, between music and the community, and between music and the self. The key contribution in this area has been to push forward the idea of performative encounters, which not only enables a consideration of the importance of specific, concrete others in performativity and performance (considered here as two interrelated concepts), but which also makes room in the concept of encounters to consider their creative potential in terms of subjectivation of self and community as well as the power relations in which they are inevitably embedded. Secondly, this book has contributed to theories of subjectivity and subjectivation to consider its multisensory dimension, through an ethnographic focus on how sound, and specifically in this case, music, can play a key role in subjectivation. An elaboration of the subtle differences between subjectivation through sight and through sound has implications for our understanding of the subject, demonstrating the influence that our anthropological frameworks (and, more specifically, whether they are based on visual or sonic bias) can have on our fundamental understanding of the human condition.

## Conclusions: 'Of course I feel Welsh'

Many years before this book was written, when I was still an anthropology undergraduate student, if anyone asked me what my ultimate research goals were, I would confidently say that my key goal was to de-romanticise and de-colonise the image of Patagonia with which this final chapter opened – the image of joy, harmony, heroic settlers and the permeation of adventure that had become so prevalent in popular media, the press and public discourse. However, this aim was based on my own bias, however subtle, that cultural performance was not 'real', or grounded in a presumption, as it has been argued in much of the literature on the anthropology of tourism, that the performative daily activities and larger performances must be connected to some other underlying reason. It is too simplistic to argue that Welsh Patagonia is not the 'little Wales beyond Wales' or the 'small slice of Wales in South America' that has been depicted in the popular imagination.

Indeed, as has been demonstrated throughout the book, for my interlocutors, an awareness of the element of performance of this image was not in conflict with their feelings of belonging. My interlocutors unproblematically switched between various subjectivities, and there was no conflict between singing in a Welsh choir or attending an eisteddfod before going home to drink *mate* and eat *asado*. As Paula simply stated, '*Sí, wrth gwrs* ...Yes, of course I feel Welsh, why do you ask?' Or, as Lucas put it, '*Dy' ni ddim yn esgus* ... We aren't pretending'. Performing Welshness in the Chubut Province was multifaceted and flexible, highlighting the ways in which a place can be both romanticised and political at the same time, the ways in which people can feel emotions of belonging whilst also being acutely aware of, and able to reflect on, the power dynamics at play, the ways in which performance can be both real and staged, the ways in which individuals taking part in performances can be aware of that duality without impacting their feelings of belonging, and the ways in which individuals can be brought into being in relation to power structures whilst also exercising their own will and even manipulating those power structures for their own advantage.

Ultimately, performing Welshness was the key to being Welsh in the Chubut Province, but being Welsh, feeling Welsh, speaking Welsh and performing Welshness in the settler colony meant different things to different people, and changed and fluctuated over time. Whilst this meaning changed and fluctuated, however, what remained consistent was that Welshness in the Chubut Province was continuously created, reproduced and maintained through a series of performative and multisensory encounters that created self and community; in doing so challenging the reliance on visual tropes that has dominated theories of subjectivation, whilst also creating and consolidating the harmonious narrative of Welsh Patagonia, which in turn was essential for its continuation. These performative encounters – in their successes and failures – generated feelings of belonging and community, moments of flow and enjoyment, moments of disgruntlement and moments of reflexivity for my interlocutors, in addition to revealing underlying power dynamics and value systems. Amid this complexity, there was no discrepancy between feeling Welsh, performing Welshness and being aware of the performance. Finally, then, in exploring these different dimensions of being Welsh in the Chubut Province, this book contributes to enriching our understanding of how exactly this Welshness came about, what it looked like, what it felt like for the individuals involved, how it changed over time and how agency and subjectivation were navigated, accepted, manipulated and challenged throughout these multisensory processes.

# Notes

## Chapter 1

1. Anthony Seeger, *Why Suyá Sing: A Musical Anthropology of an Amazonian People* (Urbana and Chicago: University of Illinois Press, 2004), p. 128.
2. Mirielle Rosello, *France and the Maghreb: Performative Encounters* (Florida: University Press of Florida, 2005); Yolanda Covington-Ward, *Gesture and Power: Religion, Nationalism and Everyday Performance in Congo* (London: Duke University Press, 2016), p. 9.
3. Jean-Paul Sartre, *Being and Nothingness* (London: Methuen & Co. Ltd, 1958); M. Foucault, 'Governmentality', in G. Burchell, C. Gordon and P. Miller (eds), *The Foucault Effect: Studies in Governmentality* (Chicago: University of Chicago Press, 1991), pp. 87–104; Louis Althusser, *Lenin and Philosophy, and Other Essays* (London: New Left Books, 1971).
4. E. Whitfield, 'Empire, Nation and the Fate of a Language: Patagonia in Argentine and Welsh Literature', *Postcolonial Studies*, 14/1 (2014), 75–93; Bryn Williams, *Cymry Patagonia* (Clwb Llyfrau Cymreig, 1942); Bryn Williams, *Gwladfa Patagonia* (Caerdydd: Gwasg Prifysgol Cymru, 1965); Bryn Williams, *Straeon Patagonia* (Gwasg y Dydd, 1946); G. Williams, 'La construcción del pasado chubutense en el discurso histórico provincial: representaciones de la experiencia exploratoria y colonizadora española en Chubut, Argentina, en textos escolares provinciales (1978–2006)', *Historia de Histogrofía* (2016).
5. INDEC, 'Censo Nacional de Población, Hogares y Viviendas 2022 (Buenos Aires: Instituto Nacional de Estadistica y Censos, 2022).
6. G. Kiff, 'Welsh language project annual report 2013, British Council of Wales (2013); G. Kiff, 'Welsh language project annual report 2014', British Council of Wales (2014); G. Kiff, 'Welsh language project annual report 2015', British Council of Wales (2014); R. Arwel, 'Welsh language project in Chubut: Annual Report 2016', British Council of Wales (2016); R. Arwel, 'Welsh language project in Chubut: Annual Report 2017', British Council of Wales (2017); R. Arwel, 'Welsh language project in Chubut: Annual Report 2018', British Council of Wales (2019); British Council, 'Report on the Welsh Language Project, Patagonia 2020', British Council of Wales (2020).
7. Waquant cited in R. Townsend and C. Cushion, 'Put that in your fucking research: Reflexivity, ethnography, and disability sport coaching', *Qualitative Research*, 21/2 (2021), 251–67, 252. See also M. Guillemin and L. Gillam, 'Ethics, reflexivity, and "ethically important moments" in research', *Qualitative Inquiry*, 10/2 (2004), 261–80.
8. M. Kaaristo, 'Everyday power dynamics and hierarchies in qualitative research: The role of humour in the field', *Qualitative Research* (2022), 22/5, 743–60, 744.

9. David Fetterman, *Ethnography: Step by Step* (London: Sage Publications, 1998); M. Funder, 'Bias, Intimacy and Power in Qualitative Fieldwork Strategies', *The Journal of Transdisciplinary Environmental Studies*, 4/1 (2005), 1–9.
10. Funder, 'Bias, Intimacy and Power in Qualitative Fieldwork Strategies', 7.
11. Kaaristo, 'Everyday power dynamics and hierarchies in qualitative research', 744.
12. J. Clifford, 'Introduction: Partial Truths', in J. Clifford and G. Marcus (eds), *Writing Culture: The Poetics and Politics of Ethnography* (Berkeley: University of California Press, 1986), pp. 1–26, 15.
13. Clifford, 'Introduction: Partial Truths', p. 11.
14. Clifford, 'Introduction: Partial Truths', p. 12.
15. Fetterman, *Ethnography: Step by Step*, p. 1.
16. Guillemin and Gillam, 'Ethics, reflexivity, and "ethically important moments" in research', 262.
17. M. Carnes, 'Machismo and gender equality in Argentina', online blog, Berkley Center for Religion, Peace, and World Affairs (2017).
18. Carol Warren and Jennifer Hackney, *Gender Issues in Ethnography* (London: Sage Publications, 2011).
19. E. Moreno, 'Rape in the Field: Reflections from a Survivor', in D. Kulick and M. Willson (eds), *Taboo: Sex, Identity, and Erotic Subjectivity in Anthropological Fieldwork* (London: Routledge, 1995), pp. 219–50, 246–7. See also D. J. Bradford, E. R. Crema, 'Risk factors for the occurrence of sexual misconduct during archaeological and anthropological fieldwork', *American Anthropologist* (2022), 548–59.
20. Will Rollason, *We Are Playing Football: Sport and Postcolonial Subjectivity: Panapompom, Papua New Guinea* (Newcastle upon Tyne: Cambridge Scholars Publishing, 2011); H. Walker, 'State of Play: The Political Ontology of Sport in Amazonian Peru', *American Ethnologist*, 40/2 (2013), 382–98; A. Diz, 'The Afterlife of Abundance: Wageless Life, Politics, and Illusion Among The Guarani of the Argentine Chaco' (unpublished PhD thesis, London School of Economics, 2016).
21. Jean-Paul Sartre, *Being and Nothingness* (London: Methuen & Co. Ltd, 1958); J. Lacan, 'The Mirror Stage as Formative of the "I" Function as Revealed in Psychoanalytic Experience', *Écrits* (1966), 93–101; Althusser, *Lenin and Philosophy, and Other Essays*.
22. Emmanuel Levinas, *Ethics and Infinity* (Pittsburgh: Duquesne University Press, 1982), p. 53; see also S. Harasym, *Levinas and Lacan: The Missed Encounter* (Albany: State University of New York Press, 1998).
23. Michael Morgan, *The Cambridge Introduction to Emmanuel Levinas* (New York: Cambridge University Press, 2011), p. 59.
24. Morgan, *The Cambridge Introduction to Emmanuel Levinas*, p. 66. See also Goffman Erving, *The Presentation of Self in Everyday Life* (Edinburgh: Social Sciences Research Centre, University of Edinburgh, 1956).
25. L. Faier and L. Rofel, 'Ethnographies of encounter', *The Annual Review of Anthropology*, 43 (2014), 363–77, 364.

26. S. Ortner, 'Subjectivity and Cultural Critique', *Anthropological Theory*, 5/1 (2005), 31–52.
27. Victor Turner, *The Anthropology of Performance* (New York: PAJ Publications, 1987); J. Lowell Lewis, 'Toward a Unified Theory of Cultural Performance: A "Reconstructive Introduction" to Victor Turner', in G. St John (ed.), *Victor Turner and Contemporary Cultural Performance* (New York: Berghahn Books, 2008), pp. 41–58; J. Lowell Lewis, *The Anthropology of Cultural Performance* (New York: Palgrave Macmillan, 2013); Erving, *The Presentation of Self in Everyday Life*; J. Butler, 'Performative acts and gender constitution: an essay in phenomenology and feminist theory', *Theatre Journal*, 40/4 (1988), 519–31; Judith Butler, *Gender Trouble: Feminism and the Subversion of Identity* (New York: Routledge, 1990).
28. Ortner, 'Subjectivity and Cultural Critique', 37.
29. Foucault, 'Governmentality'; see also M. Foucault, 'Sexual Discourse and Power', in *Culture and Society: Contemporary Debates* (Cambridge: Cambridge University Press, 1990), pp. 199–204; Michel Foucault, *The History of Sexuality, Vol. 1* (New York: Vintage, 1981).
30. Foucault, 'Governmentality'.
31. Sartre, *Being and Nothingness*.
32. Althusser, *Lenin and Philosophy, and Other Essays*.
33. Althusser, *Lenin and Philosophy, and Other Essays*.
34. Lacan, 'The Mirror Stage as Formative of the "I" Function as Revealed in Psychoanalytic Experience'.
35. See further J. Gallop, 'Lacan's "Mirror Stage": Where to Begin', *SubStance*, 11/4 (1983), 118–28.
36. Lacan, 'The Mirror Stage as Formative of the "I" Function as Revealed in Psychoanalytic Experience'.
37. J. Butler, 'Conscience doth make subjects of us all', *Yale French Studies*, 88 (1995).
38. Yolanda Covington-Ward, *Gesture and Power: Religion, Nationalism and Everyday Performance in Congo* (London: Duke University Press, 2016), p. 5.
39. R. Bianchi, 'The critical turn in tourism studies: A radical critique', *Tourism Geographies*, 11/4 (2009), 434–504; C. Gibson, 'Critical tourism studies: new directions for volatile times', *Tourism Geographies*, 3/4 (2021), 659–77.
40. Althusser, *Lenin and Philosophy, and Other Essays*; Foucault, 'Governmentality'; Sartre, *Being and Nothingness*; Lacan, 'The Mirror Stage as Formative of the "I" Function as Revealed in Psychoanalytic Experience'.
41. See further Véronique Benei, *Schooling Passions: Nation, History, and Language in Contemporary Western India* (California: Stanford University Press, 2008); C. Hirschkind, 'Hearing Modernity: Egypt, Islam, and the Pious Ear', in V. Erlmann (ed.), *Hearing Cultures: Essays on Sound, Listening and Modernity* (New York: Berg, 2004), pp. 131–51; C. Hirschkind, 'The Ethics of Listening: Cassette-Sermon Audition in Contemporary Egypt', *American Ethnologist*, 28/3 (2001), 623–49.

42. T. Rice, 'Soundselves: An Acoustemology of Sound and Self in the Edinburgh Royal Infirmary', *Anthropology Today*, 19/4 (2003), 4–9; S. Feld, and D. Brennis, 'Doing Anthropology in Sound', *American Ethnologist*, 31/4 (2004), 461–74; Gillian Siddall and Ellen Waterman, *Negotiated moments: improvisation, sound, and subjectivity* (North Carolina: Duke University Press, 2016).
43. Rice, 'Soundselves: An Acoustemology of Sound and Self in the Edinburgh Royal Infirmary', 4.
44. Susan McClary, *Feminine Endings: Music, Gender and Sexuality* (London: University of Minnesota Press, 1991); Janet Mills, *Music in the School* (Oxford: Oxford University Press, 2005); see further T. Turino, 'Habits of the Self, Identity, and Culture', in T. Turino, *Music as Social Life: The Politics of Participation* (Chicago: University of Chicago Press, 2008), pp. 93–122.
45. S. Feld, 'Aesthetics as Iconicity of Style, or "Lift-up-over-sounding": Getting into the Kaluli Groove', *Yearbook for Traditional Music*, 20 (1988), 74–113; Aaron Fox, *Real Country: Music and Language in Working Class Culture* (Durham and London: Duke University Press, 2004); V. Doubleday, 'Sounds of Power: An Overview of Musical Instruments and Gender', *Ethnomusicology Forum*, 17/1 (2008), 3–39; Smita Jassal, *Unearthing Gender: Folksongs of North India* (Durham and London: Duke University Press 2012); S. Hawkins, *Queerness in pop music: Aesthetics, gender norms, and temporality* (London: Routledge, 2015); O. Daniel, 'Songs for ordinary people: Popular music and class in post-socialist Czech society', *Communist and Post-Communist Studies*, 55/2 (2022), 84–103.
46. A. Weidman, 'Anthropology and Voice', *Annual Review of Anthropology*, 43 (2014), 37–51, 43; see further Clifford, 'Introduction: Partial Truths'.
47. See, especially, Clifford, 'Introduction: Partial Truths'; V. Erlmann, 'But What of the Ethnographic Ear? Anthropology, Sound and the Senses', in V. Erlmann (ed.), *Hearing Cultures: Essays on Sound, Listening and Modernity* (New York: Berg, 2004), pp. 1–21; D. Samuels et al., 'Soundscapes: Toward a Sounded Anthropology', *Annual Review of Anthropology*, 39 (2010), 329–45; S. Pink, 'The Future of Sensory Anthropology/The Anthropology of the Senses', *Social Anthropology*, 18/3 (2010), 331–40; Timothy Ingold, *Being Alive: Essays on Movement, Knowledge and Description* (London: Routledge, 2011).
48. F. Diaz, 'Mindfulness, Attention, and Flow During Music Listening: An Empirical Investigation', *Psychology of Music*, 41/1 (2011), 42–58; A. Chirico et al., 'When music flows: State and trait in musical performance, composition, and listening: A systematic review', *Frontiers in Psychology*, 6/906 (2015), 1–14; L. O. Harmat de Manzano and F. Ullen, 'Flow in music and arts', *Advances in Flow Research* (2021), 377–91.
49. S. Sinnamon, A. Moran and M. O'Connell, 'Flow among musicians: measuring peak experiences of student performances', *Journal of Research in Music Education*, 60/1 (2012), 6–25.
50. B. A. Hackert et al., 'Towards a reconceptualization of flow in social contexts', *Journal of Theory of Social Behaviour*, 53 (2023), 100–25, 101, 112.
51. Hackert et al., 'Towards a reconceptualization of flow in social contexts'.

## Chapter 2

1. William Rhys, *A Welsh Song in Patagonia: Memories of the Welsh Colonisation* (E.K. Vyhmeister, 2005), p. 27.
2. A. Meter, 'Argentina in the era of mass immigration', *Latin American Studies* (2010); G. Germani, 'Mass Immigration and Modernisation in Argentina', *Studies in Comparative International Development*, 2/11 (1966), 165-82; May Bletz, *Immigration and Acculturation in Brazil and Argentina 1890-1929* (New York: Palgrave MacMillan, 2010).
3. G. Lublin, 'Adjusting the focus: looking at Patagonia and the wider Argentine state through the lens of settler colonial theory', *Settler Colonial Studies*, 11/3 (2021), 386-409, 387.
4. K. Berg, 'Chubut, Argentina: a contested Welsh "first-place"', *International Journal of Heritage Studies*, 24/2 (2018), 154-66; G. Williams, 'Darllen ac ysgrifennu gorffennol y Wladfa: dadleuon am hanes a chof yn ymsefydliad Cymreig Chubut' (cyf. W. Brooks), *Gwerddon*, 36 (2023), 28-48.
5. Rhys, *A Welsh Song in Patagonia*, p. 24.
6. Geraldine Lublin, *Memoir and Identity in Welsh Patagonia: Voices from a Settler Community in Argentina* (Cardiff: University of Wales Press, 2017); F. Coronato, 'The First Welsh Footstep in Patagonia', *Welsh History Review*, 18/4 (1997), 639-66; E. Whitfield, 'Welsh Patagonian Fiction: Language and the Novel of Transnational Ethnicity', *Diaspora*, 14/2 (2005), 333-48; Susan Wilkinson, *Mimosa's Voyages: Official Logs, Crew Lists and Masters* (Ceredigion: Y Lolfa, 2007), pp. 85-90.
7. Glyn Williams, *The Desert and the Dream: A Study of Welsh Colonisation in Chubut 1815-1915* (Cardiff: University of Wales Press, 1975); Glyn Williams, *The Welsh in Patagonia: The State and the Ethnic Community* (Cardiff: University of Wales Press, 1991); G. Williams, 'Welsh Settlers and Native Americans in Patagonia', *Journal of Latin American Studies*, 11/1 (1979), 41-66; David Ross, *Wales: History of a Nation* (Scotland: Geddes & Grosset, 2008), pp. 196-200.
8. K. Morgan, 'Welsh Nationalism: The Historical Background', *Journey of Contemporary History*, 6/1 (1971), 152-72, 155.
9. Ross, *Wales: History of a Nation*; Williams, *The Desert and the Dream*; Bryn Williams, *Gwladfa Patagonia* (Caerdydd: Gwasg Prifysgol Cymru, 1965).
10. P. Manning, 'English Money and Welsh Rocks: Divisions of Language and Divisions of Labour in Nineteenth-century Welsh Slate Quarries', *Comparative Studies in Society and History*, 44/3 (2002), 481-510; P. Manning, 'Owning and Belonging: A Semiotic Investigation of the Affective Categories of a Bourgeois Society', *Comparative Studies in Society and History*, 46/2 (2004), 300-25; P. Manning, 'The Streets of Bethesda: The Slate Quarrier and the Welsh Language in the Welsh Liberal Imagination', *Language in Society*, 33/4 (2004), 517-48.
11. Rhys, *A Welsh Song in Patagonia*, p. 23; see further H. Prins, 'The Welsh in Patagonia: The State and The Ethnic Community', *The Latin American Anthropology Review*, 5/1 (1993), 29-30; G. Cohen, 'A Sense of People and Place: The Chapel and Language in Sustaining Welsh Identity,' in D. Bryceson,

12. J. Okely and J. Webber (eds), *Identity and Networks: Fashioning Gender and Ethnicity Across Cultures* (New York and Oxford: Berghahn Books, 2007).
12. Lublin, *Memoir and Identity in Welsh Patagonia*, p. 4.
13. Manning, 'The Streets of Bethesda: The Slate Quarrier and the Welsh Language in the Welsh Liberal Imagination', 527.
14. N. Coupland and P. Garrett, 'Linguistic Landscapes, Discursive Frames and Metacultural Performance: The Case of Welsh Patagonia', *International Journal of the Sociology of Language*, 2010/205 (2010), 7–36.
15. Coupland and Garrett, 'Linguistic Landscapes, Discursive Frames and Metacultural Performance: The Case of Welsh Patagonia'; E. Bowen, 'The Welsh Colony in Patagonia 1865–1885: A Study in Historical Geography', *The Geographical Journal*, 132/1 (1966), 16–27; see further Rhys, *A Welsh Song in Patagonia*; Prins, 'The Welsh in Patagonia: The State and The Ethnic Community'.
16. The Saturday Review of Politics, Literature, Science and Art, 'The Eisteddfod', 24/620 (1867), 342.
17. Lublin, *Memoir and Identity in Welsh Patagonia*, p. 4.
18. Coupland and Garrett, 'Linguistic Landscapes, Discursive Frames and Metacultural Performance: The Case of Welsh Patagonia'; Prins, 'The Welsh in Patagonia: The State and The Ethnic Community'.
19. Daniel Lewis, *History of Argentina* (Westport: Greenwood Publishing Group, 2001), p. 48.
20. Lewis, *History of Argentina*.
21. Lewis, *History of Argentina*.
22. Lewis, *History of Argentina*, p. 54.
23. A. Meter, 'Argentina in the era of mass immigration', *Latin American Studies* (2010).
24. Lewis, *History of Argentina*, p. 54.
25. Meter, 'Argentina in the era of mass immigration'.
26. Germani, 'Mass Immigration and Modernisation in Argentina'; Meter, 'Argentina in the era of mass immigration'.
27. Germani, 'Mass Immigration and Modernisation in Argentina', 181.
28. Rhys, *A Welsh Song in Patagonia*, p. 51.
29. G. Favelukes, 'Fernando Williams 2010: Entre el Desierto y el Jardín. Viaje, literature y paisaje en la colonia galesa de la Patagonia', *Registros*, 8/8 (2012), 69–71, 69; Rhys, *A Welsh Song in Patagonia*, p. 77.
30. Morgan Tomos, *Alun yr Arth ym Mhatagonia* (Ceredigion: Y Lolfa, 2013); Elizabeth Morgan, *Ticket to Paradise* (Cardiff: Opening Chapter, 2013); Cathrin Williams, *Haul ac Awyr Las* (Dinbych: Gwasg Gee, 1993); Rhys, *A Welsh Song in Patagonia*; BBC Radio Cymru, 'Gŵyl y glaniad: sgwrsio gyda rhai o ddis-gynyddion y Cymry cyntaf i lanio ym Mhatagonia' (29 July 2015); Hwb Wales, 'Film Study: Patagonia' (2016), https://hwb.gov.wales/repository/resource/616af8ba-d88a-4286-abff-c32355376cf5/overview (accessed 30 January 2024).
31. Morgan, *Ticket to Paradise*, p. 114; Wilkinson, *Mimosa's Voyages*; Sian Eirian Rees Davies, *I Fyd Sy Well* (Gomer: Ceredigion, 2005).

32. Favelukes, 'Fernando Williams 2010'; Lublin, 'Adjusting the focus'.
33. See, for example, Rhys, *A Welsh Song in Patagonia*; Atebol, 'Patagonia 150+' (2015), https://www.150patagonia.cymru/html/main/ (accessed 30 January 2024).
34. BBC Radio 4, 'Migration, Separation, and Wales' (2014).
35. E. Whitfield, 'Welsh Patagonian Fiction: Language and the Novel of Transnational Ethnicity', *Diaspora*, 14/2 (2005), 333-48, 339; see further E. Whitfield, 'Empire, Nation and the Fate of a Language: Patagonia in Argentine and Welsh Literature', *Postcolonial Studies*, 14/1 (2014), 75-93.
36. Rhys, *A Welsh Song in Patagonia*, p. 84.
37. Berg, 'Chubut, Argentina: a contested Welsh "first-place"'; Williams, 'Darllen ac ysgrifennu gorffennol y Wladfa'; emphasis mine.
38. Williams, *Haul ac Awyr Las*, pp. 16-17; emphasis mine.
39. M. Harris, 'Peasants on the Floodplain: Some Elements of the "Agrarian Question" in Riverine Amazonia', in S. Nugent and M. Harris (eds), *Some Other Amazonians: Perspectives on Modern Amazonia* (London: Institute for the Study of the Americas, 2004), pp. 81-103, 84.
40. S. Nugent, '(Some) Other Amazonians: Jewish Communities in the Lower Amazon,' in S. Nugent and M. Harris (eds), *Some Other Amazonians: Perspectives on Modern Amazonia* (London: Institute for the Study of the Americas, 2004), pp. 104-17, 107.
41. J. Bartles, 'Deserted islands for the nation: Empty land- and seascapes in three Argentine films of the Malvinas/Falkland Islands', *The Film Archipelago: Islands in Latin American Cinema*, 31 (2021).
42. Favelukes, 'Fernando Williams 2010'; Lublin, *Memoir and Identity in Welsh Patagonia*; Williams, 'Darllen ac ysgrifennu gorffennol y Wladfa'.
43. Williams, 'Darllen ac ysgrifennu gorffennol y Wladfa'.
44. L. Taylor, 'Colonial Encounters at the Margins: The Welsh/Tehuelche in Patagonia', Conceptualising IR from the margins: historically, geographically and beyond, Buenos Aires (2014); L. Taylor, 'Decolonising Citizenship: Reflections on the Coloniality of Power in Argentina', *Citizenship Studies*, 17/5 (2013), 596-610; L. Taylor, 'Decolonising International Relations: Perspectives from Latin America', *International Studies Review*, 14 (2012), 386-400; L. Taylor, 'Lifting the Veil of Kindness: "Friendship" and Settler Colonialism in Argentina's Welsh Patagonia', LSE Latin American and Caribbean blog (2017).
45. Taylor, 'Colonial Encounters at the Margins: The Welsh/Tehuelche in Patagonia', 1; see further Lublin, *Memoir and Identity in Welsh Patagonia*.
46. Lublin, *Memoir and Identity in Welsh Patagonia*, p. 7.
47. Lublin, *Memoir and Identity in Welsh Patagonia*, p. 8.
48. Taylor, 'Lifting the Veil of Kindness', p. 2.
49. Lublin, *Memoir and Identity in Welsh Patagonia*, p. 8.
50. Bletz, *Immigration and Acculturation in Brazil and Argentina 1890-1929* (London: Palgrave Macmillan, 2010).
51. Taylor, 'Lifting the Veil of Kindness'; L. Veracini, 'Settler Colonialism: Career of a Concept', *The Journal of Imperial and Commonwealth History*, 41/2

(2013), 313–33; A. Johnston and A. Lawson, 'Settler colonies', *A Companion to Postcolonial Studies* (US: Blackwell Publishing Ltd, 2005), pp. 360–76.
52. Lublin, *Memoir and Identity in Welsh Patagonia*, p. 6.
53. G. Gordillo and S. Hirsch, 'Indigenous struggles and contested identities in Argentina: histories of invisibilisation and re-emergence', *The Journal of Latin American Anthropology*, 8/3 (2003), 4–30.
54. M. Endere, 'Talking About Others: Archaeologists, Indigenous peoples and Heritage in Argentina', *Public Archaeology*, 4/2–3 (2005), 155–62; Berg, 'Chubut, Argentina: a contested Welsh "first-place"'.
55. M. Vom Hau and G. Wilde, '"We Have Always Lived Here": Indigenous Movements, Citizenship and Poverty in Argentina', *The Journal of Development Studies*, 46/7 (2010), 1283–1303.
56. Lublin, 'Adjusting the focus'.
57. Lublin, *Memoir and Identity in Welsh Patagonia*, p. 4.
58. Rhys, *A Welsh Song in Patagonia*, p. 21.
59. Berg, 'Chubut, Argentina: a contested Welsh "first-place"'.
60. Veracini, 'Settler Colonialism: Career of a Concept'; Lublin, *Memoir and Identity in Welsh Patagonia*.
61. Veracini, 'Settler Colonialism: Career of a Concept', 313.
62. Lublin, *Memoir and Identity in Welsh Patagonia*, p. 27.
63. Veracini, 'Settler Colonialism: Career of a Concept'; Lublin, *Memoir and Identity in Welsh Patagonia*.
64. Lublin, *Memoir and Identity in Welsh Patagonia*, p. 11.
65. F. Williams, 'Dŵr a Phŵer yn Nyffryn Camwy: heriau a gwrthdaro ynghylch sefydlu a rheoli system ddyfrhau', cyf. W. Brooks, *Gwerddon* (2023), 36, 1–27.
66. Meinir McDonald, *Bant i Batagonia* (Aberystwyth: Canolfan Astudiaethau Addysg, 2001); Lublin, *Memoir and Identity in Welsh Patagonia*.
67. Lublin, *Memoir and Identity in Welsh Patagonia*, p. 9.
68. Louis Althusser, *Lenin and Philosophy, and Other Essays* (London: New Left Books, 1971), p. 89.
69. Olwyn Blouet and John Blouet, *Latin America and the Caribbean: A Systematic and Regional Survey* (US: Wiley, 2015).
70. H. Griffiths, 'Flooding, Draught and Adaptation in the Hydrographic Society of Welsh Patagonia', lecture delivered at the National Eisteddfod of Llanelli (2014).
71. Germani, 'Mass Immigration and Modernisation in Argentina'.
72. Lublin, *Memoir and Identity in Welsh Patagonia*.
73. Lublin, *Memoir and Identity in Welsh Patagonia*, p. 11.
74. D. Lenton, 'The Malon de la Paz of 1946: Indigenous Descamisados at the Dawn of Peronism', in M. Karush and O. Chamosa (eds), *The New Cultural History of Peronism: Power and Identity in Mid-Twentieth Century Argentina* (Durham and London: Duke University Press, 2010), pp. 85–111, 92.
75. A. Adkin, 'The Paradox of Transnational Indigenous Identities in Argentina', *Core Seminar: Fall 2006* (2006), 11; emphasis mine.
76. Lenton, 'The Malon de la Paz of 1946', p. 92.
77. Lenton, 'The Malon de la Paz of 1946', p. 85.

78. Adkin, 'The Paradox of Transnational Indigenous Identities in Argentina'.
79. Lublin, *Memoir and Identity in Welsh Patagonia*, p. 13.
80. W. Brooks and G. Lublin, 'The Eisteddfod of Chubut, or How the Reinvention of Tradition has Contributed to the Preservation of a Language and Culture', *Beyond Philology*, 4 (2007), 245-59; BBC Magazine, 'Viewpoint: the Argentines who speak Welsh – Wyn Jones' (2014).
81. Lublin, *Memoir and Identity in Welsh Patagonia*, p. 13.
82. Lublin, *Memoir and Identity in Welsh Patagonia*; Brooks and Lublin, 'The Eisteddfod of Chubut'.
83. Lublin, *Memoir and Identity in Welsh Patagonia*, p. 15.
84. R. Arwel, 'Welsh language project in Chubut: Annual Report 2016', British Council of Wales (2016); R. Arwel, 'Welsh language project in Chubut: Annual Report 2017', British Council of Wales (2017); R. Arwel, 'Welsh language project in Chubut: Annual Report 2018', British Council of Wales (2018); G. Kiff, 'Welsh language project annual report 2013', British Council of Wales (2013); G. Kiff, 'Welsh language project annual report 2014', British Council of Wales (2014); G. Kiff, 'Welsh language project annual report 2015', British Council of Wales (2014).
85. Welsh Government, 'Cymraeg 2050: A million Welsh speakers: Action plan 2019-20' (Cardiff: Welsh Government, 2019), p. 23.
86. Gordillo and Hirsch, 'Indigenous struggles and contested identities in Argentina', 18.
87. Vom Hau and Wilde, 'We Have Always Lived Here', 1288.
88. A. Barreiro et al., '"They are not truly Indigenous people": Social Representations and Prejudice against Indigenous people in Argentina', *Papers on Social Representations*, 29 (2020), 6.1-6.24, 6.3.
89. Adkin, 'The Paradox of Transnational Indigenous Identities in Argentina', 1.
90. INDEC, 'Censo Nacional de Población, Hogares y Viviendas 2010' (Buenos Aires: Instituto Nacional de Estadistica y Censos, 2012).
91. INDEC, 'Censo Nacional de Población, Hogares y Viviendas 2010'; fieldwork personal communications; Arwel, 'Welsh language project in Chubut: Annual Report 2018'.
92. Arwel, 'Welsh language project in Chubut: Annual Report 2018'.
93. INDEC, 'Censo Nacional de Población, Hogares y Viviendas 2010'.
94. INDEC, 'Censo Nacional de Población, Hogares y Viviendas 2010'.
95. INDEC, 'Censo Nacional de Población, Hogares y Viviendas 2010'.
96. Gobierno Chubut, 'Introducción de la Secretaría de Ciencia, Tecnología e Innovación Productiva Del Chubut' (Rawson: Gobierno Chubut, 2015); Dirreción Nacional de Asuntos Provinciales, 'Informe Sintético de Caracterización Socio-Productiva' (2013).
97. Dirreción Nacional de Asuntos Provinciales, 'Informe Sintético de Caracterización Socio-Productiva'.
98. G. Lublin, 'The War of the Tea-houses, or How Welsh Heritage in Patagonia Became a Valuable Commodity', *Journal of Interdisciplinary Celtic studies*, 1/3 (2009), 69-92.
99. BBC News, 'Cash boost for Patagonia Welsh project considered' (2015).

100. Lublin, 'The War of the Tea-houses'.
101. G. Lublin, 'Adjusting the focus: looking at Patagonia and the wider Argentine state through the lens of settler colonial theory', *Settler Colonial Studies*, 11/3 (2021), 386–409.
102. A. Fabre, 'Diccionario Etnolinguistico y Guia Bibliografica de los Pueblos Indigenas Sudamericanos' (2005), *http://www.ling.fi/Diccionario%20etnoling.htm* (accessed 24 October 2024), 8.
103. Fabre, 'Diccionario Etnolinguistico y Guia Bibliografica de los Pueblos Indigenas Sudamericanos', 8; see further C. Aliga, 'The land "wars" in twenty-first century Patagonia', *Journal of Latin American Cultural Studies*, 28/1 (2019), 139–51.
104. A. Lazzari and D. Lenton, 'Etnologia y Nación: facetas del concepto de araucanización', in R. Guber and L. Ferrero (eds), *Antropologías hechas en la Argentina*, Associacion Latinoamericana de Antropología (2020), 53–76.
105. Adkin, 'The Paradox of Transnational Indigenous Identities in Argentina', 15.
106. Lublin, 'Adjusting the focus', 389.
107. Berg, 'Chubut, Argentina: a contested Welsh "first-place"'.
108. Berg, 'Chubut, Argentina: a contested Welsh "first-place"'; G. Williams, 'La construcción del pasado chubutense en el discurso histórico provincial: representaciones de la experiencia exploratoria y colonizadora española en Chubut, Argentina, en textos escolares provinciales (1978–2006)', *Historia de Histogrofia* (2016).
109. P. Garrett et al., 'Diasporic ethnolinguistic subjectivities: Patagonia, North America and Wales', *International Journal of the Sociology of Language*, 195 (2009), 173–200; I. Johnson, 'Revitalising Welsh in the Chubut Province, Argentina: The Role of the Welsh Language Project', in M. Newton (ed.), *Celts in the Americas* (Nova Scotia: Cape Breton University Press, 2013), pp. 144–58; Welsh Government, 'Cymraeg 2050'; Welsh Government, 'Cymraeg 2050: Work Programme 2021–2026', *https://www.gov.wales/sites/default/files/pdf-versions/2022/2/4/1643896220/cymraeg-2050-work-programme-2021-2026.pdf* (accessed 23 September 2024); Welsh Government, 'Welsh Language Data from the Annual Population Survey: July 2022 to June 2023' (2023), *https://www.gov.wales/welsh-language-data-annual-population-survey-july-2022-june-2023* (accessed 23 September 2024).
110. Welsh Government, 'Cymraeg 2050: Work Programme 2021–2026'.
111. Constructed from data presented in Arwel, 'Welsh language project in Chubut: Annual Report 2018'.
112. British Council, 'Report on the Welsh Language Project, Patagonia 2020', British Council of Wales (2020).
113. INDEC, 'Censo Nacional de Poblacion, Hogares y Viviendas 2022' (Buenos Aires: Instituto Nacional de Estadistica y Censos, 2023).
114. British Council, 'Report on the Welsh Language Project, Patagonia 2020'.
115. Lublin, 'The War of the Tea-houses'.
116. F. Mallimaci, 'What do Argentine people believe in? Religion and Social Structure in Argentina', *Social Compass*, 62/2 (2015), 255–77.

117. Gabriela Nouzeilles and Graciela Montaldo (eds), *The Argentina Reader: History, Culture, Politics* (Durham: Duke University Press, 2002), p. 1.
118. O. Chamosa, 'Criollo and Peronist: The Argentine Folklore Movement during the First Peronism, 1943-1945', in M. Karush and O. Chamosa (eds), *The New Cultural History of Peronism: Power and Identity in Mid-Twentieth Century Argentina* (Durham and London: Duke University Press, 2010), pp. 113-42; Lublin, 'Adjusting the focus'.
119. E. Guano, 'A Colour for the Modern Nation: The Discourse on Class, Race, and Education in the Porteno Middle Class', *The Journal of Latin American Anthropology*, 8/1 (2003), 148-71; J. Hooker, 'Indigenous Inclusion/Black Exclusion: Rage, Ethnicity and Multicultural Citizenship in Latin America', *Journal of Latin American Studies*, 37 (2005), 285-310, 285.
120. Lublin, 'Adjusting the focus', 387.
121. Lublin, *Memoir and Identity in Welsh Patagonia*, p. 25; for an account of the Danes in the Argentine Pampas see also M. Bjerg, 'The Danes in the Argentine Pampa: the role of ethnic leaders in the creation of an ethnic community', in S. Baily and E. Miguez (eds), *Mass Migration to Modern Latin America* (USA: Scholarly Resources Inc., 2003), pp. 147-67.
122. E. Hu-DeHart and López, K., 'Asian Diasporas in Latin America and the Caribbean: An Historical Overview', *Afro-Hispanic Review*, 27/1 (2008), 9-21; L. Denardi, 'Ser Chino en Buenos Aires: Historia, moralidades y cambios en la diaspora China en Argentina', *Horizontes Antropologicas*, 21/43 (2015), 79-103.
123. T. Boas, 'The Arab Diaspora in Latin America', in B. Vinson, *Oxford Bibliographies in Latin American Studies* (New York: Oxford University Press, 2017); V. Beaume, 'Politics resettled: The Case of the Palestinian Diaspora in Chile', Refugees Studies Centre, University of Oxford (2019), 1-23.
124. George Andrews, *Afro-Latin America 1800-2000* (Oxford: Oxford University Press, 2004); L. Gorofolo, 'The Shape of a Diaspora: The Movement of Afro-Iberians to Colonial Spanish America', in S. Bryant, R. S. O'Toole and B. Vinson III (eds), *Africans to Spanish America: Expanding the Diaspora* (Chicago: University of Illinois Press, 2012), pp. 27-49; F. Proctor, 'African Diasporic Ethnicity in Mexico City to 1650', in S. Bryant, R. S. O'Toole and B. Vinson III (eds), *Africans to Spanish America: Expanding the Diaspora* (Chicago: University of Illinois Press, 2012), pp. 50-72.
125. Gorofolo, 'The Shape of a Diaspora', p. 34.
126. Guano, 'A Colour for the Modern Nation', p. 160; see further C. Briones and R. Guber, 'Argentina: contagious marginalities', in D. Poole (ed.), *A Companion to Latin American Anthropology* (Oxford: Blackwell Publishing, 2008), pp. 11-31.
127. Hu-DeHart and López, 'Asian Diasporas in Latin America and the Caribbean: An Historical Overview', 11.
128. Hu-DeHart and López, 'Asian Diasporas in Latin America and the Caribbean: An Historical Overview'; Denardi, 'Ser Chino en Buenos Aires'.
129. Hu-DeHart and López, 'Asian Diasporas in Latin America and the Caribbean: An Historical Overview'.

130. T. Boas, 'The Arab Diaspora in Latin America', in B. Vinson, *Oxford Bibliographies in Latin American Studies* (New York: Oxford University Press, 2017); for an analysis of the more recent wave of Palestinian migration to Chile, see Beaume, 'Politics resettled: The Case of the Palestinian Diaspora in Chile', 1-23.
131. Beaume, 'Politics resettled: The Case of the Palestinian Diaspora in Chile', 5.
132. Boas, 'The Arab Diaspora in Latin America', p. 1.
133. Denardi, 'Ser Chino en Buenos Aires'.
134. P. Wade, 'Blackness, Indigeneity, Multiculturalism and Genomics in Brazil, Colombia and Mexico', *Journal of Latin American Studies*, 45/2 (2013), 205-33; P. Wade, 'Rethinking Mestizaje: Ideology and Lived Experience', *Journal of Latin American Studies*, 37/2 (2005), 239-57; P. Wade, 'Skin colour and race as analytic concepts', *Ethnic and Racial Studies*, 35/7 (2012), 1169-73; Peter Wade, *Race and Ethnicity in Latin America* (London: Pluto Press, 1997).
135. J. Hooker, 'Indigenous Inclusion/Black Exclusion: Rage, Ethnicity and Multicultural Citizenship in Latin America', *Journal of Latin American Studies*, 37 (2005), 285-310.
136. P. Richards, 'Of Indians and Terrorists: How the State and Local Elites Construct the Mapuche in Neoliberal Multicultural Chile', *Journal of Latin American Studies*, 42/1 (2010), 59-90; S. Warren, 'A Nation Divided: Building the Cross-Border Mapuche Nation in Chile and Argentina', *Journal of Latin American Studies*, 45/2 (2013), 235-64.
137. Guano, 'A Colour for the Modern Nation'.
138. O. Chamosa, 'Criollo and Peronist: The Argentine Folklore Movement during the First Peronism, 1943-1945', in M. Karush and O. Chamosa (eds), *The New Cultural History of Peronism: Power and Identity in Mid-Twentieth Century Argentina* (Durham and London: Duke University Press, 2010), pp. 113-42, 114.

## Chapter 3

1. Mathijs Pelkmans, *Fragile Conviction: Changing Ideological Landscapes in Urban Kyrgyzstan* (USA: Cornell University Press, 2017), p. 170.
2. BBC Cymru Fyw, '89,943 yn ymweld ag Eisteddfod yr Urdd 2017', 3 June 2017; El Chubut, '14 edicion del Eisteddfod Mimosa Porth Madryn', 24 August 2017; El Chubut, 'Comienza en Trevelin el 40 Eisteddfod', 27 April 2017; El Chubut, 'Eisteddfod de la juventud en Gaiman', 1 September 2016; El Chubut, 'Hoy comienza el Eisteddfod Mimosa Porth Madryn 2015', 1 August 2015; El Chubut, 'Inauguran hoy en Gaiman el Eisteddfod de la juventud', 9 September 2016; El Chubut, 'Invitan al Eisteddfod Mimosa Porth Madryn 2017', 1 August 2017; El Chubut, 'Se inauguro el Eisteddfod de la Juventud 2015', 4 September 2015; Kathryn Jones, Carol Tully and Heather Williams, *Hidden Texts, Hidden Nations: (Re)discoveries of Wales in Travel Writing in French and German (1780-2018)* (Liverpool: Liverpool University Press, 2020).
3. W. Brooks and G. Lublin, 'The Eisteddfod of Chubut, or How the Reinvention of Tradition has Contributed to the Preservation of a Language and Culture' (2007), https://www.researchgate.net/publication/276204417 (accessed 27 October 2024).

4. Yolanda Covington-Ward, *Gesture and Power: Religion, Nationalism and Everyday Performance in Congo* (London: Duke University Press, 2016), p. 9.
5. Webb Keane, *Signs of Recognition: Power and Hazards of Representation in an Indonesian Society* (Berkeley: University of California Press, 1997), p. 18; see further S. O'Connor et al., 'Ideology, ritual performance, and its manifestations in the rock art of Timor-Leste and Kisar Island, Island Southeast Asia', *Cambridge Archaeological Journal*, 28/2 (2018), 225-41.
6. Covington-Ward, *Gesture and Power*, p. 7.
7. Keane, *Signs of Recognition*, p. 95.
8. Pelkmans, *Fragile Conviction*, p. 171.
9. Pelkmans, *Fragile Conviction*, p. 183.
10. Keane, *Signs of Recognition*, p. 95.
11. Victor Turner, *The Anthropology of Performance* (New York: PAJ Publications, 1987), p. 124; see further G. St John, 'Victor Turner and Contemporary Cultural Performance: An Introduction', in G. St John (ed.), *Victor Turner and Contemporary Cultural Performance* (New York: Berghahn Books, 2008), pp. 1-40; J. Lowell Lewis, 'Toward a Unified Theory of Cultural Performance: A "Reconstructive Introduction" to Victor Turner', in G. St John (ed.), *Victor Turner and Contemporary Cultural Performance* (New York: Berghahn Books, 2008), pp. 41-58; J. Lowell Lewis, *The Anthropology of Cultural Performance* (New York: Palgrave Macmillan, 2013).
12. Turner, *The Anthropology of Performance*; Lewis, *The Anthropology of Cultural Performance*, p. 6.
13. Lowell Lewis, 'Toward a Unified Theory of Cultural Performance'.
14. W. Beeman, 'The Anthropology of Theatre and Spectacle', *Annual Review of Anthropology*, 22 (1993), 369-93, 380; D. Kapchan, 'Performance', *The Journal of American Folklore*, 108/430 (1995), 479-508, 479; see further Lowell Lewis, 'Toward a Unified Theory of Cultural Performance'; C. Trosset, 'Triangulation and confirmation in the study of Welsh concepts of personhood', *Journal of Anthropological Research*, 57/1 (2001), 61-81; Carol Trosset, *Welshness Performed: Welsh Concepts of Person and Society* (Tuscon: University of Arizona Press, 1993).
15. Michael Billig, *Banal Nationalism* (London: Sage Publications, 1995).
16. Goffman, *The Presentation of Self in Everyday Life*; J. Butler, 'Conscience doth make subjects of us all', *Yale French Studies*, 88 (1995), 6-26; J. Butler, 'Performative acts and gender constitution: an essay in phenomenology and feminist theory', *Theatre Journal*, 40/4 (1988), 519-31; Judith Butler, *Gender Trouble: Feminism and the Subversion of Identity* (New York: Routledge, 1990); Judith Butler, *Excitable Speech: A Politics of the Performative* (New York and London: Routledge, 1997); Judith Butler, *The Psychic Life of Power* (Stanford: Stanford University Press, 1997).
17. Turner, *The Anthropology of Performance*, p. 81.
18. Goffman, *The Presentation of Self in Everyday Life*; see further M. Pedelty, 'Teaching Anthropology through Performance', *Anthropology and Education Quarterly*, 32/2 (2001), 244-53, 246; W. Beeman, 'The Anthropology of Theatre and Spectacle', *Annual Review of Anthropology*, 22 (1993), 369-93.

19. Goffman, *The Presentation of Self in Everyday Life*.
20. Goffman, *The Presentation of Self in Everyday Life*, pp. 150-1.
21. Butler, 'Performative acts and gender constitution: an essay in phenomenology and feminist theory'.
22. John Austin, *How to Do Things with Words* (Cambridge, MA: Harvard University Press, 1962); Butler, 'Performative acts and gender constitution: an essay in phenomenology and feminist theory'; see further P. Ebron, 'Constituting Subjects through Performative Acts', in C. Cole et al. (eds), *Africa after Gender?* (Indiana: Indiana University Press, 2007), pp. 171-90.
23. Will Rollason, *We Are Playing Football: Sport and Postcolonial Subjectivity: Panapompom, Papua New Guinea* (Newcastle upon Tyne: Cambridge Scholars Publishing, 2011), p. 43.
24. Goffman, *The Presentation of Self in Everyday Life*.
25. Butler, 'Performative acts and gender constitution: an essay in phenomenology and feminist theory'.
26. Ebron, 'Constituting Subjects through Performative Acts', p. 177.
27. Keane, *Signs of Recognition*, p. 18.
28. *The Musical Herald*, 'The Eisteddfod', 631 (1 October 1990), 296-9.
29. Tom Parryand Cynan, *Yr Eisteddfod/The Eisteddfod* (Liverpool: National Eisteddfod Court, 1956).
30. *The Musical World*, 'The Eisteddfod', 50/35 (7 September 1872), 559; *The Musical World*, 'The Welsh National Eisteddfod', 47/1 (2 January 1869), 10; *The Musical World*, 'Wrexham National Eisteddfod', 54/35 (26 August 1876), 582-3; *The Magazine of Music*, 'The Eisteddfod', 3/31 (1886), 127.
31. K. Morgan, 'Welsh Nationalism: The Historical Background', *Journey of Contemporary History*, 6/1 (1971), 152-72; P. Manning, 'English Money and Welsh Rocks: Divisions of Language and Divisions of Labour in Nineteenth-century Welsh Slate Quarries', *Comparative Studies in Society and History*, 44/3 (2002), 481-510; P. Manning, 'Owning and Belonging: A Semiotic Investigation of the Affective Categories of a Bourgeois Society', *Comparative Studies in Society and History*, 46/2 (2004), 300-25; P. Manning, 'The Streets of Bethesda: The Slate Quarrier and the Welsh Language in the Welsh Liberal Imagination', *Language in Society*, 33/4 (2004), 517-48.
32. *The Musical World*, 'The Eisteddfod', 65 (13 August 1888), 629-30, 629.
33. *The Musical World*, 'The Eisteddfod', 65, 630.
34. *The Saturday Review of Politics, Literature, Science and Art*, 'The Eisteddfod', 24/620 (1867), 341-2, 341.
35. *The Musical Herald*, 'The National Eisteddfod', 810 (1 September 1915), 403.
36. *The Guardian*, 'Wrestling and rock at Eisteddfod', 5 August 1985, 3.
37. *The Guardian*, 'In praise of ... the national Eisteddfod', 8 August 2008; BBC Cymru Fyw, '89,943 yn ymweld ag Eisteddfod yr Urdd 2017'.
38. K. Barnard, 'Visible Welshness: Performing Welshness at the National Eisteddfod in the Twentieth Century' (unpublished PhD thesis, University of Wales Swansea, 2004), 1.
39. Parry and Cynan, *Yr Eisteddfod/The Eisteddfod*, p. 39.

40. Brooks and Lublin, 'The Eisteddfod of Chubut, or How the Reinvention of Tradition has Contributed to the Preservation of a Language and Culture', 3.
41. Brooks and Lublin, 'The Eisteddfod of Chubut, or How the Reinvention of Tradition has Contributed to the Preservation of a Language and Culture'.
42. Brooks and Lublin, 'The Eisteddfod of Chubut, or How the Reinvention of Tradition has Contributed to the Preservation of a Language and Culture'.
43. C. Ap Aeron Jones, 'Appendix 2: The Eisteddfod in Chubut', in D. Rhys, *A Welsh Song in Patagonia: Memories of the Colonisation* (E.K. Vyhmeister, 2005), pp. 182–6, 184.
44. Brooks and Lublin, 'The Eisteddfod of Chubut, or How the Reinvention of Tradition has Contributed to the Preservation of a Language and Culture', 5.
45. Ap Aeron Jones, 'Appendix 2: The Eisteddfod in Chubut', pp. 185–6.
46. Keane, *Signs of Recognition*, p. 18.
47. Kelly Askew, *Performing the Nation: Swahili Music and Cultural Politics in Tanzania* (Chicago: University of Chicago Press, 2002), p. 26.
48. Pelkmans, *Fragile Conviction*, p. 170.
49. J. Zigon, 'Moral Breakdown and the Ethical Demand: A Theoretical Framework for an Anthropology of Moralities', *Anthropological Theory*, 7/2 (2007), 131–50, 137, 133; J. Zigon, 'An Ethics of Dwelling', in *Disappointment* (New York: Fordham University Press, 2017), pp. 102–28; see further J. Zigon, 'Moral Breakdown and the Ethical Demand: A Theoretical Framework for an Anthropology of Moralities', *Anthropological Theory*, 7/2 (2007), pp. 131–50.
50. Brooks and Lublin, 'The Eisteddfod of Chubut, or How the Reinvention of Tradition has Contributed to the Preservation of a Language and Culture', 10.
51. E. Hobsbawm, 'Introduction: Inventing Traditions', in E. Hobsbawm and T. Ranger (eds), *The Invention of Tradition* (Cambridge: Cambridge University Press, 1983), pp. 1–14; Brooks and Lublin, 'The Eisteddfod of Chubut, or How the Reinvention of Tradition has Contributed to the Preservation of a Language and Culture', 5.
52. Keane, *Signs of Recognition*, p. 95.
53. Brooks and Lublin, 'The Eisteddfod of Chubut, or How the Reinvention of Tradition has Contributed to the Preservation of a Language and Culture', 7.
54. Parry and Cynan, *Yr Eisteddfod/The Eisteddfod*, p. 44.
55. Keane, *Signs of Recognition*, p. 115.
56. Louis Althusser, *Lenin and Philosophy, and Other Essays* (London: New Left Books, 1971); Pierre Bourdieu, *Distinction: A Social Critique of the Judgement of Taste* (London: Routledge, 1984); D. Foley, 'The rise of Class Culture Theory in Educational Anthropology', *Anthropology and Education Quarterly*, 41/3 (2010), 215–27; J. Collins, 'Social Reproduction in Classrooms and Schools', *Annual Review of Anthropology*, 38 (2009), 33–48.
57. Butler, 'Conscience doth make subjects of us all', 7.
58. Butler, *The Psychic Life of Power*, p. 9.
59. Keane, *Signs of Recognition*, p. 95.
60. Parry and Cynan, *Yr Eisteddfod/The Eisteddfod*, p. 44.
61. Keane, *Signs of Recognition*.

62. Pelkmans, *Fragile Conviction*.
63. Alfred Gell, *Art and Agency: An Anthropological Theory* (Oxford: Clarendon Press, 1998), p. 7.
64. F. Diaz, 'Mindfulness, Attention, and Flow During Music Listening: An Empirical Investigation', *Psychology of Music*, 41/1 (2011), 42–58, 42.
65. T. Turino, *Music as Social Life: The Politics of Participation* (Chicago: University of Chicago Press, 2008), p. 4.
66. S. Cohen and E. Bodner, 'The Relationship Between Flow and Music Performance Anxiety amongst Professional Classical Orchestral Musicians', *Psychology of Music*, 47/3 (2019), 420–35, 421; see further J. Mowitt, '(I Can't Get No) Affect', in M. Thompson and I. Biddle (eds), *Sound, Music, Affect: Theorising Sonic Experience* (London: Bloomsbury, 2013), pp. 91–100.
67. Butler, 'Conscience doth make subjects of us all', 626.
68. Keane, *Signs of Recognition*.
69. See further William Rhys, *A Welsh Song in Patagonia: Memories of the Colonisation* (E.K. Vyhmeister, 2005), p. 144.
70. BBC News, 'How inclusive is the National Eisteddfod?' (2022), https://www.bbc.co.uk/news/av/uk-wales-62438410 (accessed 30 January 2024).
71. Althusser, *Lenin and Philosophy, and Other Essays*.
72. Keane, *Signs of Recognition*.

## Chapter 4

1. John Urry, *The Tourist Gaze: Second Edition* (London: Sage Publications, 2002), p. 3.
2. Jean-Paul Sartre, *Being and Nothingness* (London: Methuen and Co Ltd, 1958); R. Bianchi, 'The critical turn in tourism studies: A radical critique', *Tourism Geographies*, 11/4 (2009), 434–504.
3. Bianchi, 'The critical turn in tourism studies: A radical critique'
4. J. Carty and Y. Musharbash, 'You've Got to be Joking: Asserting the Analytical Value of Humour and Laughter in Contemporary Anthropology', *Anthropological Forum*, 18/3 (2008), 209–17.
5. C. Gibson, 'Critical tourism studies: new directions for volatile times', *Tourism Geographies*, 3/4 (2021), 659–77, 667.
6. K. Price, 'What was the Velindre Patagonia Trek really like? This trekker's diary gets to heart of gruelling challenge' (11 December 2015).
7. BBC Radio Cymru, 'Gŵyl y glaniad: sgwrsio gyda rhai o ddisgynyddion y Cymry cyntaf i lanio ym Mhatagonia', 29 July 2015.
8. BBC News, 'Patagonia 150 years on: a "little Wales beyond Wales"', 30 May 2015; BBC News, '150th anniversary of Welsh emigration to Patagonia', 28 July 2015; BBC News, 'Welsh settlers' "path of friendship" in Patagonia', 2 August 2016; BBC News, 'Can the Welsh language survive in Patagonia?', 30 July 2015; BBC News, 'How is the Welsh language being preserved in Patagonia?', 28 July 2015; BBC News, 'Welsh connection important boost for Patagonia's economy', 29 July 2015; BBC News, 'BBC National Orchestra of Wales first for Patagonia',

22 October 2015; BBC News, 'Record number of Welsh learners in Patagonia, Argentina', 7 June 2017.
9. K. Berg, 'Chubut, Argentina: a contested Welsh "first-place"', *International Journal of Heritage Studies*, 24/2 (2018), 154–66, 156.
10. M. Benson, 'Living the "real" dream in la France profonde? Lifestyle migration, social distinction, and the authenticities of everyday life', *Anthropological Quarterly*, 86/2 (2013), 501–25, 502, 509; see further Michaela Benson, *The British in Rural France: Lifestyle Migration and the Ongoing Quest for a Better Way of Life* (Manchester: Manchester University Press, 2011).
11. M. Novoa, 'Gendered nostalgia: grassroots heritage tourism and (de) industrialization in Lota, Chile', *Journal of Heritage Tourism* (2021), 1–19, 1, 12.
12. B. Lashua, K. Sprachlen and P. Long, 'Introduction to the special issue: music and tourism', *Tourism Studies*, 14/1 (2014), 3–9, 4.
13. A. Gillespie, 'Tourist Photography and the Reverse Gaze', *Ethos*, 34 (2006), 343–66, 344.
14. Judith Butler and Gayatri Spivak, *Who Sings the Nation-State? Language, politics, belonging* (London, New York and Calcutta: Seagull Books, 2007), p. 58.
15. Butler and Spivak, *Who Sings the Nation-State?*, pp. 58–9.
16. E. Whitfield, 'Welsh Patagonian Fiction: Language and the Novel of Transnational Ethnicity', *Diaspora*, 14/2 (2005), 333–48.
17. Morgan Tomos, *Alun yr Arth ym Mhatagonia* (Ceredigion: Y Lolfa, 2013), pp. 3–4, 22.
18. Sartre, *Being and Nothingness*, pp. 282–4.
19. Sartre, *Being and Nothingness*, p. 280.
20. John Urry, *The Tourist Gaze* (London: Sage Publications, 1990).
21. J. Urry, 'Globalising the Tourist Gaze', Department of Sociology, Lancaster University (2001), 1–9, 3; Urry, *The Tourist Gaze*.
22. H. Perkins and D. Thorns, 'Gazing or performing? Reflecting on Urry's Tourist Gaze in the Context of Contemporary Experience in the Antipodes', *International Sociology*, 16/2 (2001), 185–204; A. Guneratne, 'Shaping the Tourist's Gaze: Representing Ethnic Difference in a Nepali Village', *The Journal of the Royal Anthropological Institute*, 7/3 (2001), 527–43; D. Moaz, 'The mutual gaze', *Annual of Tourism Research*, 33/1 (2005), 221–39.
23. C. Cater, K. Poguntke and W. Morris, 'Y Wladfa Gymreig: Outbound diasporic tourism and contribution to identity', *Tourism Geographies*, 21/4 (2019), 665–86.
24. L. Stone and G. Nyaupane, 'The tourist gaze: Domestic versus international tourists', *Journal of Travel Research*, 58/5 (2019), 877–91.
25. B. Zhihong, 'Ethnic Identities Under the Tourist Gaze', *Asian Ethnicity*, 8/3 (2007), 245–59; see also T. Volkman, 'Visions and Revisions: Taraja Culture and the Tourist Gaze', *American Ethnologist*, 17/1 (1990), 91–110.
26. E. Korstanje, 'Passage from the Tourist Gaze to the Wicked Gaze: A Case Study on COVID-19 with special reference to Argentina', *International case studies in the management of disasters* (2020), 197–211.

27. Kathryn Jones, Carol Tully and Heather Williams, *Hidden Texts, Hidden Nations: (Re)discoveries of Wales in Travel Writing in French and German (1780–2018)* (Liverpool: Liverpool University Press, 2020).
28. M. Walsh et al., 'The social media tourist gaze: social media photography and its disruption at the zoo', *Information Technology & Tourism*, 21/3 (2019), 391–412; E. Fälton, 'The romantic tourist gaze on Swedish national parks: tracing ways of seeing the non-human world through representations in tourists' Instagram posts', *Tourism Recreation Research* (2021), 1–24.
29. Bianchi, 'The critical turn in tourism studies: A radical critique'.
30. BBC News, 'BBC National Orchestra of Wales first for Patagonia'.
31. BBC News, 'BBC National Orchestra of Wales first for Patagonia'.
32. Sartre, *Being and Nothingness*.
33. G. Waitt and M. Duffy, 'Listening and Tourism studies', *Annals of Tourism Research*, 37/2 (2009), 457–77, 460.
34. Sartre, *Being and Nothingness*, p. 285.
35. M. Rosaldo, 'The Shame of Headhunters and The Autonomy of Self', *Ethos*, 11/3 (1983), 135–51; J. Fajans, 'Shame, Social Action and the Person Among the Baining', *Ethos*, 11/3 (1983), 166–80.
36. L. Dolezal, 'Shame, vulnerability and belonging: reconsidering Sartre's account of shame', *Human Studies*, 40/3 (2017), 421–38, 423.
37. E. Anderson, 'Sartre's Affective Turn: Shame as Recognition in "The Look"', *Philosophy Today* (2021).
38. *Golwg 360*, 'Cynnal Gŵyl y Glaniad ym Mhorth Madryn', 28 July 2015.
39. Cymru Fyw, 'Darlithydd ar drywydd hanes Gŵyl y Glaniad', 16 December 2015.
40. Welsh Government, 'Written Statement – First Minister's Visit to Patagonia' (2015), https://www.gov.wales/written-statement-first-ministers-visit-patagonia (accessed 31 January 2024); emphasis mine.
41. M. Kaaristo, 'Everyday power dynamics and hierarchies in qualitative research: The role of humour in the field', *Qualitative Research* (2022), 22/5, 743–60, 744.
42. K. Alexeyeff, 'Are you being served? Sex, humour and globalisation in the Cook Islands', *Anthropological Forum*, 18/3 (2008), 287–93, 288.
43. Carty and Musharbash, 'You've Got to be Joking: Asserting the Analytical Value of Humour and Laughter in Contemporary Anthropology'.
44. B. McCullough, 'Poor Black Bastard Can't Shake-A-Leg: Humour and Laughter in Urban Aboriginal North Queensland, Australia', *Anthropological Forum*, 18/3 (2008), 279–85, 284.
45. Alexeyeff, 'Are you being served? Sex, humour and globalisation in the Cook Islands', 292.
46. Donna Goldstein, *Laughter Out of Place: Race, Class, Violence, and Sexuality in a Rio Shantytown* (London: University of California Press, 2013), p. 5.
47. M. Yoshida, 'Joking, gender, power, and professionalism among Japanese inn workers', *Ethnology* (2001), 361–9.
48. Kaaristo, 'Everyday power dynamics and hierarchies in qualitative research', 744.

49. Kaaristo, 'Everyday power dynamics and hierarchies in qualitative research', 748, 747.
50. John Morreall, *The Philosophy of Laughter and Humour* (Albany: State University of New York Press, 1987).
51. J. Butler, 'Conscience doth make subjects of us all', *Yale French Studies*, 88 (1995), 626; Judith Butler, *Excitable Speech: A Politics of the Performative* (New York and London: Routledge, 1997); Judith Butler, *The Psychic Life of Power* (Stanford: Stanford University Press, 1997).
52. Sartre, *Being and Nothingness*, pp. 300–1.
53. M. Foucault, 'Governmentality', in G. Burchell, C. Gordon and P. Miller (eds), *The Foucault Effect: Studies in Governmentality* (Chicago: University of Chicago Press, 1991), pp. 87–104.
54. D. Moaz, 'The mutual gaze', *Annual of Tourism Research*, 33/1 (2005), 221–39, 222.

## Chapter 5

1. V. Crapanzano, '"Hermes" Dilemma: The Masking of Subversion in Ethnographic Description' in J. Clifford and G. Marcus (eds), *Writing Culture: The Poetics and Politics of Ethnography* (Berkeley: University of California Press, 1986), pp. 51–76, 52.
2. Crapanzano, '"Hermes" Dilemma'.
3. P. Lichterman, 'Interpretive reflexivity in ethnography', *Ethnography*, 18/1 (2017), 35–45, 36.
4. L. Schindler and H. Schäfer, 'Practices of writing in ethnographic work', *Journal of Contemporary Ethnography*, 50/1 (2021), 11–32; see also J. Clifford, 'Introduction: Partial Truths', in J. Clifford and G. Marcus (eds), *Writing Culture: The Poetics and Politics of Ethnography* (Berkeley: University of California Press, 1986), pp. 1–26.
5. J. Ruby, 'The last 20 years of Visual Anthropology – A Critical Review', *Visual Studies*, 20/2 (2005), 159–70, 165.
6. John Urry, *The Tourist Gaze* (London: Sage Publications, 1990); Jean-Paul Sartre, *Being and Nothingness* (London: Methuen and Co. Ltd, 1958).
7. Noel Salazar and Nelson Graburn, *Tourism Imaginaries, Anthropological Approaches* (New York and Oxford: Berghahn Books, 2010), p. 8; see also D. Moaz, 'The mutual gaze', *Annual of Tourism Research*, 33/1 (2005), 221–39; B. Zhihong, 'Ethnic Identities Under the Tourist Gaze', *Asian Ethnicity*, 8/3 (2007), 245–59.
8. Moaz, 'The mutual gaze', 229.
9. R. Elliott, 'So Transported: Nina Simone, "My Sweet Lord", and the (Un)folding of Affect', in M. Thompson and I. Biddle (eds), *Sound Music Affect* (London: Bloomsbury, 2013), pp. 76–90, 87.
10. J. Geiger, 'Virtual travels and the tourist gaze', in *American Documentary Film: Projecting the Nation* (Edinburgh: Edinburgh University Press, 2011), pp. 40–61, 40.

11. Kaja Silverman, *The Acoustic Mirror: The Female Voice in Psychoanalysis and Cinema* (Bloomington: Indiana University Press, 1988), p. 6.
12. J. Lacan, 'The Mirror Stage as Formative of the "I" Function as Revealed in Psychoanalytic Experience', *Écrits* (1966), 93–101.
13. Christian Metz, *The imaginary signifier: Psychoanalysis and the cinema* (Indiana: Indiana University Press, 1982); Silverman, *The Acoustic Mirror*; L. Mulvey, 'Visual Pleasure and Narrative Cinema', in *Visual and Other Pleasures* (London: Macmillan Press, 1989), pp. 14–18; Frances Restuccia, *The Blue Box: Kristevan/Lacanian Readings of Contemporary Cinema* (London: Continuum, 2012).
14. Glen Gabbard, *Psychoanalysis and film* (London: Routledge, 2018), pp. 1–2.
15. Metz, *The imaginary signifier*, p. 48.
16. A. Schneider, 'A Black Box for Participatory Cinema: Movie-Making with "Neighbours" in Saladillo, Argentina', *Visual Anthropology*, 29/4–5 (2016), 406–31.
17. Ed Gold, *Patagonia: Byd Arall; Otro Mundo; Another World* (Llandysul: Gwasg Gomer, 2012).
18. G. Gibbard, 'Gwenan in Patagonia 2015', interview with Wales Arts International (May 2015).
19. René Griffiths, *Ramblings of a Patagonian* (Cardiff: Artisan Media Publishing, 2014), pp. 290–1.
20. L. Faier and L. Rofel, 'Ethnographies of encounter', *The Annual Review of Anthropology*, 43 (2014), 363–77.
21. Ruby, 'The last 20 years of Visual Anthropology – A Critical Review', 163.
22. See also Sian Eirian Rees Davies, *I Fyd Sy Well* (Ceredigion: Gomer, 2005).
23. Yolanda Covington-Ward, *Gesture and Power: Religion, Nationalism and Everyday Performance in Congo* (London: Duke University Press, 2016), p. 7.
24. Sartre, *Being and Nothingness*.
25. P. Santos, 'The imagined nation: The mystery of the endurance of the colonial imaginary in postcolonial times', in N. Salazar and N. Graburn (eds), *Tourism Imaginaries, Anthropological Approaches* (New York and Oxford: Berghahn Books, 2010), p. 211.
26. Bazin, quoted in Restuccia, *The Blue Box*, p. 39.
27. Lacan, 'The Mirror Stage as Formative of the "I" Function as Revealed in Psychoanalytic Experience'.
28. J. Butler, 'Conscience doth make subjects of us all', *Yale French Studies*, 88 (1995), 626
29. L. Abu-Lughod, 'The Interpretation of Culture(s) After Television', *Representations*, 59 (1997), 109–34; Ruby, 'The last 20 years of Visual Anthropology – A Critical Review', 7.
30. Abu-Lughod, 'The Interpretation of Culture(s) After Television', 110, 120.
31. Schneider, 'A Black Box for Participatory Cinema', 407.
32. Schneider, 'A Black Box for Participatory Cinema', 409.
33. P. Ebron, 'Constituting Subjects through Performative Acts', in C. Cole et al. (eds), *Africa after gender?* (Indiana: Indiana University Press, 2007), pp. 171–90, 172–3.

34. P. Jain, 'Sara Jahan Homare: Indian films and their portrayal of foreign destinations', *Visual Anthropology*, 32/3-4 (2019), 343-52.
35. M. Karush, 'Populism, Melodrama, and the Market', in M. Karush and O. Chamosa (eds), *The New Cultural History of Peronism* (USA: Duke University Press, 2010), pp. 21-52, 25.
36. L. Baldassar, 'Missing kin and longing to be together: emotions and the construction of co-presence in transnational relationships', *Journal of Intercultural Studies*, 29/3 (2008), 247-66, 248; see also Loretta Baldassar, *Visits Home: Migration Experiences Between Italy and Australia* (Melbourne: University of Melbourne Press, 2001).
37. C. Baldock, 'Migrants and their parents: caregiving at a distance', *Journal of Family Issues*, 21/2 (2000), 205-24; see further J. Agullo, 'The Spanish Diaspora in Latin America: an "Unknown" geopolitical case', *Diaspora Studies*, 5/1 (2012), 79-95.
38. Schneider, 'A Black Box for Participatory Cinema', 416.
39. Lacan, 'The Mirror Stage as Formative of the "I" Function as Revealed in Psychoanalytic Experience'.
40. J. Gallop, 'Lacan's "Mirror Stage": Where to Begin', *SubStance*, 11/4 (1983), 118-28, 120.
41. Gallop, 'Lacan's "Mirror Stage": Where to Begin'; L. Kodre, 'Psychoanalysis for Anthropology: An Introduction to Lacanian Anthropology', *Anthropological Notebooks*, 17/1 (2011), 53-72; D. Leader, 'Lacan and the Subject', *Philosophy, Psychiatry, and Psychology*, 21/4 (2014), 367-8.
42. S. Rubenstein, 'On the Importance of Visions among the Amazonian Shuar', *Current Anthropology*, 53/1 (2012), 39-79, 44.
43. L. Mulvey, 'Visual Pleasure and Narrative Cinema', in *Visual and Other Pleasures* (London: Macmillan Press, 1989), pp. 14-18, 18.
44. Rubenstein, 'On the Importance of Visions among the Amazonian Shuar'.
45. Goffman Erving, *The Presentation of Self in Everyday Life* (Edinburgh: Social Sciences Research Centre, University of Edinburgh, 1956); Althusser, *Lenin and Philosophy, and Other Essays*; Butler, 'Conscience doth make subjects of us all'.
46. W. Bukowski and D. Raufelder, 'Peers and the self', in W. Bukowski, B. Laursen and K. Rubin (eds), *Handbook of peer interactions, relationships and groups* (New York: The Guilford Press, 2018), pp. 141-56; G. Moore et al., 'School, peer and family relationships and adolescent substance use, subjective wellbeing and mental health symptoms in Wales: A cross sectional study', *Child indicators research*, 11/6 (2018), 1951-65; M. Maulyda and M. Erfan, 'Do Social Interactions with Peers Affect Student Identity?', *Qalam: Jurnal Ilmu Kependidikan*, 9/2 (2020), 60-5.
47. S. Winkler-Reid, '"Looking Good" and "Good Looking" in School: Beauty Ideals, Appearance, and Enskilled Vision Among Girls in a London Secondary School', *Anthropology and Education Quarterly*, 48/3 (2017), 284-300; see further C. Grasseni, 'Skilled Vision: on Apprenticeship in Breeding Aesthetics', *Social Anthropology*, 12/1 (2004), 41-55.
48. Sartre, *Being and Nothingness*.

49. P. Messier, 'Cameras at Work: Dusty Lenses and Processed Videos in the Quarries of Hyderabad', *Visual Anthropology*, 32/3-4 (2019), 287-308, 289.

## Chapter 6

1. A. Kassabian, 'Music for Sleeping', in M. Thompson and I. Biddle (eds), *Sound, Music, Affect: Theorising Sonic Experience* (London: Bloomsbury, 2013), p. 179.
2. Kassabian, 'Music for Sleeping'.
3. S. Feld, 'Aesthetics as Iconicity of Style, or "Lift-up-over-sounding": Getting into the Kaluli Groove', *Yearbook for Traditional Music*, 20 (1988), 74-113.
4. V. Doubleday, 'Sounds of Power: An Overview of Musical Instruments and Gender', *Ethnomusicology Forum*, 17/1 (2008), 3-39.
5. M. Course, 'Why Mapuche Sing', *Journal of the Royal Anthropological Institute*, 15/2 (2009), 295-313.
6. N. Violinsky, 'Standing Up: Violin Performance Technique and Ethnic Resurgence in Saraguro, Ecuador', *Visual Anthropology*, 16/2-3 (2010), 315-40.
7. K. Bridge, 'Music and Identity in Paraguay: Expressing National, Racial and Class Identity in Guitar Music Culture', *Journal of the Royal Musical Association* (2022), 1-49.
8. M. Foucault, 'Governmentality', in G. Burchell, C. Gordon and P. Miller (eds), *The Foucault Effect: Studies in Governmentality* (Chicago: University of Chicago Press, 1991), pp. 87-104; Jean-Paul Sartre, *Being and Nothingness* (London: Methuen and Co. Ltd, 1958); Louis Althusser, *Lenin and Philosophy, and Other Essays* (London: New Left Books, 1971).
9. J. Clifford, 'Introduction: Partial Truths', in J. Clifford and G. Marcus (eds), *Writing Culture: The Poetics and Politics of Ethnography* (Berkeley: University of California Press, 1986), pp. 1-26, 12.
10. T. Ingold, *The Perception of the Environment: Essays on Livelihood, Dwelling, and Skill* (London: Routledge, 2000), p. 407.
11. Clifford, 'Introduction: Partial Truths', p. 12.
12. S. Feld and D. Brennis, 'Doing Anthropology in Sound', *American Ethnologist*, 31/4 (2004), 461-74; D. Samuels et al., 'Soundscapes: Toward a Sounded Anthropology', *Annual Review of Anthropology*, 39 (2010), 329-45.
13. S. Doxat-Pratt, 'Musical communities in the society of captives: Exploring the impact of music making on the social world of prison', *Musicae Scientiae*, 25/3 (2021), 290-302; K. Kulkarni, '"Like a Cosmic, Invisible Umbilical Cord": Soul Summit and the Haptic Arrangements of Black Social Life', *Journal of Popular Music Studies*, 33/4 (2021), 171-202; T. Jääskeläinen, '"Music is my life": Examining the connections between music students' workload experiences in higher education and meaningful engagement in music', *Research Studies in Music Education* (2022), 1-21.
14. Samuels et al., 'Soundscapes: Toward a Sounded Anthropology'.
15. R. Alsina-Pagès et al., 'Changes in the soundscape of Girona during the COVID lockdown', *The Journal of the Acoustical Society of America*, 149/5 (2021), 3416-23; A. Ednie et al., 'Connecting protected area visitor experiences, wellness

motivations, and soundscape perceptions in Chilean Patagonia', *Journal of Leisure Research*, 53/3 (2022), 377–403.
16. Timothy Ingold, *Being Alive: Essays on Movement, Knowledge and Description* (London: Routledge, 2011), p. 138.
17. Feld, 'Aesthetics as Iconicity of Style, or "Lift-up-over-sounding"'; Michael Bull, *Sounding Out the City: Personal Stereos and the Management of Everyday Life* (Oxford: Berg, 2000).
18. S. Merlino et al., 'Walking through the city soundscape: an audio-visual analysis of sensory experience for people with psychosis', *Visual Communication*, 22/1 (2023), 71–95.
19. D. Dratsky and J. Goldschmidt, 'P103 The Power of Music: Creating a Pleasurable Eating Experience for Adults with Intellectual and Developmental Disabilities', *Journal of Nutrition Education and Behavior*, 53/7 (2021), 72–3; M. Vassallo, 'Mobilising the masses through music and songs: the global phenomenon of music and politics', in M. Vassallo and A. Debattista (eds), *The Different Faces of Politics: A Handbook of Political Thought and Artistic Expression* (UK: Routledge, 2022).
20. A. Hofman, 'The Affective turn in Ethnomusicology', *Muzikologija*, 18 (2015), 35–55, 26.
21. M. Thompson and I. Biddle, 'Somewhere Between the Signifying and the Sublime', in M. Thompson and I. Biddle (eds), *Sound Music Affect: Theorising Sonic Experience* (London: Bloomsbury, 2013), pp. 2–24, 5.
22. F. Jarman, 'Relax, Feel Good, Chill Out: The Affective Distribution of Classical Music', in M. Thompson and I. Biddle (eds), *Sound, Music, Affect: Theorising Sonic Experience* (London: Bloomsbury, 2013), pp. 183–204, 189.
23. M. Bloch, 'Symbols song, dance and features of articulation: is religion an extreme form of traditional authority?', *European Journal of Sociology*, 15/1 (1974), 54–81, 71.
24. K. Avenburg, 'Interpellation and performance: the construction of identities through musical experience in the Virgen del Rosario Fiesta, Iruya, Argentina', *Latin American Perspectives*, 39/2 (2012), 134–49, 143.
25. See, for example, Susan McClary, *Feminine Endings: Music, Gender and Sexuality* (London: University of Minnesota Press, 1991); Tia DeNora, *Music in Everyday Life* (Cambridge: Cambridge University Press, 2000).
26. See further Thompson and Biddle, 'Somewhere Between the Signifying and the Sublime'.
27. DeNora, *Music in Everyday Life*; Jarman, 'Relax, Feel Good, Chill Out'; A. Cabedo-Mas et al., 'Uses and perceptions of music in times of COVID-19: a Spanish population survey', *Frontiers in Psychology*, 11 (2021), 1–13; Kassabian, 'Music for Sleeping'.
28. J. Butler, 'Conscience doth make subjects of us all', *Yale French Studies*, 88 (1995), 626.
29. S. Kang, 'An Exploratory Study of Music Teachers' Flow Experiences Between Performing and Teaching Music', *Journal of Research in Music Education* (2022), 162–79; T. Loepthien and B. Leipold, 'Flow in music performance

30. and music-listening: differences in intensity, predictors, and the relationship between flow and subjective well-being', *Psychology of Music*, 50/1 (2022), 111–26; R. Antonini Philippe et al., 'Flow and music performance: professional musicians and music students' views', *Psychology of Music*, 50/4 (2022), 1023–38.
30. S. Cohen and E. Bodner, 'The Relationship Between Flow and Music Performance Anxiety amongst Professional Classical Orchestral Musicians', *Psychology of Music*, 47/3 (2019), 420–35.
31. Kassabian, 'Music for Sleeping', p. 165.
32. Michel Foucault, *The Care of the Self: The History of Sexuality, Vol. 3* (London: Penguin Books, 1984); Michel Foucault, *The Use of Pleasure: The History of Sexuality, Vol. 2* (London: Penguin Books, 1984).
33. Foucault, *The Use of Pleasure*, p. 27; see further D. Smith, 'Foucault on Ethics and Subjectivity: Care of the Self and Aesthetics of Existence', *Foucault Studies*, 19 (2015), 135–50.
34. Mercédès Pavlicevic and Gary Ansdell, *Community Music Therapy* (London: Jessica Kingsley, 2004); B. Ahessy, 'The use of a music therapy choir to reduce depression and improve quality of life in older adults – a randomised control trial', *Music and Medicine*, 8/1 (2016), 17–28.
35. R. MacDonald, 'Music, Health, and Well-being: A Review', *International Journal of Qualitative Studies in Health and Well-being* (2013), 1–13, 13.
36. Deborah James, *Songs of the Women Migrants: Performance and Identity in South Africa* (Edinburgh: Edinburgh University Press, 1999).
37. Anthony Seeger, *Why Suya Sing: A Musical Anthropology of an Amazonian People* (Urbana and Chicago: University of Illinois Press, 2004), p. 6.
38. Kelly Askew, *Performing the Nation: Swahili Music and Cultural Politics in Tanzania* (Chicago: University of Chicago Press, 2002), p. 155.
39. Sartre, *Being and Nothingness*.
40. F. Diaz, 'Mindfulness, Attention, and Flow During Music Listening: An Empirical Investigation', *Psychology of Music*, 41/1 (2011), 42.
41. Mihaly Csikszentmihalyi, *Beyond Boredom and Anxiety* (US: Jossey-Bass, 2000).
42. A. Chirico et al., 'When music flows: state and trait in musical performance, composition, and listening: A systematic review', *Frontiers in Psychology*, 6/906 (2015), 1.
43. See, for example, Chirico et al., 'When music flows'; S. Sinnamon, A. Moran and M. O'Connell, 'Flow among musicians: measuring peak experiences of student performances', *Journal of Research in Music Education*, 60/1 (2012), 6–25.
44. B. Hackert et al., 'Towards a reconceptualization of flow in social contexts', *Journal of Theory of Social Behaviour*, 53 (2023), 100–25, 114.
45. P. Laukka, 'Uses of Music and Psychological Well-Being Among the Elderly', *Journal of Happiness Studies*, 8 (2007), 215–41, 232.
46. MacDonald, 'Music, Health, and Well-being: A Review'.
47. Pavlicevic and Ansdell, *Community Music Therapy*; Ahessy, 'The use of a music therapy choir to reduce depression and improve quality of life in older adults – a randomised control trial'.

48. E. Costa-Giomi, 'Music Instruction and Children's Intellectual Development: The Educational Context of Music Participation', in R. MacDonald et al. (eds), *Music, Health and Wellbeing* (Oxford: Oxford University Press, 2012), pp. 339-56.
49. F. Baker et al., 'Therapeutic Songwriting in Music Therapy, Part 1: Who Are the Therapists, Who are the Clients, and Why is Songwriting Used?', *Nordic Journal of Music Therapy*, 17/2 (2008), 105-23; Q. Tang et al., 'Effects of music therapy on depression: A meta-analysis of randomized controlled trials', *PloS one*, 15/11 (2020), 1-23; Michael Silverman, *Music therapy in mental health for illness management and recovery* (Oxford: Oxford University Press, 2022).
50. P. Elvers, T. Fischinger and J. Steffens, 'Music Listening as Self-enhancement: Effects of Empowering Music on Momentary Explicit and Implicit Self-esteem', *Psychology of Music*, 46/3 (2018), 307-25; A. van Rooyen and A. dos Santos, 'Exploring the Lived Experiences of Teenagers in a Children's Home Participating in a Choir: A Community Music Therapy Perspective', *International Journal of Community Music*, 13/1 (2020), 81-101; G. Harpaz and T. Vaizman, 'Music self-efficacy, self-esteem, and help-seeking orientation among amateur musicians who use online music tutorials', *Psychology of Aesthetics, Creativity, and the Arts* (2021), 17/5 (2023), 598-607.
51. MacDonald, 'Music, Health, and Well-being: A Review', 2.
52. L. Zhang, 'Cultivating the Therapeutic Self in China', *Medical Anthropology*, 37/1 (2018), 45-58, 54; G. Klyve and R. Rolvsjord, 'Moments of fun: narratives of children's experiences of music therapy in mental health care', *Nordic Journal of Music Therapy* (2022), 1-21.
53. Foucault, *The Care of the Self*, p. 53.
54. Zhang, 'Cultivating the Therapeutic Self in China', 46.
55. C. Stafford, 'Be Careful What You Wish For: The Case of Happiness in China', in I. Kavedžija and H. Walker (eds), *Values of Happiness* (Chicago: Hau Books Special Issues in Ethnographic Theory Series (Volume 2), 2016), pp. 59-81, 69.
56. W. Jock et al., 'Differential Client Perspectives on Therapy in Argentina and the United States: A Cross-Cultural study', *Psychotherapy*, 50/4 (2013), 517-24; A. Dagfal, 'Psychology and Psychoanalysis in Argentina: Politics, French Thought and the University Connection 1955-1976', *History of Psychology*, 21/3 (2018), 254-72; C. Fierro, J. Álvarez and G. Manzo, 'A Century of Psychotherapy in Argentina: Clinical Psychology, Psychoanalysis and Recent Developments', *Revista de Psicologia*, 27/2 (2018), 1-27.
57. V. Koç and G. Kafa, 'Cross-cultural Research on Psychotherapy: The Need for Change', *Journal of Cross-Cultural Psychology*, 50/1 (2019), 100-15, 102.
58. Dagfal, 'Psychology and Psychoanalysis in Argentina'.
59. J. Stagnaro, 'The Current State of Psychiatric and Mental Healthcare in Argentina', *BJPsych Advances*, 22 (2016), 260-2, 260.
60. H. Farndon, 'HCPC registered psychoanalysts in the UK', The British Psychological Society (2016); G. Thornicroft, 'Improving access to psychological therapies in England', *The Lancet*, 391 (2018), 636-7.

61. F. Giovannetti et al., 'Psychological science in Argentina: current state & future directions', *Discover Psychology*, 2/1 (2022), 1–7.
62. Jock et al., 'Differential Client Perspectives on Therapy in Argentina and the United States'; Dagfal, 'Psychology and Psychoanalysis in Argentina'; Fierro, Álvarez and Manzo, 'A Century of Psychotherapy in Argentina'; Koç and Kafa, 'Cross-cultural Research on Psychotherapy'.
63. Dagfal, 'Psychology and Psychoanalysis in Argentina', 254.
64. A. Lakoff, 'The Lacan Ward: Pharmacology and Subjectivity in Buenos Aires', *Social Analysis: The International Journal of Social and Cultural Practice*, 47/2 (2003), 82–101, 85.
65. Koç and Kafa, 'Cross-cultural Research on Psychotherapy', 104.
66. Foucault, *The Care of the Self*, p. 43.
67. J. Bergen and P. Verbeek, 'To-do is to be: Foucault, Levinas, and technologically mediated subjectivation', *Philosophy & Technology*, 34/2 (2021), 325–48.
68. DeNora, *Music in Everyday Life*, p. 47.
69. Foucault, *The Care of the Self*, p. 53.
70. R. White, 'Foucault on the Care of the Self as an Ethical Project and a Spiritual Goal', *Human Studies*, 37/4 (2014), 489–504, 498.
71. Ahessy, 'The use of a music therapy choir to reduce depression and improve quality of life in older adults – a randomised control trial'.
72. van Rooyen and dos Santos, 'Exploring the Lived Experiences of Teenagers in a Children's Home Participating in a Choir'.
73. K. McFerran and M. Hunt, 'Music, adversity and flourishing: Exploring experiences of a community music therapy group for Australian youth', *British Journal of Music Therapy*, 36/1 (2022), 37–47, 45.
74. H. Walker and I. Kavedžija, 'Introduction: Values of Happiness', in I. Kavedžija and H. Walker (eds), *Values of Happiness* (Chicago: Hau Books Special Issues in Ethnographic Theory Series (Volume 2), 2016), pp. 1–28, 21.
75. I. Kavedžija and H. Walker (eds), *Values of Happiness* (Chicago: Hau Books Special Issues in Ethnographic Theory Series (Volume 2), 2016), p. 285.
76. D. Graeber, 'It is Value that Brings Universes into Being', *HAU: Journal of Ethnographic Theory*, 3/2 (2013), 219–43, 226; see also David Graeber, *Toward an Anthropological Theory of Value: The False Coin of Our Own Dreams* (New York: Palgrave, 2001); Arjun Appadurai, *The social life of things: commodities in cultural perspective* (Cambridge: Cambridge University Press, 1986).
77. Foucault, *The Care of the Self*.
78. L. Flood, 'Instrument in Tow: Bringing Musical Skills to the Field', *Ethnomusicology*, 61/3 (2017), 486–505, 486; see also Paul Rabinow, *Reflections on Fieldwork in Morocco* (California: University of California Press, 1977).
79. White, 'Foucault on the Care of the Self as an Ethical Project and a Spiritual Goal', 499.
80. Chirico et al., 'When music flows', 1.
81. Sartre, *Being and Nothingness*, p. 317.

82. Lacan, 'The Mirror Stage as Formative of the "I" Function as Revealed in Psychoanalytic Experience'; Sartre, *Being and Nothingness*; Althusser, *Lenin and Philosophy, and Other Essays*.
83. Althusser, *Lenin and Philosophy, and Other Essays*, p. 117.
84. A. Hofman, 'The Affective Turn in Ethnomusicology', *Muzikologija*, 18 (2015), 35–55, 47.
85. Butler, 'Conscience doth make subjects of us all', 626.
86. DeNora, *Music and Everyday Life*, p. 105.
87. Foucault, *The Care of the Self*; Foucault, *The Use of Pleasure*; Graeber, 'It is Value that Brings Universes into Being'; Graeber, *Toward an Anthropological Theory of Value*.
88. Bourdieu Pierre, *Distinction: a social critique of the judgement of taste* (London: Routledge, 1984), p. 1.

## Chapter 7
1. S. Ortner, 'Subjectivity and Cultural Critique', *Anthropological Theory*, 5/1 (2005), 31–52, 41.
2. Louis Althusser, *Lenin and Philosophy, and Other Essays* (London: New Left Books, 1971); Jean-Paul Sartre, *Being and Nothingness* (London: Methuen and Co. Ltd, 1958); J. Lacan, 'The Mirror Stage as Formative of the "I" Function as Revealed in Psychoanalytic Experience', *Écrits* (1966), 93–101; M. Foucault, "Governmentality", in G. Burchell, C. Gordon and P. Miller (eds), *The Foucault Effect: Studies in Governmentality* (Chicago: University of Chicago Press, 1991), pp. 87–104.
3. F. Diaz, 'Mindfulness, Attention, and Flow During Music Listening: An Empirical Investigation', *Psychology of Music*, 41/1 (2011), 42–58.
4. A. Chirico et al., 'When music flows: State and trait in musical performance, composition, and listening: A systematic review', *Frontiers in Psychology*, 6/906 (2015), 1–14.
5. S. Sinnamon, A. Moran and M. O'Connell, 'Flow among musicians: measuring peak experiences of student performances', *Journal of Research in Music Education*, 60/1 (2012), 6.
6. Diaz, 'Mindfulness, Attention, and Flow During Music Listening: An Empirical Investigation'; Sinnamon, Moran and O'Connell, 'Flow among musicians: measuring peak experiences of student performances'.
7. B. A. Hackert et al., 'Towards a reconceptualization of flow in social contexts', *Journal of Theory of Social Behaviour*, 53 (2023), 100–25, 101.
8. Hackert et al., 'Towards a reconceptualization of flow in social contexts', 112.
9. Hackert et al., 'Towards a reconceptualization of flow in social contexts', 114.
10. S. Cohen and E. Bodner, 'The Relationship Between Flow and Music Performance Anxiety amongst Professional Classical Orchestral Musicians', *Psychology of Music*, 47/3 (2019), 422.
11. Diaz, 'Mindfulness, Attention, and Flow During Music Listening: An Empirical Investigation'; Cohen and Bodner, 'The Relationship Between Flow and Music Performance Anxiety amongst Professional Classical Orchestral Musicians'.

12. J. Butler, 'Conscience doth make subjects of us all', *Yale French Studies*, 88 (1995), 626.
13. Althusser, *Lenin and Philosophy, and Other Essays*.
14. T. Matthews, J. Stupacher and P. Vuust, 'The Pleasurable Urge to Move to Music Through the Lens of Learning Progress', *Journal of Cognition*, 6/1 (2023), 1–22.
15. O. McDermott et al., 'The importance of music for people with dementia: the perspectives of people with dementia, family carers, staff and music therapists', *Aging & Mental Health*, 18/6 (2014), 706–16; G. Barradas et al., 'Emotional Reactions to Music in Dementia Patients and Healthy Controls: Differential Responding Depends on the Mechanism', *Music & Science*, 4 (2021); T. Amano et al., 'Strategies for implementing music-based interventions for people with dementia in long-term care facilities: A systematic review', *International Journal of Geriatric Psychiatry*, 37/1 (2022).
16. R. Dowlen et al., 'In the moment with music: an exploration of the embodied and sensory experiences of people living with dementia during improvised music-making', *Ageing & Society* (2021), 1–23.
17. M. D. Schulkind, 'Is memory for music special?', *Annals of the New York Academy of Science*, 1169/1 (2009), 216–24.
18. Marilyn Strathern, *The Gender of the Gift: Problems with Women and Problems with Society in Melanesia* (Berkeley: University of California Press, 1988); see further N. Bird-David, '"Animism" revisited: personhood, environment, and relational epistemology', *Current Anthropology*, 40/51 (1999), 67–91.
19. Charles Taylor, *A Secular Age* (Cambridge, MA: The Belknap Press of Harvard University Press, 2007); K. Smith, 'From Dividual and Individual Selves to Porous Subjects', *TAJA The Australian Journal of Anthropology*, 23 (2012), 50–64.
20. C. Trosset, 'Triangulation and confirmation in the study of Welsh concepts of personhood', *Journal of Anthropological Research*, 57/1 (2001), 61–81; Carol Trosset, *Welshness Performed: Welsh Concepts of Person and Society* (Tuscon: University of Arizona Press, 1993).

# Works Cited

Abu-Lughod L., 'The Interpretation of Culture(s) After Television', *Representations*, 59 (1997), pp. 109-34.

Adkin, A., 'The Paradox of Transnational Indigenous Identities in Argentina', *Core Seminar: Fall 2006* (2006).

Agullo, J., 'The Spanish Diaspora in Latin America: an "Unknown" geopolitical case', *Diaspora Studies*, 5/1 (2012), 79-95.

Ahessy, B., 'The use of a music therapy choir to reduce depression and improve quality of life in older adults – a randomised control trial', *Music and Medicine*, 8/1 (2016), 17-28.

Alexeyeff, K., 'Are you being served? Sex, humour and globalisation in the Cook Islands', *Anthropological Forum*, 18/3 (2008), 287-93.

Aliga, C, 'The land 'wars' in twenty-first century Patagonia', *Journal of Latin American Cultural Studies*, 28/1 (2019), 139-51.

Alsina-Pagès R. et al., 'Changes in the soundscape of Girona during the COVID lockdown', *The Journal of the Acoustical Society of America*, 149/5 (2021), 3416-23.

Althusser, Louis, *Lenin and Philosophy, and Other Essays* (London: New Left Books, 1971).

Amano T. et al., 'Strategies for implementing music-based interventions for people with dementia in long-term care facilities: A systematic review', *International Journal of Geriatric Psychiatry*, 37/1 (2022).

Amit, V., 'Introduction: Constructing the field', in V. Amit (ed.), *Constructing the Field: Ethnographic Fieldwork in the Contemporary World* (London: Routledge, 1999), pp. 1-18.

Anderson, E., 'Sartre's Affective Turn: Shame as Recognition in "The Look"', *Philosophy Today* (2021).

Andrews, George, *Afro-Latin America 1800-2000* (Oxford: Oxford University Press, 2004).

Antonini R. et al., 'Flow and music performance: professional musicians and music students' views', *Psychology of Music*, 50/4 (2022), 1023-38.

Ap Aeron Jones, C., 'Appendix 2: The Eisteddfod in Chubut', in D. Rhys, *A Welsh Song in Patagonia: Memories of the Colonisation* (E.K. Vyhmeister, 2005), pp. 182-6.

Appadurai, Arjun, *The social life of things: commodities in cultural perspective* (Cambridge: Cambridge University Press, 1986).

Arwel, R., 'Welsh language project in Chubut: Annual Report 2016', British Council of Wales (2016).
Arwel, R., 'Welsh language project in Chubut: Annual Report 2017', British Council of Wales (2017).
Arwel, R., 'Welsh language project in Chubut: Annual Report 2018', British Council of Wales (2019).
Askew, Kelly, *Performing the Nation: Swahili Music and Cultural Politics in Tanzania* (Chicago: University of Chicago Press, 2002).
Austin, John, *How To Do Things with Words* (Cambridge, MA: Harvard University Press, 1962).
Avenburg, K., 'Interpellation and performance: the construction of identities through musical experience in the Virgen del Rosario Fiesta, Iruya, Argentina', *Latin American Perspectives*, 39/2 (2012), 134–49.
Baker, F. et al., 'Therapeutic Songwriting in Music Therapy, Part I: Who Are the Therapists, Who are the Clients, and Why is Songwriting Used?', *Nordic Journal of Music Therapy*, 17/2 (2008), 105–23.
Baldassar, L., 'Missing kin and longing to be together: emotions and the construction of co-presence in transnational relationships', *Journal of Intercultural Studies*, 29/3 (2008), 247–66.
Baldassar, Loretta, *Visits Home: Migration Experiences Between Italy and Australia* (Melbourne: University of Melbourne Press, 2001).
Baldock, C., 'Migrants and their parents: caregiving at a distance', *Journal of Family Issues*, 21/2 (2000), 205–24.
Barradas, G. et al., 'Emotional Reactions to Music in Dementia Patients and Healthy Controls: Differential Responding Depends on the Mechanism', *Music & Science*, 4 (2021).
Barreiro, A. et al., '"They are not truly Indigenous people": Social Representations and Prejudice against Indigenous People in Argentina', *Papers on Social Representations*, 29 (2020), 6.1–6.24.
Bartles J., 'Deserted islands for the nation: Empty land-and seascapes in three Argentine films of the Malvinas/Falkland Islands', *The Film Archipelago: Islands in Latin American Cinema*, 31 (2021).
BBC Cymru Fyw, '89,943 yn ymweld ag Eisteddfod yr Urdd 2017', 3 June 2017.
*BBC Magazine*, 'Viewpoint: the Argentines who speak Welsh – Wyn Jones' (2014).
BBC News, 'Cash boost for Patagonia Welsh project considered' (2015).
BBC News, 'Patagonia 150 years on: a "little Wales beyond Wales"', 30 May 2015.
BBC News, '150th anniversary of Welsh emigration to Patagonia', 28 July 2015.

BBC News, 'How is the Welsh language being preserved in Patagonia?', 28 July 2015.
BBC News, 'Welsh connection important boost for Patagonia's economy', 29 July 2015.
BBC News, 'Can the Welsh language survive in Patagonia?', 30 July 2015.
BBC News, 'BBC National Orchestra of Wales first for Patagonia', 22 October 2015.
BBC News, 'Welsh settlers path of friendship in Patagonia', 2 August 2016.
BBC News, 'Record number of Welsh learners in Patagonia, Argentina', 7 June 2017.
BBC Radio 4, 'Migration, Separation, and Wales' (2014).
BBC Radio Cymru, 'Gŵyl y glaniad: sgwrsio gyda rhai o ddisgynyddion y Cymry cyntaf i lanio ym Mhatagonia', 29 July 2015.
Beaume, V., 'Politics resettled: The Case of the Palestinian Diaspora in Chile', Refugees Studies Centre, University of Oxford (2019), 1-23.
Beeman, W., 'The Anthropology of Theatre and Spectacle', *Annual Review of Anthropology*, 22 (1993), 369-93.
Benei, Véronique, *Schooling Passions: Nation, History, and Language in Contemporary Western India* (California: Stanford University Press, 2008).
Benson, M., 'Living the "real" dream in la France profonde? Lifestyle migration, social distinction, and the authenticities of everyday life', *Anthropological Quarterly*, 86/2 (2013), 501-25.
Benson, Michaela, *The British in Rural France: Lifestyle Migration and the Ongoing Quest for a Better Way of Life* (Manchester: Manchester University Press, 2011).
Berg, K., 'Chubut, Argentina: a contested Welsh "first-place"', *International Journal of Heritage Studies*, 24/2 (2018), 154-66.
Bergen, J. and P. Verbeek, 'To-do is to be: Foucault, Levinas, and technologically mediated subjectivation', *Philosophy & Technology*, 34/2 (2021), 325-48.
Bianchi, R., 'The critical turn in tourism studies: A radical critique', *Tourism Geographies*, 11/4 (2009), 434-504.
Billig, Michael, *Banal Nationalism* (London: Sage Publications, 1995).
Bird-David, N., '"Animism" revisited: personhood, environment, and relational epistemology', *Current Anthropology*, 40/51 (1999), 67-91.
Bjerg, M., 'The Danes in the Argentine Pampa: the role of ethnic leaders in the creation of an ethnic community', in S. Baily and E. Miguez (eds), *Mass migration to modern Latin America* (US: Scholarly Resources Inc., 2003), pp. 147-67.

Bloch, M., 'Symbols song, dance and features of articulation: is religion an extreme form of traditional authority?', *European Journal of Sociology*, 15/1 (1974), 54-81.

Blouet, Olwyn and John Blouet, *Latin America and the Caribbean: A Systematic and Regional Survey* (US: Wiley, 2015).

Boas, T., 'The Arab Diaspora in Latin America', in B. Vinson (ed.), *Oxford Bibliographies in Latin American Studies* (New York: Oxford University Press, 2017).

Bourdieu Pierre, *Distinction: A Social Critique of the Judgement of Taste* (London: Routledge, 1984).

Bowen, E., 'The Welsh Colony in Patagonia 1865-1885: A Study in Historical Geography', *The Geographical Journal*, 132/1 (1966), 16-27.

Bradford, D. J. and E. R. Crema, 'Risk factors for the occurrence of sexual misconduct during archaeological and anthropological fieldwork', *American Anthropologist* (2022), 548-59.

Bridge, K., 'Music and Identity in Paraguay: Expressing National, Racial and Class Identity in Guitar Music Culture', *Journal of the Royal Musical Association* (2022) 1-49.

Briones C. and R. Guber, 'Argentina: contagious marginalities', in D. Poole (ed.), *A Companion to Latin American Anthropology* (Oxford: Blackwell Publishing, 2008), pp. 11-31.

British Council, 'Report on the Welsh Language Project, Patagonia 2020', British Council of Wales (2020).

Brooks, W. and G. Lublin, 'The Eisteddfod of Chubut, or How the Reinvention of Tradition has Contributed to the Preservation of a Language and Culture' (2007), *https://www.researchgate.net/publication/276204417* (accessed 27 October 2024).

Bukowski, W. and D. Raufelder, 'Peers and the self', in K. Rubin, W. Bukowski and B. Laursen (eds), *Handbook of peer interactions, relationships and groups* (New York: The Guilford Press, 2018), pp. 141-56.

Bull, M., *Sounding Out the City: Personal Stereos and the Management of Everyday Life* (Oxford: Berg, 2000).

Burrell, J., 'The field site as a network: A strategy for locating ethnographic research', *Field Methods*, 21/2 (2009), 181-99.

Burrell, Jenna, 'The fieldsite as a network: a strategy for locating ethnographic research' in L. Hjorth, H. Horst, A. Galloway and G. Bell (eds), *The Routledge companion to digital ethnography* (London: Routledge, 2017), pp. 51-60.

Butler, J., 'Performative acts and gender constitution: an essay in phenomenology and feminist theory', *Theatre Journal*, 40/4 (1988), 519-31.

Butler, J., 'Conscience doth make subjects of us all', *Yale French Studies*, 88 (1995), 626.

Butler, Judith, *Gender Trouble: Feminism and the Subversion of Identity* (New York: Routledge, 1990).

Butler, Judith, *Excitable Speech: A Politics of the Performative* (New York and London: Routledge, 1997).

Butler, Judith, *The Psychic Life of Power* (Stanford: Stanford University Press, 1997).

Butler, Judith and Gayatri Spivak, *Who Sings the Nation-State? Language, Politics, Belonging* (London, New York and Calcutta: Seagull Books, 2007).

Stafford, C., 'Be Careful What You Wish for: The Case of Happiness in China', in I. Kavedžija and H. Walker (eds), *Values of Happiness* (Chicago: Hau Books Special Issues in Ethnographic Theory Series (Volume 2), 2016), pp. 59-81.

Cabedo-Mas, A. et al., 'Uses and perceptions of music in times of COVID-19: a Spanish population survey', *Frontiers in psychology*, 11 (2021), 1-13.

Candea, M., 'Arbitrary Locations: In Defence of the Bounded Fieldsite', *The Journal of the Royal Anthropological Institute*, 13/1 (2007), 167-84.

Carnes, M., 'Machismo and gender equality in Argentina', Berkley Center for Religion, Peace, and World Affairs (2017).

Carty, J. and Y. Musharbash, 'You've Got to be Joking: Asserting the Analytical Value of Humour and Laughter in Contemporary Anthropology', *Anthropological Forum*, 18/3 (2008), 209-17.

Chamosa, O., 'Criollo and Peronist: The Argentine Folklore Movement during the First Peronism, 1943-1945', in M. Karush and O. Chamosa (eds), *The New Cultural History of Peronism: Power and Identity in Mid-Twentieth Century Argentina* (Durham and London: Duke University Press, 2010), pp. 113-142.

Chirico A. et al., 'When music flows: State and trait in musical performance, composition, and listening: A systematic review', *Frontiers in Psychology*, 6/906 (2015), 1-14.

Clifford, J., 'Introduction: Partial Truths', in J. Clifford and G. Marcus (eds), *Writing Culture: The Poetics and Politics of Ethnography* (Berkeley: University of California Press, 1986), pp. 1-26.

Cohen, G., 'A Sense of People and Place: The Chapel and Language in Sustaining Welsh Identity', in D. Bryceson, J. Okely and J. Webber (eds), *Identity and Networks: Fashioning Gender and Ethnicity across Cultures* (New York and Oxford: Berghahn Books, 2007).

Cohen, S. and E. Bodner, 'The Relationship between Flow and Music Performance Anxiety amongst Professional Classical Orchestral Musicians', *Psychology of Music*, 47/3 (2019), 420–35.

Collins, J., 'Social Reproduction in Classrooms and Schools', *Annual Review of Anthropology*, 38 (2009), 33–48.

Coronato, F., 'The First Welsh Footstep in Patagonia', *Welsh History Review*, 18/4 (1997), 639–66.

Costa-Giomi, E., 'Music Instruction and Children's Intellectual Development: The Educational Context of Music Participation', in R. MacDonald et al. (eds), *Music, Health and Wellbeing* (Oxford: Oxford University Press, 2012), pp. 339–56.

Coupland, N. and P. Garrett, 'Linguistic Landscapes, Discursive Frames and Metacultural Performance: The Case of Welsh Patagonia', *International Journal of the Sociology of Language*, 2010/205 (2010), 7–36.

Course, M., 'Why Mapuche Sing', *Journal of the Royal Anthropological Institute*, 15/2 (2009), 295–313.

Covington-Ward, Yolanda, *Gesture and Power: Religion, Nationalism and Everyday Performance in Congo* (London: Duke University Press, 2016).

Crapanzano, V., 'Hermes' Dilemma: The Masking of Subversion in Ethnographic Description', in J. Clifford and G. Marcus (eds), *Writing Culture: The Poetics and Politics of Ethnography* (Berkeley: University of California Press, 1986), pp. 51–76.

Dagfal, A., 'Psychology and Psychoanalysis in Argentina: Politics, French Thought and the University Connection 1955–1976', *History of Psychology*, 21/3 (2018), 254–72.

Daniel, O., 'Songs for ordinary people: Popular music and class in post-socialist Czech society', *Communist and Post-Communist Studies*, 55/2 (2022), 84–103.

Denardi, L., 'Ser Chino en Buenos Aires: Historia, moralidades y cambios en la diaspora China en Argentina', *Horizontes Antropologicas*, 21/43 (2015), 79–103.

DeNora, Tia, *Music in Everyday Life* (Cambridge: Cambridge University Press, 2000).

Diaz, F., 'Mindfulness, Attention, and Flow During Music Listening: An Empirical Investigation', *Psychology of Music*, 41/1 (2011), 42–58.

Dirreción Nacional de Asuntos Provinciales, 'Informe Sintético de Caracterización Socio-Productiva' (2013).

Diz, A., 'The Afterlife of Abundance: Wageless Life, Politics, and Illusion among the Guarani of the Argentine Chaco' (unpublished PhD thesis, London School of Economics, 2016).

Dolezal, L., 'Shame, vulnerability and belonging: reconsidering Sartre's account of shame', *Human Studies*, 40/3 (2017), 421–38.

Doubleday, V., 'Sounds of Power: An Overview of Musical Instruments and Gender', *Ethnomusicology Forum*, 17/1 (2008), 3–39.

Dowlen, R. et al., 'In the moment with music: an exploration of the embodied and sensory experiences of people living with dementia during improvised music-making', *Ageing & Society* (2021), 1–23.

Doxat-Pratt, S., 'Musical communities in the society of captives: Exploring the impact of music making on the social world of prison', *Musicae Scientiae*, 25/3 (2021), 290–302.

Dratsky, D. and J. Goldschmidt, 'P103 The Power of Music: Creating a Pleasurable Eating Experience for Adults with Intellectual and Developmental Disabilities', *Journal of Nutrition Education and Behavior*, 53/7 (2021), 72–3.

Ebron, P., 'Constituting Subjects through Performative Acts', in C. Cole et al. (eds), *Africa after gender?* (Bloomington and Indianapolis: Indiana University Press, 2007), pp. 171–90.

Ednie A. et al., 'Connecting protected area visitor experiences, wellness motivations, and soundscape perceptions in Chilean Patagonia', *Journal of Leisure Research*, 53/3 (2022), 377–403.

El Chubut, 'Hoy comienza el Eisteddfod Mimosa Porth Madryn 2015', 1 August 2015.

El Chubut, 'Se inauguro el Eisteddfod de la Juventud 2015', 4 September 2015.

El Chubut, 'Eisteddfod de la juventud en Gaiman', 1 September 2016.

El Chubut, 'Inauguran hoy en Gaiman el Eisteddfod de la juventud', 9 September 2016.

El Chubut, 'Comienza en Trevelin el 40 Eisteddfod', 27 April 2017.

El Chubut, 'Invitan al Eisteddfod Mimosa Porth Madryn 2017', 1 August 2017.

El Chubut, '14 edicion del Eisteddfod Mimosa Porth Madryn', 24 August 2017.

Elliott, R., 'So Transported: Nina Simone, "My Sweet Lord", and the (Un)folding of Affect', in M. Thompson and I. Biddle (eds), *Sound, Music, Affect* (London: Bloomsbury, 2013), pp. 76–90.

Elvers P., T. Fischinger and J. Steffens, 'Music Listening as Self-enhancement: Effects of Empowering Music on Momentary Explicit and Implicit Self-esteem', *Psychology of Music*, 46/3 (2018), 307–25.

Endere, M., 'Talking About Others: Archaeologists, Indigenous peoples and Heritage in Argentina', *Public Archaeology*, 4/2–3 (2005), 155–62.

Erlmann, V., 'But What of the Ethnographic Ear? Anthropology, Sound and the Senses', in V. Erlmann (ed.), *Hearing Cultures: Essays on Sound, Listening and Modernity* (New York: Berg, 2004), pp. 1-21.

Fabre, A., 'Diccionario Etnolinguistico y Guia Bibliografica de los Pueblos Indigenas Sudamericanos', http://www.ling.fi/Diccionario%20etnoling. htm (2005) (accessed 24 October 2024).

Faier, L. and L. Rofel, 'Ethnographies of encounter', *The Annual Review of Anthropology* 43 (2014), 363-77.

Fajans, J., 'Shame, Social Action and the Person Among the Baining', *Ethos*, 11/3 (1983), 166-80.

Fälton, E., 'The romantic tourist gaze on Swedish national parks: tracing ways of seeing the non-human world through representations in tourists' Instagram posts', *Tourism Recreation Research* (2021), 1-24.

Farndon, H., 'HCPC registered psychoanalysts in the UK', The British Psychological Society (2016).

Feld, S., 'Aesthetics as Iconicity of Style, or "Lift-up-over-sounding": Getting into the Kaluli Groove', *Yearbook for Traditional Music*, 20 (1988), 74-113.

Feld, S. and D. Brennis, 'Doing Anthropology in Sound', *American Ethnologist*, 31/4 (2004), 461-74.

Fetterman, David, *Ethnography: Step-by-Step* (London: Sage Publications, 1998).

Fierro C., J. Álvarez and G. Manzo, 'A Century of Psychotherapy in Argentina: Clinical Psychology, Psychoanalysis and Recent Developments', *Revista de Psicologia*, 27/2 (2018), 1-27.

Flood, L., 'Instrument in Tow: Bringing Musical Skills to the Field', *Ethnomusicology*, 61/3 (2017), 486-505.

Foley, D., 'The Rise of Class Culture Theory in Educational Anthropology', *Anthropology and Education Quarterly*, 41/3 (2010), 215-27.

Foucault, Michel, *The History of Sexuality, Vol. 1* (New York: Vintage, 1981).

Foucault, Michel, *The Care of the Self: The History of Sexuality, Vol. 3* (London: Penguin Books, 1984).

Foucault, Michel, *The Use of Pleasure: The History of Sexuality, Vol. 2* (London: Penguin Books, 1984).

Foucault, M., 'Sexual Discourse and Power', in *Culture and Society: Contemporary Debates* (Cambridge: Cambridge University Press, 1990), pp. 199-204.

Foucault, M., 'Governmentality', in G. Burchell, C. Gordon and P. Miller (eds), *The Foucault Effect: Studies in Governmentality* (Chicago: University of Chicago Press, 1991), pp. 87-104.

Fox, Aaron, *Real Country: Music and Language in Working Class Culture* (Durham and London: Duke University Press, 2004).

Funder, M., 'Bias, Intimacy and Power in Qualitative Fieldwork Strategies', *The Journal of Transdisciplinary Environmental Studies*, 4/1 (2005), 1–9.

Gabbard, Glen, *Psychoanalysis and film* (London: Routledge, 2018).

Gallop, J., 'Lacan's "Mirror Stage": Where to Begin', *SubStance*, 11/4 (1983), 118–28.

Garrett, P. et al., 'Diasporic ethnolinguistic subjectivities: Patagonia, North America and Wales', *International Journal of the Sociology of Language*, 195 (2009), 173–200.

Geiger, J., 'Virtual travels and the tourist gaze', in *American Documentary Film: Projecting the Nation* (Edinburgh: Edinburgh University Press, 2011), pp. 40–61.

Gell, Alfred, *Art and Agency: An Anthropological Theory* (Oxford: Clarendon Press, 1998).

Gibbard, G., 'Gwenan in Patagonia 2015', interview with Wales Arts International (May 2015).

Gibson, C., 'Critical tourism studies: new directions for volatile times', *Tourism Geographies*, 3/4 (2021), 659–77.

Giovannetti F. et al., 'Psychological science in Argentina: current state & future directions', *Discover Psychology*, 2/1 (2022), 1–7.

Gobierno Chubut, *Introducción de la Secretaría de Ciencia, Tecnología e Innovación Productiva Del Chubut* (Rawson: Gobierno Chubut, 2015).

Goffman, Erving, *The Presentation of Self in Everyday Life* (Edinburgh: University of Edinburgh, 1956).

Gold, Ed, *Patagonia: Byd Arall; Otro Mundo; Another World* (Llandysul: Gwasg Gomer, 2012).

Goldstein, Donna, *Laughter Out of Place: Race, Class, Violence, and Sexuality in a Rio Shantytown* (London: University of California Press, 2013).

*Golwg 360*, 'Cynnal Gŵyl y Glaniad ym Mhorth Madryn', 28 July 2015.

Gordillo, G. and S. Hirsch, 'Indigenous struggles and contested identities in Argentina: histories of invisibilization and reemergence', *The Journal of Latin American Anthropology*, 8/3 (2003), 4–30.

Gorofolo, L., 'The Shape of a Diaspora: The Movement of Afro-Iberians to Colonial Spanish America', in S. Bryant, R. S. O'Toole and B. Vinson III (eds), *Africans to Spanish America: Expanding the Diaspora* (Chicago: University of Illinois Press, 2012), pp. 27–49.

Graeber, D., 'It is Value that Brings Universes into Being', *HAU: Journal of Ethnographic Theory*, 3/2 (2013), 219–43.

Graeber, David, *Toward an Anthropological Theory of Value: The False Coin of Our Own Dreams* (New York: Palgrave, 2001).

Grasseni, C., 'Skilled Vision: on Apprenticeship in Breeding Aesthetics', *Social Anthropology*, 12/1 (2004), 41–55.

Griffiths, H., 'Flooding, Draught and Adaptation in the Hydrographic Society of Welsh Patagonia', lecture delivered at the National Eisteddfod of Llanelli (2014).

Griffiths, René, *Ramblings of a Patagonian* (Cardiff: Artisan Media Publishing, 2014).

Guano, E., 'A Colour for the Modern Nation: The Discourse on Class, Race, and Education in the Porteno Middle Class', *The Journal of Latin American Anthropology*, 8/1 (2003), 148–71.

Guillemin, M and L. Gillam, 'Ethics, reflexivity, and "ethically important moments" in research', *Qualitative Inquiry*, 10/2 (2004), 261–80.

Guneratne, A., 'Shaping the Tourist's Gaze: Representing Ethnic Difference in a Nepali Village', *The Journal of the Royal Anthropological Institute*, 7/3 (2001), 527–43.

Hackert, B. A. et al., 'Towards a reconceptualization of flow in social contexts', *Journal of Theory of Social Behaviour*, 53 (2023), 100–25.

Harasym, S., *Levinas and Lacan: The Missed Encounter* (Albany: State University of New York Press, 1998).

Harmat L., O. de Manzano and F. Ullen, 'Flow in music and arts', *Advances in Flow Research* (2021), 377–91.

Harpaz, G. and T. Vaizman, 'Music self-efficacy, self-esteem, and help-seeking orientation among amateur musicians who use online music tutorials', *Psychology of Aesthetics, Creativity, and the Arts* (2021), 17/5 (2023), 598–607.

Harris, M., 'Peasants on the Floodplain: Some Elements of the "Agrarian Question" in Riverine Amazonia', in S. Nugent and M. Harris (eds), *Some other Amazonians: Perspectives on Modern Amazonia* (London: Institute for the Study of the Americas, 2004), pp. 81–103.

Hawkins, S., *Queerness in pop music: Aesthetics, gender norms, and temporality* (London: Routledge, 2015).

Hirschkind, C., 'Hearing Modernity: Egypt, Islam, and the Pious Ear', in V. Erlmann (ed.), *Hearing Cultures: Essays on Sound, Listening and Modernity* (New York: Berg, 2004), pp. 131–51.

Hirschkind, C., 'The Ethics of Listening: Cassette-Sermon Audition in Contemporary Egypt', *American Ethnologist*, 28/3 (2001), 623–49.

Hobsbawm, Eric, 'Introduction: Inventing Traditions', in E. Hobsbawm and T. Ranger (eds), *The Invention of Tradition* (Cambridge: Cambridge University Press, 1983), pp. 1–14.

Hofman, A., 'The Affective turn in Ethnomusicology', *Muzikologija*, 18 (2015), 35–55.

Hooker, J., 'Indigenous Inclusion/Black Exclusion: Rage, Ethnicity and Multicultural Citizenship in Latin America', *Journal of Latin American Studies*, 37 (2005), 285-310.

Hu-DeHart, E. and López, K., 'Asian Diasporas in Latin America and the Caribbean: An Historical Overview', *Afro-Hispanic Review*, 27/1 (2008), 9-21.

INDEC, 'Censo Nacional de Población, Hogares y Viviendas 2010' (Buenos Aires: Instituto Nacional de Estadistica y Censos, 2012).

INDEC, 'Censo Nacional de Poblacion, Hogares y Viviendas 2022' (Buenos Aires: Instituto Nacional de Estadistica y Censos, 2023).

Ingold, T., *The Perception of the Environment: Essays on Livelihood, Dwelling, and Skill* (London: Routledge, 2000).

Ingold, Timothy, *Being Alive: Essays on Movement, Knowledge and Description* (London: Routledge, 2011).

Jääskeläinen, T., '"Music is my life": Examining the connections between music students' workload experiences in higher education and meaningful engagement in music', *Research Studies in Music Education* (2022), 1-21.

James, Deborah, *Songs of the Women Migrants: Performance and Identity in South Africa* (Edinburgh: Edinburgh University Press, 1999).

Jarman, F., 'Relax, Feel Good, Chill Out: The Affective Distribution of Classical Music', in M. Thompson and I. Biddle (eds), *Sound, Music, Affect: Theorising Sonic Experience* (London: Bloomsbury, 2013), pp. 183-204.

Jassal, Smita, *Unearthing Gender: Folksongs of North India* (Durham and London: Duke University Press, 2012).

Jock, W. et al., 'Differential Client Perspectives on Therapy in Argentina and the United States: A Cross-Cultural study', *Psychotherapy*, 50/4 (2013), 517-24.

Johnson, I., 'Revitalising Welsh in the Chubut Province, Argentina: The Role of the Welsh Language Project', in M. Newton (ed.), *Celts in the Americas* (Nova Scotia: Cape Breton University Press, 2013), pp. 144-58.

Johnston, A. and A. Lawson, 'Settler colonies', in *A Companion to Postcolonial Studies* (US: Blackwell Publishing Ltd, 2005), pp. 360-76.

Jones, Kathryn, Carol Tully and Heather Williams, *Hidden Texts, Hidden Nations: (Re)discoveries of Wales in Travel Writing in French and German (1780-2018)* (Liverpool: Liverpool University Press, 2020).

Kaaristo, M., 'Everyday power dynamics and hierarchies in qualitative research: The role of humour in the field', *Qualitative Research*, 22/5 (2022), 743-60.

Kaltefleiter, C. and K. Alexander, 'Self-care and community: Black girls saving themselves', in A. Halliday, *The Black Girlhood Studies Collection* (Toronto: Women's Press, 2019), pp. 191–208.

Kang, S., 'An Exploratory Study of Music Teachers' Flow Experiences between Performing and Teaching Music', *Journal of Research in Music Education* (2022), 162–79.

Kapchan, D., 'Performance', *The Journal of American Folklore*, 108/430 (1995), 479–508.

Karush, M., 'Populism, Melodrama, and the Market: The Mass Cultural Origins of Peronism', in M. Karush and O. Chamosa (eds), *The New Cultural History of Peronism: Power and Identity in Mid-Twentieth Century Argentina* (Durham and London: Duke University Press, 2010), pp. 21–51.

Kassabian, A., 'Music for Sleeping', in M. Thompson and I. Biddle (eds), *Sound, Music, Affect: Theorising Sonic Experience* (London: Bloomsbury, 2013), pp. 165–81.

Keane, Webb, *Signs of Recognition: Power and Hazards of Representation in an Indonesian Society* (Berkeley: University of California Press, 1997).

Kiff, G., 'Welsh language project annual report 2013, British Council of Wales (2013).

Kiff, G., 'Welsh language project annual report 2015', British Council of Wales (2014).

Klyve, G. and R. Rolvsjord, 'Moments of fun: Narratives of children's experiences of music therapy in mental health care', *Nordic Journal of Music Therapy* (2022), 1–21.

Koc, V. and G. Kafa, 'Cross-cultural Research on Psychotherapy: The Need for Change', *Journal of Cross-Cultural Psychology*, 50/1 (2019), 100–15.

Konig, V. et al., 'Psychotherapists' experiences of telepsychotherapy during the COVID-19 pandemic in Argentina: Impact on therapeutic relationship and burden', *Research in Psychotherapy: Psychopathology, Process, and Outcome*, 26/632 (2023).

Korstanje, E., 'Passage from the Tourist Gaze to the Wicked Gaze: A case study on COVID-19 with special reference to Argentina', *International case studies in the management of disasters* (2020), 197–211.

Koskela, M., 'Middle-class Music Making? Social Class, "Race", and their Intersections in the Practice of School Popular Music', *International Journal of Education & the Arts*, 23/7 (2022), 1–18.

Kulkarni, K., '"Like a Cosmic, Invisible Umbilical Cord" Soul Summit and the Haptic Arrangements of Black Social Life', *Journal of Popular Music Studies*, 33/4 (2021), 171-202.

Lacan, J., 'The Mirror Stage as Formative of the "I" Function as Revealed in Psychoanalytic Experience', *Écrits* (1966), 93–101.

Lakoff, A., 'The Lacan Ward: Pharmacology and Subjectivity in Buenos Aires', *Social Analysis: The International Journal of Social and Cultural Practice*, 47/2 (2003), 82–101.

Lashua, B., K. Sprachlen and P. Long, 'Introduction to the special issue: music and tourism', *Tourism Studies*, 14/1 (2014), 3–9.

Laukka, P., 'Uses of Music and Psychological Well-Being Among the Elderly', *Journal of Happiness Studies*, 8 (2007), 215–41.

Lenton, D., 'The Malon de la Paz of 1946: Indigenous Descamisados at the Dawn of Peronism', in M. Karush and O. Chamosa (eds), *The New Cultural History of Peronism: Power and Identity in Mid-Twentieth Century Argentina* (Durham and London: Duke University Press, 2010), pp. 85–111.

Levinas, Emmanuel, *Ethics and Infinity* (Pittsburgh: Duquesne University Press, 1982).

Lewis, Daniel, *History of Argentina* (Westport: Greenwood Publishing Group, 2001).

Lowell Lewis, J., 'Toward a Unified Theory of Cultural Performance: A "Reconstructive Introduction" to Victor Turner', in G. St John (ed.), *Victor Turner and Contemporary Cultural Performance* (New York: Berghahn Books, 2008), pp. 41–58.

Lowell Lewis, J., *The Anthropology of Cultural Performance* (New York: Palgrave Macmillan, 2013).

Lichterman, P., 'Interpretive reflexivity in ethnography', *Ethnography*, 18/1 (2017), 35–45.

Loepthien, T. and B. Leipold, 'Flow in music performance and music-listening: Differences in intensity, predictors, and the relationship between flow and subjective well-being', *Psychology of Music*, 50/1 (2022), 111–26.

Lublin, G., 'The War of the Tea-houses, or How Welsh Heritage in Patagonia Became a Valuable Commodity', *Journal of Interdisciplinary Celtic Studies*, 1/3 (2009), 69–92.

Lublin, G., 'Adjusting the focus: looking at Patagonia and the wider Argentine state through the lens of settler colonial theory', *Settler Colonial Studies*, 11/3 (2021), 386–409.

Lublin, Geraldine, *Memoir and Identity in Welsh Patagonia: Voices from a Settler Community in Argentina* (Cardiff: University of Wales Press, 2017).

MacDonald, R., 'Music, Health, and Well-being: A Review', *International Journal of Qualitative Studies in Health and Well-being* (2013), 1–13.

McClary Susan, *Feminine Endings: Music, Gender and Sexuality* (London: University of Minnesota Press, 1991).

McDermott, O. et al., 'The importance of music for people with dementia: the perspectives of people with dementia, family carers, staff and music therapists', *Aging & Mental Health*, 18/6 (2014), 706-16.

McDonald, Meinir, *Bant i Batagonia* (Aberystwyth: Canolfan Astudiaethau Addysg, 2001).

McFerran, K. and M. Hunt, 'Music, adversity and flourishing: Exploring experiences of a community music therapy group for Australian youth', *British Journal of Music Therapy*, 36/1 (2022), 37-47.

Mallimaci, F., 'What do Argentine People Believe in? Religion and Social Structure in Argentina', *Social Compass*, 62/2 (2015), 255-77.

Manning, P., 'English Money and Welsh Rocks: Divisions of Language and Divisions of Labour in Nineteenth-century Welsh Slate Quarries', *Comparative Studies in Society and History*, 44/3 (2002), 481-510.

Manning, P., 'Owning and Belonging: A Semiotic Investigation of the Affective Categories of a Bourgeois Society', *Comparative Studies in Society and History*, 46/2 (2004), 300-25.

Manning, P., 'The Streets of Bethesda: The Slate Quarrier and the Welsh Language in the Welsh Liberal Imagination', *Language in Society*, 33/4 (2004), 517-48.

Maulyda, M. and M. Erfan, 'Do Social Interactions with Peers Affect Student Identity?', *Qalam: Jurnal Ilmu Kependidikan*, 9/2 (2020), 60-5.

Merlino, S. et al., 'Walking through the city soundscape: an audio-visual analysis of sensory experience for people with psychosis', *Visual Communication*, 22/1 (2023), 71-95.

Messier, P., 'Cameras at Work: Dusty Lenses and Processed Videos in the Quarries of Hyderabad', *Visual Anthropology*, 32/3-4 (2019), 287-308.

Metz, Christian, *The imaginary signifier: Psychoanalysis and the cinema* (Bloomington and Indianapolis: Indiana University Press, 1982).

Mills, Janet, *Music in the School* (Oxford: Oxford University Press, 2005).

Ministerio de Educación Gobierno del Chubut, '30 de Abril: Día de la conmemoración del plebiscite del Valle 16 de Octubre 1902' (Centro Provincial de Informatión Educativa, 2019).

Moaz, D., 'The mutual gaze', *Annual of Tourism Research*, 33/1 (2005), 221-39.

Moore, G. et al., 'School, peer and family relationships and adolescent substance use, subjective wellbeing and mental health symptoms in Wales: A cross sectional study', *Child indicators research*, 11/6 (2018), 1951-65.

Moreno, E., 'Rape in the Field: Reflections from a Survivor', in D. Kulick and M. Willson (eds), *Taboo: Sex, Identity, and Erotic Subjectivity in Anthropological Fieldwork* (London: Routledge, 1995), pp. 219-50.

Morgan, Elizabeth, *Ticket to Paradise* (Cardiff: Opening Chapter, 2013).

Morgan, K., 'Welsh Nationalism: The Historical Background', *Journey of Contemporary History*, 6/1 (1971), 152-72.

Morgan, Michael, *The Cambridge Introduction to Emmanuel Levinas* (New York: Cambridge University Press, 2011).

Morreall, John, *The Philosophy of Laughter and Humour* (Albany: State University of New York Press, 1987).

Mowitt, J., '(I Can't Get No) Affect', in M. Thompson and I. Biddle (eds), *Sound, Music, Affect: Theorising Sonic Experience* (London: Bloomsbury, 2013), pp. 91-100.

Mulvey, L., 'Visual Pleasure and Narrative Cinema', in *Visual and Other Pleasures* (London: Macmillan Press, 1989), pp. 14-18.

Nouzeilles, Gabriela and Graciela Montaldo (eds), *The Argentina Reader: History, Culture, Politics* (Durham: Duke University Press, 2002).

Novoa, M., 'Gendered nostalgia: grassroots heritage tourism and (de) industrialization in Lota, Chile', *Journal of Heritage Tourism* (2021), 1-19.

Nugent, S., '(Some) Other Amazonians: Jewish Communities in the Lower Amazon', in S. Nugent and M. Harris (eds), *Some Other Amazonians: Perspectives on Modern Amazonia* (London: Institute for the Study of the Americas, 2004), pp. 104-17.

O'Connor, S. et al., 'Ideology, ritual performance and its manifestations in the rock art of Timor-Leste and Kisar Island, Island Southeast Asia', *Cambridge Archaeological Journal*, 28/2 (2018), 225-41.

Ortner, S., 'Subjectivity and Cultural Critique', *Anthropological Theory*, 5/1 (2005), 31-52.

Parry, Tom, *Yr Eisteddfod/The Eisteddfod* (Liverpool: National Eisteddfod Court, 1956).

Pavlicevic, Mercedes and Gary Ansdell, *Community Music Therapy* (London: Jessica Kingsley, 2004).

Pedelty, M., 'Teaching Anthropology through Performance', *Anthropology and Education Quarterly*, 32/2 (2001), 244-53.

Pelkmans, Mathijs, *Fragile Conviction: Changing Ideological Landscapes in Urban Kyrgyzstan* (USA: Cornell University Press, 2017).

Perkins, H. and D. Thorns, 'Gazing or performing? Reflecting on Urry's Tourist Gaze in the Context of Contemporary Experience in the Antipodes', *International Sociology*, 16/2 (2001), 185-204.

Perry, R., 'Argentina and Chile: The Struggle for Patagonia 1843-1881', *The Americas*, 36/3 (1980), 347-63.

Pink, S., 'The Future of Sensory Anthropology/The Anthropology of the Senses', *Social Anthropology*, 18/3 (2010), 331–40.

Price, K., 'What was the Velindre Patagonia Trek really like? This trekker's diary gets to heart of gruelling challenge', 11 December 2015.

Prichard, Hesketh, *Through the Heart of Patagonia* (Thomas Nelson, 1911).

Prins, H., 'The Welsh in Patagonia: The State and The Ethnic Community', *The Latin American Anthropology Review*, 5/1 (1993), 29–30.

Proctor, F., 'African Diasporic Ethnicity in Mexico City to 1650', in S. Bryant, R. S. O'Toole and B. Vinson III (eds), *Africans to Spanish America: Expanding the Diaspora* (Chicago: University of Illinois Press, 2012), pp. 50–72.

Rabinow, Paul, *Reflections on Fieldwork in Morocco* (California: University of California Press, 1977).

Restuccia, Frances, *The Blue Box: Kristevan/Lacanian Readings of Contemporary Cinema* (London: Continuum, 2012).

Rice, T., 'Soundselves: An Acoustemology of Sound and Self in the Edinburgh Royal Infirmary', *Anthropology Today*, 19/4 (2003), 4–9.

Richards, P., 'Of Indians and Terrorists: How the State and Local Elites Construct the Mapuche in Neoliberal Multicultural Chile', *Journal of Latin American Studies*, 42/1 (2010), 59–90.

Rollason, Will, *We Are Playing Football: Sport and Postcolonial Subjectivity: Panapompom, Papua New Guinea* (Newcastle upon Tyne: Cambridge Scholars Publishing, 2011).

Rosaldo, M., 'The Shame of Headhunters and the Autonomy of Self', *Ethos*, 11/3 (1983), 135–51.

Rosello, Mirielle, *France and the Maghreb: Performative Encounters* (USA: University Press of Florida, 2005).

Ross, David, *Wales: History of a Nation* (Scotland: Geddes and Grosset, 2008).

Rubenstein, S., 'On the Importance of Visions Among the Amazonian Shuar', *Current Anthropology*, 53/1 (2012), 39–79.

Ruby, J., 'The last 20 years of Visual Anthropology – A Critical Review', *Visual Studies*, 20/2 (2005), 159–70.

Salazar, Noel and Nelson Graburn, *Tourism Imaginaries, Anthropological Approaches* (New York: Berghahn Books, 2010).

Samuels, D. et al., 'Soundscapes: Toward a Sounded Anthropology', *Annual Review of Anthropology*, 39 (2010), 329–45.

Santos, P., 'The imagined nation: The mystery of the endurance of the colonial imaginary in postcolonial times', in N. Salazar and N. Graburn (eds), *Tourism Imaginaries, Anthropological Approaches* (New York: Berghahn Books, 2010).

Sartre, Jean-Paul, *Being and Nothingness* (London: Methuen and Co. Ltd, 1958).
Schenider, Arnd, *Expanded Visions: A New Anthropology of the Moving Image* (London: Routledge, 2022).
Schindler, L. and H. Schäfer, 'Practices of writing in ethnographic work', *Journal of Contemporary Ethnography*, 50/1 (2021), 11–32.
Schulkind, M. D., 'Is memory for music special?', *Annals of the New York Academy of Science*, 1169/1 (2009), 216–24.
Seeger, Anthony, *Why Suyá Sing: A Musical Anthropology of an Amazonian People* (Urbana and Chicago: University of Illinois Press, 2004).
Siddall, Gillian and Ellen Waterman, *Negotiated moments: improvisation, sound, and subjectivity* (North Carolina: Duke University Press, 2016).
Silverman, Kaja, *The Acoustic Mirror: The Female Voice in Psychoanalysis and Cinema* (Bloomington: Indiana University Press, 1988).
Silverman, Michael, *Music therapy in mental health for illness management and recovery* (Oxford: Oxford University Press, 2022).
Sinnamon, S., A. Moran and M. O'Connell, 'Flow among musicians: measuring peak experiences of student performances', *Journal of Research in Music Education*, 60/1 (2012), 6–25.
St John, G., 'Victor Turner and Contemporary Cultural Performance: An Introduction', in G. St John (ed.), *Victor Turner and Contemporary Cultural Performance* (New York: Berghahn Books, 2008), pp. 1–40.
Stagnaro, J., 'The Current State of Psychiatric and Mental Healthcare in Argentina', *BJPsych Advances*, 22 (2016), 260–2.
Stone, L. and G. Nyaupane, 'The tourist gaze: Domestic versus international tourists', *Journal of Travel Research*, 58/5 (2019), 877–91.
Strathern, Marilyn, *The Gender of the Gift: Problems with Women and Problems with Society in Melanesia* (Berkeley: University of California Press, 1988).
Tang, Q. et al., 'Effects of music therapy on depression: A meta-analysis of randomized controlled trials', *PloS one*, 15/11 (2020), 1–23.
Taylor, Charles, *A Secular Age* (Cambridge, MA: The Belknap Press of Harvard University Press, 2007).
Taylor, L., 'Decolonising International Relations: Perspectives from Latin America', *International Studies Review*, 14 (2012), 386–400.
Taylor, L., 'Decolonising Citizenship: Reflections on the Coloniality of Power in Argentina', *Citizenship Studies*, 17/5 (2013), 596–610.
Taylor, L., 'Colonial Encounters at the Margins: The Welsh/Tehuelche in Patagonia', *Conceptualising IR from the margins: historically, geographically and beyond*, Buenos Aires (2014).

Taylor, L., 'Lifting the Veil of Kindness: "Friendship" and Settler Colonialism in Argentina's Welsh Patagonia', LSE Latin American and Caribbean blog (2017).
*The Guardian*, 'Wrestling and rock at Eisteddfod', 5 August 1985, 3.
*The Guardian*, 'In praise of ... the national Eisteddfod', 8 August 2008.
*The Magazine of Music*, 'The Eisteddfod', 3/31 (1886), 127.
*The Musical Herald*, 'The Eisteddfod', 1 October, 631 (1890), 296-9.
*The Musical Herald*, 'The Eisteddfod', 1 October, 535 (1892), 296-7.
*The Musical Herald*, 'The National Eisteddfod', 1 September, 810 (1915), 403.
*The Musical World*, 'The Welsh National Eisteddfod', 2 January, 47/1 (1869), 10.
*The Musical World*, 'The Eisteddfod', 7 September, 50/35 (1872), 559.
*The Musical World*, 'Wrexham National Eisteddfod', 26 August, 54/35 (1876), 582-3.
*The Saturday Review of Politics, Literature, Science and Art*, 'The Eisteddfod', 24/620 (1867), 341-2.
Thompson, M. and I. Biddle, 'Somewhere between the Signifying and the Sublime', in M. Thompson and I. Biddle (eds), *Sound Music Affect: Theorising Sonic Experience* (Bloomsbury: London, 2013), pp. 2-24.
Thornicroft, G., 'Improving access to psychological therapies in England', *The Lancet*, 391 (2018), 636-7.
Tomos, Morgan, *Alun yr Arth ym Mhatagonia* (Ceredigion: Y Lolfa, 2013).
Townsend, R. and C. Cushion, 'Put that in your fucking research: Reflexivity, ethnography, and disability sport coaching', *Qualitative Research*, 21/2 (2021), 251-67.
Trosset, C., 'Triangulation and confirmation in the study of Welsh concepts of personhood', *Journal of Anthropological Research*, 57/1 (2001), 61-81.
Trosset, Carol, *Welshness Performed: Welsh Concepts of Person and Society* (Tuscon: University of Arizona Press, 1993).
Turino, T., *Music as Social Life: The Politics of Participation* (Chicago: University of Chicago Press, 2008).
Turner, Victor, *The Anthropology of Performance* (New York: PAJ Publications, 1987).
United Nations, 'Reports of international arbitral awards: the Cordillera of the Andes Boundary Case (Argentina, Chile)', 20 November 1902 (2006).
Urry, J., 'Globalising the Tourist Gaze', Department of Sociology, Lancaster University (2001), 1-9.
Urry, John, *The Tourist Gaze* (London: Sage Publications, 1990).
Urry, John, *The Tourist Gaze: Second Edition* (London: Sage Publications, 2002).

Vaillancourt, G. et al., 'An intergenerational singing group: A community music therapy qualitative research project and graduate student mentoring initiative', *Voices: A World Forum for Music Therapy*, 18/1 (2018), 1–17.

van Rooyen, A. and dos Santos, A., 'Exploring the Lived Experiences of Teenagers in a Children's Home Participating in a Choir: A Community Music Therapy Perspective', *International Journal of Community Music*, 13/1 (2020), 81–101.

Vassallo, M., 'Mobilising the masses through music and songs: the global phenomenon of music and politics', in M. Vassallo and A. DeBattista (eds), *The Different Faces of Politics: A Handbook of Political Thought and Artistic Expression* (Oxford: Routledge, 2024).

Veracini, L., 'Settler Colonialism: Career of a Concept', *The Journal of Imperial and Commonwealth History*, 41/2 (2013), 313–33.

Violinsky, N., 'Standing Up: Violin Performance Technique and Ethnic Resurgence in Saraguro, Ecuador', *Visual Anthropology*, 16/2–3 (2010), 315–40.

Volkman, T., 'Visions and Revisions: Taraja Culture and the Tourist Gaze', *American Ethnologist*, 17/1 (1990), 91–110.

Vom Hau, M. and G. Wilde, '"We Have Always Lived Here": Indigenous Movements, Citizenship and Poverty in Argentina', *The Journal of Development Studies*, 46/7 (2010), 1283–303.

Wade, P., 'Rethinking Mestizaje: Ideology and Lived Experience', *Journal of Latin American Studies*, 37/2 (2005), 239–57.

Wade, P., 'Skin colour and race as analytic concepts', *Ethnic and Racial Studies*, 35/7 (2012), 1169–73.

Wade, P., 'Blackness, Indigeneity, Multiculturalism and Genomics in Brazil, Colombia and Mexico', *Journal of Latin American Studies*, 45/2 (2013), 205–33.

Wade, Peter, *Race and Ethnicity in Latin America* (London: Pluto Press, 1997).

Waitt, G. and M. Duffy, 'Listening and Tourism studies', *Annals of Tourism Research*, 37/2 (2009), 457–77.

Walker, H., 'State of Play: The Political Ontology of Sport in Amazonian Peru', *American Ethnologist*, 40/2 (2013), 382–8.

Walker, H. and I. Kavedžija, 'Introduction: Values of Happiness', in I. Kavedžija and H. Walker (eds), *Values of Happiness* (Chicago: Hau Books Special Issues in Ethnographic Theory Series (Volume 2), 2016), pp. 1–28.

Walsh, M. et al., 'The social media tourist gaze: social media photography and its disruption at the zoo', *Information Technology & Tourism*, 21/3 (2019), 391–412.

Warren, Carol and Jennifer Hackney, *Gender Issues in Ethnography* (UK: Sage Publications, 2011).

Warren, S., 'A Nation Divided: Building the Cross-Border Mapuche Nation in Chile and Argentina', *Journal of Latin American Studies*, 45/2 (2013), 235–64.

Weidman, A., 'Anthropology and Voice', *Annual Review of Anthropology*, 43 (2014), 37–51.

Welsh Government, 'Cymraeg 2050: A Million Welsh speakers: Action Plan 2019-20' (Cardiff: Welsh Government, 2019).

Welsh Government, 'Cymraeg 2050: Work Programme 2021 to 2026' (2021), https://www.gov.wales/cymraeg-2050-work-programme-2021-2026-html (accessed 27 October 2024).

Welsh Government, 'Welsh Language Data from the Annual Population Survey: July 2022 to June 2023' (2023), https://www.gov.wales/welsh-language-data-annual-population-survey-july-2022-june-2023#:~:text=For%20the%20year%20ending%2030,to%20around%209%2C800%20fewer%20people (accessed 27 October 2024).

White, R., 'Foucault on the Care of the Self as an Ethical Project and a Spiritual Goal', *Human Studies*, 37/4 (2014), 489–504.

Whitfield, E., 'Welsh Patagonian Fiction: Language and the Novel of Transnational Ethnicity', *Diaspora*, 14/2 (2005), 333–48.

Whitfield, E., 'Empire, Nation and the Fate of a Language: Patagonia in Argentine and Welsh Literature', *Postcolonial Studies*, 14/1 (2014), 75–93.

Wilkinson, Susan, *Mimosa's Voyages: Official Logs, Crew Lists and Masters* (Ceredigion: Y Lolfa, 2007).

William, Rhys, *A Welsh Song in Patagonia: Memories of the Welsh Colonisation* (E.K. Vyhmeister, 2005).

Williams, Bryn, *Cymry Patagonia* (Clwb Llyfrau Cymreig, 1942).

Williams, Bryn, *Straeon Patagonia* (Gwasg y Dydd, 1946).

Williams, Bryn, *Gwladfa Patagonia* (Caerdydd: Gwasg Prifysgol Cymru, 1965).

Williams, Cathrin, *Haul ac Awyr Las* (Dinbych: Gwasg Gee, 1993).

Williams, F., 'Dŵr a Phŵer yn Nyffryn Camwy: heriau a gwrthdaro ynghylch sefydlu a rheoli system ddyfrhau', *Gwerddon*, 36 (2023), 1–27, https://doi.org/10.61257/MOPO4816.

Williams, G., 'Welsh Settlers and Native Americans in Patagonia', *Journal of Latin American Studies*, 11/1 (1979), 41–66.

Williams, G., 'La construcción del pasado chubutense en el discurso histórico provincial: representaciones de la experiencia exploratoria y colonizadora española en Chubut, Argentina, en textos escolares provinciales (1978–2006)', *Historia de Histografía* (2016).

Williams, G., 'Darllen ac ysgrifennu gorffennol y Wladfa: dadleuon am hanes a chof yn ymsefydliad Cymreig Chubut', *Gwerddon*, 36 (2023), 28–48, https://doi.org/10.61257/GIST9419.

Williams, Glyn, *The Desert and the Dream: A Study of Welsh Colonisation in Chubut 1815–1915* (Cardiff: University of Wales Press, 1975).

Williams, Glyn, *The Welsh in Patagonia: The State and the Ethnic Community* (Cardiff: University of Wales Press, 1991).

Winkler-Reid, S., 'Looking Good and Good Looking in School: Beauty Ideals, Appearance, and Enskilled Vision Among Girls in a London Secondary School', *Anthropology and Education Quarterly*, 48/3 (2017), 284–300.

Yoshida, M., 'Joking, gender, power, and professionalism among Japanese inn workers', *Ethnology* (2001), 361–9.

Zhang, L., 'Cultivating the Therapeutic Self in China', *Medical Anthropology*, 37/1 (2018), 45–58.

Zhihong, B., 'Ethnic Identities Under the Tourist Gaze', *Asian Ethnicity*, 8/3 (2007), 245–59.

Zigon, J., 'Moral Breakdown and the Ethical Demand: A Theoretical Framework for an Anthropology of Moralities', *Anthropological Theory*, 7/2 (2007), pp. 131–50.

Zigon, J., 'An Ethics of Dwelling', in *Disappointment* (New York: Fordham University Press, 2017), pp. 102–28.

# Index

## A
Aberystwyth 1-3, 48, 51, 62, 92, 98, 100
Accessibility 54, 79, 82-3, 155, 176-7
Affect theory 11, 182-3
Agency 75, 85, 90, 112-13, 119, 131, 182, 192, 195
  *see also* Gell, Alfred
Althusser, Louis 12-13, 32, 69-70, 83-4, 152, 180
  *see also* interpellation
Amazonia 26, 139, 141, 159
Andes 5, 18, 30, 40-1, 61, 66, 92, 128, 139
Araucanization 39
Argentine Ministry of Tourism and Sports 38

## B
BBC National Orchestra of Wales 87-8, 91, 93-5, 102-5, 115
Belonging 14, 52, 73-7, 82-3, 96, 105, 108, 146, 159, 165-6, 181, 194
  *see also* identity
Bolivia/Bolivians 36, 38
Bourdieu, Pierre 183
British Council 34, 40, 122
Buenos Aires 23, 41, 44, 66
Butler, Judith 56-7, 70, 96-7, 112-13, 130-1, 155, 190
  *see also* gender

## C
Canada 32
Capel Bethel 42, 71, 107, 117, 123, 187
Cardiff 6, 51, 70, 90, 124, 125, 132, 133
Cardiff University 67
Casa de Cultura 13, 41, 120, 132
Catholicism 21, 32, 43
Chinese/China 36, 38, 44-5, 169

Choele-Choel 32
Chubut Eisteddfod 48, 50, 61-2, 65-6, 75, 78, 81, 127
Chubut Eisteddfod Association 61
Chubut Province 4-6, 32-5, 38-9, 40-1, 90-1, 176
Chubut River 30-3
Chubut Valley 22, 34
Columbus Day 39
Comodoro 40, 110
Conquest of the Desert 26-30, 35, 46
  *see also* historical narrative
Covid-19 40-1, 82
Covington-Ward, Yolanda 13, 52, 129
  *see also* performative encounters
Cultural independence 21-3, 32-4
Cultural performance 54-7, 87-90, 99-102

## D
Day of Race 39
Day of Respect for Cultural Diversity 39
DeNora, Tia 154, 171, 182
Desert 24, 26
Diaspora 29
Documentary film 120-7, 139-41
Dolavon 5, 36, 40

## E
Eisteddfod
  Ceremonies 64-73
  De la Juventud 61
  Del Chubut 48-51, 61, 78-82
  History 58-62
  Llangollen 60
  Main discussion 47-63
  Mimosa 47-9
  Yr Urdd 60
England/English 21-3, 46, 58-9, 92-3

Escuela 100 41, 66
Esquel 5-6, 52-3, 61, 73
Ethnography 6-9, 117-19
   *see also* methodology
Europe 23-4, 34, 43-6, 44, 45-6

**F**
Film theory 120-6, 139-41
   *see also* Mulvey, Laura
Flow 73-7, 155, 164-6, 188-91
Foucault, Michel 11-12, 32, 167-8, 171-2, 187-93
   *see also* panopticon
French/France 43-4

**G**
Gaiman 5-6, 17-18, 33, 36-43
Gaiman Music School 49-51
Gaze 89, 99-102, 114-16, 119-20, 187-90, 193
Gell, Alfred 75
   *see also* agency
Gender 8-9, 56, 153
   *see also* Butler, Judith
Gibbard, Gwenan 122-5
Goffman, Erving 56, 141
Gorsedd 51-2, 70-6
Graeber, David 173-4
Gŵyl y Glaniad 33, 90, 111

**H**
Historical narrative 21-5, 30-5
   *see also* settler colonialism

**I**
Identity
   Welsh identity 55-7
   *see also* belonging
Immigration policy 23-4
Indigenous peoples 24-9, 33-5, 39
Ingold, Tim 152-3
International Day of Indigenous People 39
Interpellation 69-70, 83, 180, 191-2
   *see also* Althusser, Louis

Ireland 111
Italian descent 36, 43-4

**K**
Keane, Webb 52-3, 57, 64-5, 69, 77
   *see also* slippages

**L**
La Pampa 39
Lacan, Jacques 12-13, 120, 130-1, 139-40, 179-80
   *see also* mirror stage theory
Language 21-3, 32, 39-42
Latin America 26, 28, 44-6
Levinas, Emmanuel 10
Liverpool 21, 32
London 58, 153

**M**
Mapuche 20, 36, 39, 151
Mapuche Tehuelche Trelew Community 39
Mate 48, 74, 87, 107, 128-9
Menter Patagonia 40, 79, 91, 118
Methodology 6-9
   *see also* ethnography
Mexico 28, 45
Mimosa 21-2
Mirror stage theory 12-13, 120-1, 130-1, 139-40, 180
   *see also* Lacan, Jacques
Moments of disgruntlement 53, 73, 84-5
Multisensory 14-15, 187-9, 191
Mulvey, Laura 140
Music 149-83
   Musical analysis 159-62
Myth of whiteness 44-6

**N**
Namuncura Syhueque Community 39
National anthem 94-7
National Library of Wales 51
Neuquen 41

New York 22
North America 21-2

## O
Ohio 22
Ortner, Sherry 11, 187

## P
Palestinians 44-5
Panopticon 11-12, 114-15
Patagonia Welsh Language Project 34, 39-40
Pennsylvania 22
Performance theory 54-7
  Performativity 55-7
  Performative encounter 9-11, 193-5
Peron 33-4
Playa Union 66, 172
Power relations 9-10, 56-7, 78-82, 112-14
Psychoanalysis/therapy 166-73
Puerto Madryn 5, 47-8

## R
Rawson 5-6, 60
Recognition 13, 68-70, 180-2, 189-91
Representation 19, 119-27
Research ethics 6-9
Rice, Tom 14
Rio Negro 32, 96
Ritual performance 52-4, 64-6
Roca, General Julio Argentino 27
Rosas, Juan Manuel de 23
Rubenstein, Steven 139-40

## S
Santa Cruz 39
Saraguro (Ecuador) 151
Sartre, Jean-Paul 9-10, 12, 99-102, 179-80
Seeger, Anthony 159
Self-cultivation 169-75
Senses 14-15, 152-3
Settler colonialism/settler colony 29-30

Shame 12, 104-5
  *see also* Sartre, Jean-Paul
Siop Bara 41, 49, 117
Slippages 64-73
  *see also* Keane, Webb
Social media 91-2
Sonic interpellation 14-15, 191-3
Soundscape 153-4
St David's Hall 51
Strathern, Marilyn 192
Subjectivity 11-15, 191-5

## T
Taylor, Lucy 27
Tehuelche 24-9, 39
Teithiau Tango 62, 92
Tourism 87-116
Traditional Argentinian music 162
  Tango 62
  Zamba 62, 149-50, 162-3
Trelew 5-6, 17-18
Trevelin 5-6, 41-2, 61-2
Turner, Victor 54-5
  *see also* performance

## U
United States 96, 107
Urry, John 101

## V
Veintiocho de Julio 36
Veracini, Lorenzo 28
Villa Dique Florentino 36

## W
Wade, Peter 45-6
Welsh Settler's Square 51, 71

## Y
Y Wladfa 4-6
Ysgol Camwy 41, 67
Ysgol Gymraeg y Gaiman 18, 41, 48, 67, 141
Ysgol Meithrin Gaiman 41
Ysgol yr Hendre 39-40